# Badger Key St...
# Science Starters

# Year 7

# John Parker

Badger Publishing Limited
26 Wedgwood Way, Pin Green Industrial Estate, Stevenage, Hertfordshire SG1 4QF
Telephone: 01438 356907  Fax: 01438 747015.

Cover photograph: Educational Solutions Ltd.

# Introduction

The **Badger** *Science Starters* have been specially written for the KS3 Science Framework. The contents follow through the QCA scheme of work sequentially. The key ideas, considered fundamental to KS3 Science, are also highlighted. These are:

- **Investigational skills** (Sc1)
- **Cells**
- **Interdependence**
- **Particles**
- **Forces**
- **Energy**

Understanding of the key ideas is considered to be instrumental in the access of all other Science concepts and skills.

These books contain a series of lively *Starters*, each of which can be completed within a 5 - 10 minute timeframe. Each Starter is an energetic interaction at the beginning of a lesson, designed to stimulate pupils of all abilities. Activities will elicit a wide range of responses:

- **recall** of previously learned concepts
- **links** to what is about to be encountered
- **modern** , **relevant**, relating to **everyday life**, **linking** to what pupils already know

The Year 7 Starters begin from a KS2 baseline. Awakening of a KS2 concept via a Starter will carry more pupils with the teacher and maximise achievement across the whole class. Where pupils participate in Starter activities above baseline level, **concept transfer** may be achieved by **team work** so that concepts pass from one pupil to another.

Following the **Starter**, the pupils receive the **main course**. A short **plenary** brings the lesson to a successful conclusion.

The resources provide a **collection** of **exciting activities** that complement lesson content. They constitute a **menu** from which teachers can **select**. Implementing a Starter will kick-start a lesson and catalyse the raising of standards required by the government.

*John Parker*

# Contents

# Investigating: suggest a question (1)

### Objective:

To be able to frame questions which are testable and appropriate to scientific enquiry.

### Teaching point:

It is important to build on Key Stage 2 investigational skills and develop them into those appropriate to Key Stage 3. Activity 1 is to frame *the* question which has been scientifically investigated by another pupil, Gemma. It is important for the pupils to be aware that questions need to be in a form suitable for scientific investigation.

**What you will need:**
Enough copies of Copymaster 1, pupils to work in pairs.

**Time:**
10 minutes

### Activity:

Explain that each pair of pupils will be given a copy of part of Gemma's investigation.

Ask pupils to look carefully at the diagram and results, then write down a question they think Gemma has tried to answer by doing her investigation.

A good question would be "Does the height of the ramp affect the distance travelled by a toy car?"

"Does a toy car move down a ramp?" This type of response may be given but falls short of what Gemma was investigating holistically.

Discuss with the class the importance of beginning with a suitable question when planning an investigation.

The first part of the Copymaster shows a diagram of Gemma's investigation, together with a results table. The pupils analyse information given to enable them to work out what was the question Gemma was trying to answer in her investigation.

**Challenge:** Ask pupils to give THREE ways that Gemma could have made sure that her investigation was a fair test.

**Links to plenary:** Discuss the importance of beginning an investigation with a suitable question which can be tested.

**Badger Key Stage 3 Science Starters**

# Investigating: suggest a question (1)

Gemma measured the distance travelled by her toy car after she released it down a ramp.

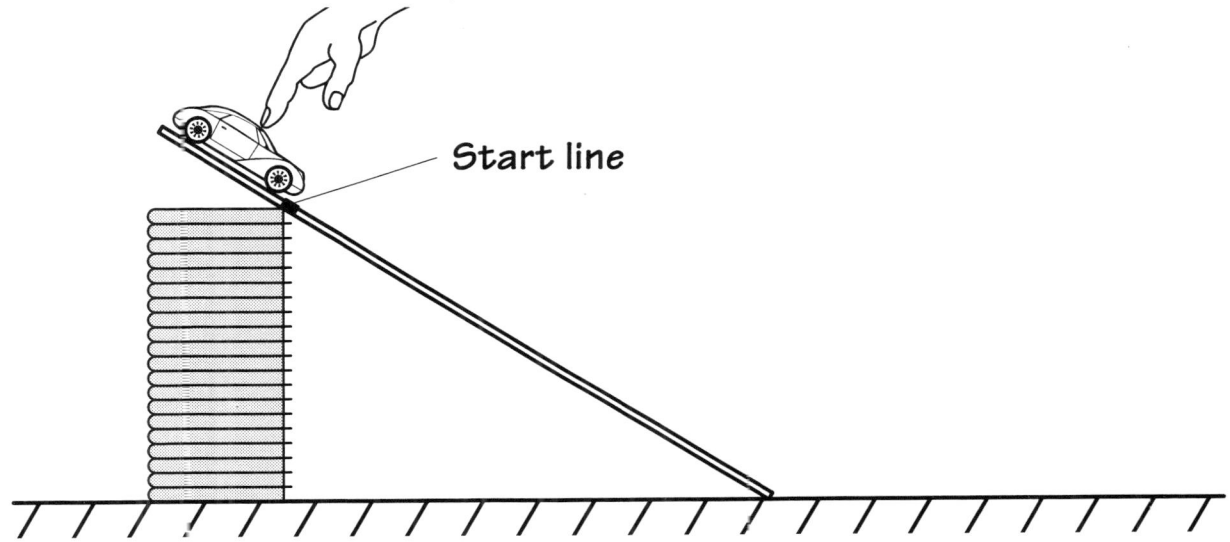

Start line

For each run
- she used the same toy car.
- she released the car from the same position behind the start line.
- she measured the distance travelled by the car down the ramp and along the table.

She changed the height of the ramp, going up one book each time. Each book was 2cm in width.

| Height of ramp (cm) | Distance travelled by car (cm) |
|---|---|
| 40 | 94 |
| 42 | 106 |
| 44 | 119 |
| 46 | 132 |

From the information given, write down the question which Gemma investigated.

# Investigating: suggest a question (2)

### Objective:

To be able to pose a suitable question which could help them to plan a scientific investigation effectively.

### Teaching point:

Each scenario has an underlying relationship which the pupils may be able to identify. From the given information, pupils can predict a possible relationship which can be tested by applying their question.

**What you will need:**
Scenario cards from Copymaster 2. Pupils to work in pairs.

**Time:**
10 minutes

### Activity:

Explain that cards will be given out to pairs. On each card is a scenario. Give one scenario at a time.

In pairs the pupils discuss the main **relationship** shown after their analysis of each scenario.

Ask the pupils to write down a question which is testable. The question should enable the pupils to find out if the relationship they suggest is true or false.

Logical questions which they may give:

**Woodlice**
Do more woodlice live under rocks or logs?

**Dandelions**
Do more dandelions grow on a path or the rest of a field?

**Sugar and water**
Does sugar disappear more quickly in warm water than cold water?

**Football**
Does a football travel further across a cut lawn than one with longer grass (from the same power of kick)?

**Challenge:** Can the pupils list possible reasons for the relationships they suggest?

**Links to plenary:** Discuss the importance of the question to planning an investigation well.

**Badger Key Stage 3 Science Starters**

# Investigating: suggest a question (2)

## Woodlice

- Billy searched around his garden looking for woodlice.
- He found some woodlice under some rocks and some under old logs.
- There seemed to be more woodlice under the logs.

## Dandelions

- Nita looked across a field and saw a herd of cows grazing.
- Ramblers regularly walked across a path through the field.
- There appeared to be more dandelions growing on the path than on the rest of the field.

## Sugar and water

- Jayne put a spoonful of sugar in a beaker of cold water then another spoonful in a beaker of warm water.
- She stirred the contents of each beaker.
- She thought that the sugar disappeared more quickly in the warm water compared to the cold water.

## Football

- Raj kicked a football across a field before and after the grass was cut.
- After he kicked the ball, he thought that it travelled further after the grass was cut even though he had given the same power to his kicks.

# Investigating: can you spot the key factors?

### Objective:

To be able to identify and control key factors before planning an investigation.

### Teaching point:

The pupils should analyse the given information and identify as many factors which affect the time it takes the parachutes to fall as possible.

**What you will need:**
Copymaster 3 as OHT.
Whole class activity.

**Time:**
10 minutes

### Activity:

Project Copymaster OHT.

Explain that the OHT shows a class of pupils who are timing how long it takes for their parachutes to fall.

Ask the pupils to write down the factors which affect how quickly the parachutes fall to the floor.

They may include:

- Type of material from which the canopy of the parachute is made.
- Type of material from which the strings of the parachute are made.
- Area of parachute canopy.
- Length of strings.
- Weight / density of load.
- Height of release.
- Atmospheric conditions of room.

Class 7P released their parachutes from different heights.

The Copymaster asks this question, "Can you write down the factors which affect how quickly

**Challenge:** Using the factors identified by class and teacher how could class 7P make every parachute and drop comparable with those of each pupil?

**Links to plenary:** Discuss importance of identifying all factors before planning an investigation.

**Badger Key Stage 3 Science Starters**

# How quickly *do model* parachutes fall?

The pupils of 7P are seen above. Their homework was to make a parachute and you can see them timing how long it takes to fall to the floor.

Can you write down the factors which affect how quickly the parachutes fall to the floor?

# Investigating: controlling the key factors

### Objective:

To be able to control all key factors whilst changing just one, the experimental factors.

### Teaching point:

Linked to previous Starter, pupils learn what to do with the factors once they have identified them. Only the experimental factor should be changed. All other factors remain the same, being controlled. By the end of the activity, pupils should readily exchange the terms **factors** with **variables**.

**What you will need:**
Copymaster 4 supplied as a worksheet to all pupils. They can share ideas in pairs.

**Time:**
5 - 10 minutes

**Key terms:** Controlled factors (variables), Experimental factors (variables)

### Activity:

Give out a Copymaster worksheet to each pupil.

Ask pupils to look at the worksheet. After reading the title of the investigation and looking at the diagram, they should complete the table.

Recall of previous Starter will give the factors which they need to insert.

Which factor should be changed in this investigation? **(Experimental variable/ factor)**
*(Surface) Area of parachute canopy.*

Which factors should be kept the same? **(Controlled factors)**

1   *Type of material from which the canopy of parachute is made.*

2   *Type of material from which the strings of parachute are made.*

3   *Length of parachute strings.*

4   *Weight / density of load.*

5   *Height of release.*

6   *Conditions of room / laboratory.*

**Challenge:** Ask pupils how they would investigate the effect of string length on the time it takes for a parachute to descend.

**Links to plenary:** Discuss the importance of changing just one factor whilst keeping the others controlled.

**Badger Key Stage 3 Science Starters**

# Investigating: controlling the key factors

Does the surface area of the canopy affect how quickly model parachutes fall?

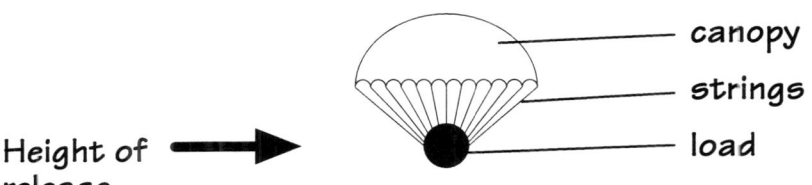

Height of release →

canopy

strings

load

**LABORATORY**

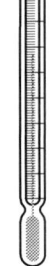

stop clock

5.3

Complete the table below to help plan a fair test.

| Which factor should be changed in this investigation? (Experimental factor) |
| --- |
| . . . . . . . . . . . . . . . . . . . . . . . . . . . . . . . . . . . . . . . . . |

| Which factors should be kept the same? (Controlled factors) |
| --- |
| 1 . . . . . . . . . . . . . . . . . . . . . . . . . . . . . . . . . . . . . . . |
| 2 . . . . . . . . . . . . . . . . . . . . . . . . . . . . . . . . . . . . . . . |
| 3 . . . . . . . . . . . . . . . . . . . . . . . . . . . . . . . . . . . . . . . |
| 4 . . . . . . . . . . . . . . . . . . . . . . . . . . . . . . . . . . . . . . . |
| 5 . . . . . . . . . . . . . . . . . . . . . . . . . . . . . . . . . . . . . . . |
| 6 . . . . . . . . . . . . . . . . . . . . . . . . . . . . . . . . . . . . . . . |

# Can you choose suitable apparatus? (1)

**Objective:**

To be able to select appropriate apparatus for their investigations.

**Teaching point:**

Pupils need to select apparatus carefully for investigations.

**What you will need:**
Copymaster 5a supplied
as a worksheet to
all pupils. Pupils to
work individually.

**Time:**
10 minutes

**Activity:**

Give a Copymaster worksheet to each pupil.

Ask the pupils to draw a line from the correct apparatus to the correct statement. Tell pupils that one has been done for them.

Answers are provided on Copymaster 5b OHT.

Discuss with the class the advantage of using computers plus probes: e.g. using an active oxygen probe + computer, pupils can track the variation in a pond over 24 hours. The apparatus remains active long after they have gone home from school. Pupils can take readings and record them even whilst they sleep. What an advantage!

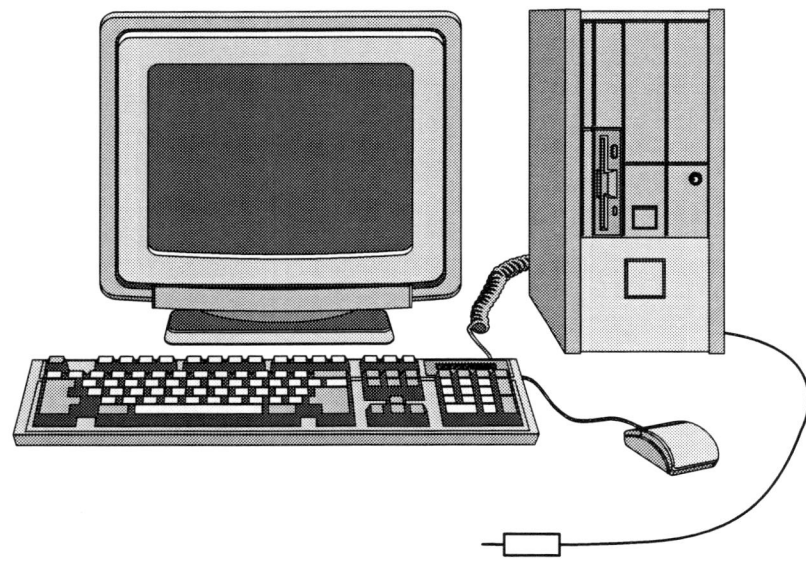

**Challenge:** Can pupils give the units they could use for the measuring apparatus in the activity? Magnification could be mentioned, linked to the microscope.

**Links to plenary:** Discuss the importance of choosing suitable apparatus and recording the units correctly.

**Badger Key Stage 3 Science Starters**

# Can you choose suitable apparatus? (1)

## Apparatus

## Statement

Balance

measure the amount of a gas in pond water over 24 hours

Thermometer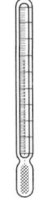

measure the force of pulling along a toy car

Force meter

measure the volume of water

Measuring cylinder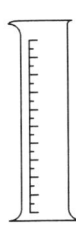

measure the mass of iron filings

Computer + oxygen probe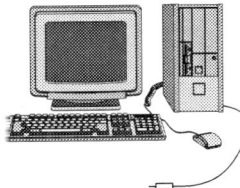

see the parts of an onion cell

Microscope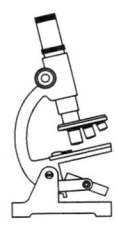

measure temperature of water

## Answers:
## Apparatus

## Statement

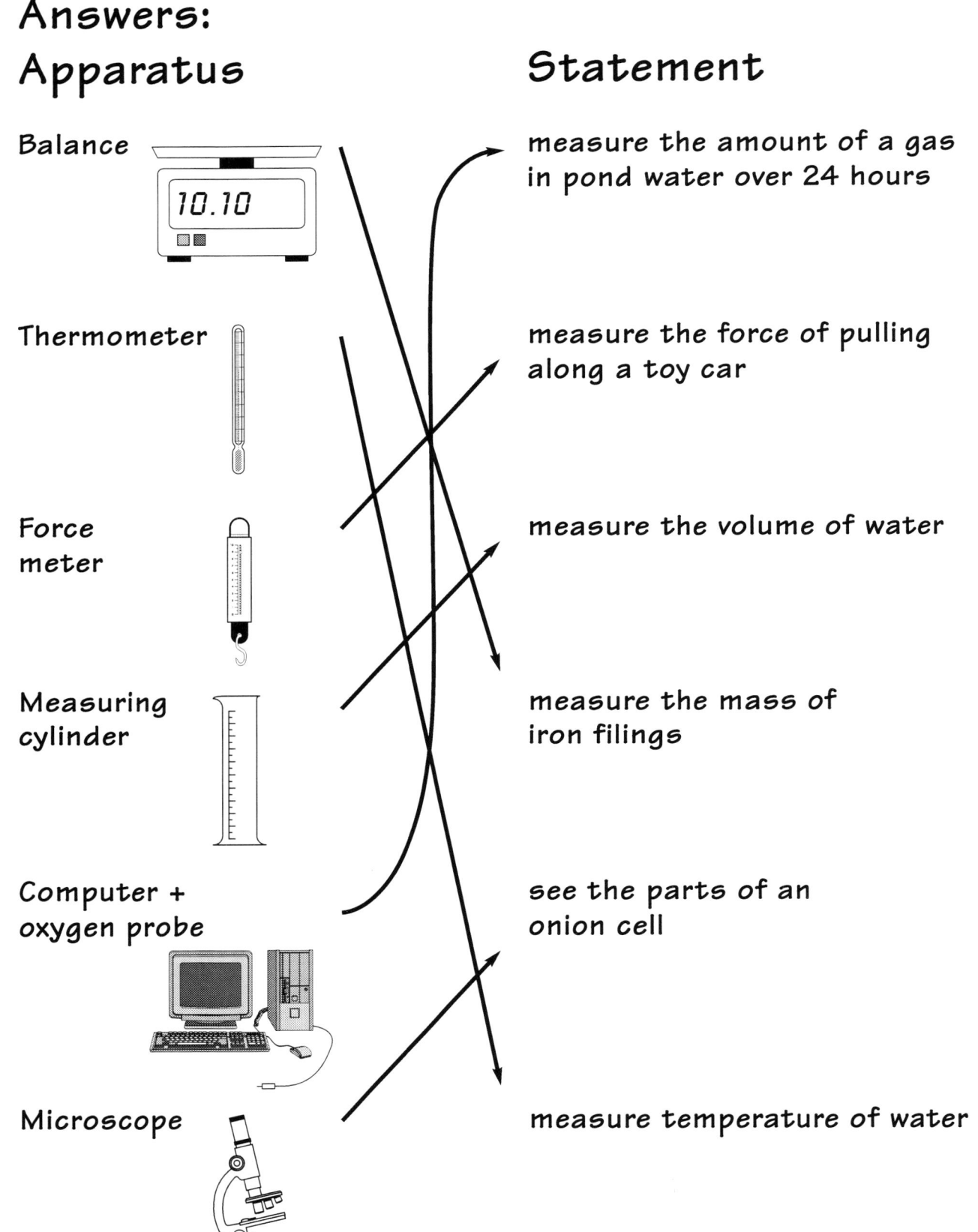

Balance

measure the amount of a gas in pond water over 24 hours

Thermometer

measure the force of pulling along a toy car

Force meter

measure the volume of water

Measuring cylinder

measure the mass of iron filings

Computer + oxygen probe

see the parts of an onion cell

Microscope

measure temperature of water

# Can you choose suitable apparatus? (2)

### Objective:

Given a range of sizes of the same piece of apparatus, to be able to select the piece appropriate to the task.

### Teaching point:

In a laboratory there may a number of pieces of apparatus which range in accuracy. The activity is based on different sizes of measuring cylinder and allows the pupils to choose the most appropriate for a task.

### Activity:

Project the Copymaster OHT.

It shows a choice of three different measuring cylinders which can be used to measure the volume of an irregular rock.

Ask the pupils to analyse the diagram and choose the most appropriate measuring cylinder.

Pupils should write down the letter of the most suitable measuring cylinder. They should give a reason for their choice.

The correct choice is C because this measuring cylinder allows you to read the water level most accurately. It is the level which moves up highest and each graduation is for a smaller volume. Easier to see!

### What you will need:

Copymaster 6 as OHT. Whiteboards and pens. Whole class activity.

### Time:
5 minutes

**Challenge:** Ask pupils to explain how the measuring cylinder can be used to measure the volume of the rock. They could sequence this in bullet points.

**Links to plenary:** Discuss the fact that other instruments also require careful selection, e.g. thermometers which measure to 1°C, 5°C, 10°C. (If a doctor used a thermometer which measured to nearest 5°C then he would not be able to detect the difference between a fever and normal human temperature. Dangerous!)

**Badger Key Stage 3 Science Starters**

# Can you choose suitable apparatus? (2)

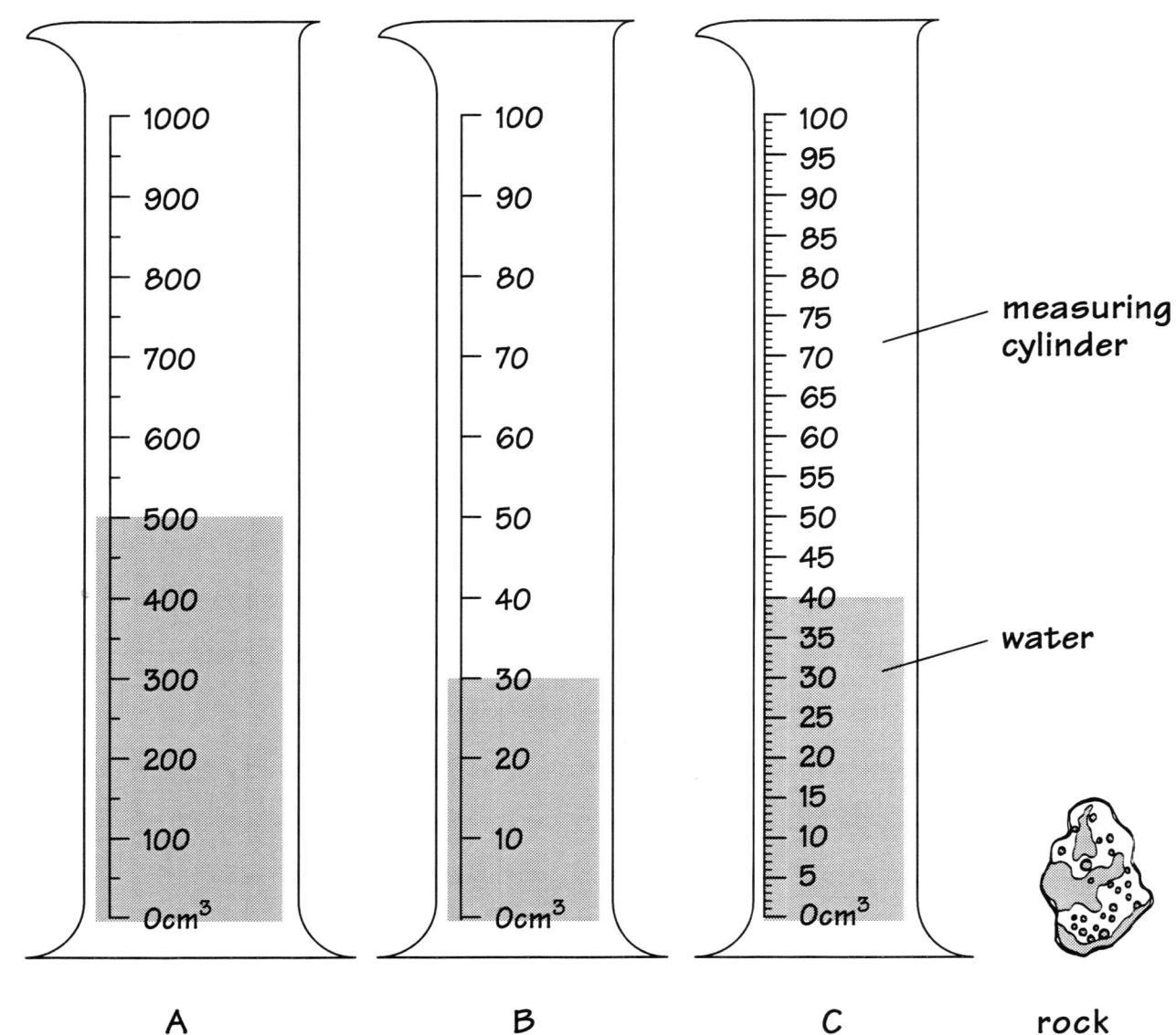

| A | B | C | rock |

When a rock is dropped into a measuring cylinder the water level rises.

Which of the measuring cylinders is the best for measuring the volume of the rock shown?

Write down a reason for your choice.

# Why do we repeat measurements?

**Objective:**

To know that repeat measurements improve reliability.

**What you will need:**
Copymaster 7 as
worksheets for each
pupil. Pupils to work
in pairs.

**Time:**
10 minutes

**Teaching point:**

If pupils take isolated measurements then they may be atypical and give the wrong impression. The activity will show that repeating the number of measurements will give more reliable results.

**Activity:**

Give a Copymaster worksheet to each pupil. Allow them to work in pairs or groups.

A lawn is shown (10m x 10m) with the positions and results of 5 random quadrats. Each quadrat shows the number of dandelions counted by a group of pupils.

A results table is shown and a sample calculation shows the atypical number of dandelions in the lawn estimated using quadrat 1.

Ask the pupils to work out the number of plants in the lawn if quadrat 2 had been used. (100 x 15 = 1500)

Lead to their calculation of the number of plants in the lawn if the average number of 8·4 dandelions had been used. (100 x 8·4 = 840)

Inform the class that the more we repeat our readings the more reliable and representative the results become.

**Challenge:** Ask how the survey could be improved further.

**Links to plenary:** Discuss why repeated readings give more reliable results.

**Badger Key Stage 3 Science Starters**

# Why do we repeat measurements?

## How many dandelions are there in a lawn?

A group of pupils tried to find out how many dandelions there were in a lawn.

- They threw a wooden square, called a quadrat, randomly on the lawn.
- Where the square landed, they counted the number of dandelions in it.
- Each square was an area of 1m² (one square metre).
- They repeated this 5 times.

The diagram shows the lawn and results of each count.

10m

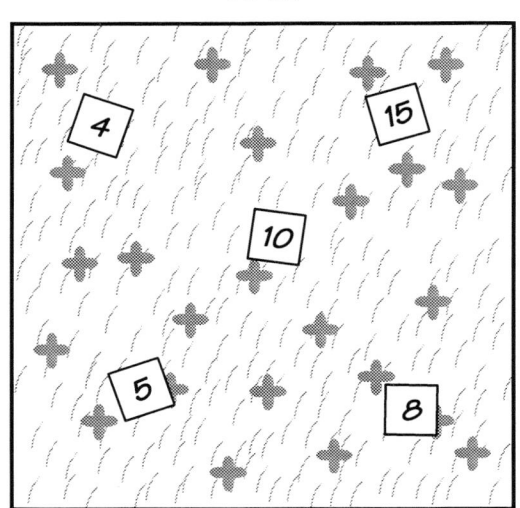

Area of lawn = 10m x 10m
= 100m²

10m

| Quadrat no. | No. of dandelions (in 1m²) |
|---|---|
| 1 | 4 |
| 2 | 15 |
| 3 | 8 |
| 4 | 10 |
| 5 | 5 |
| Total        5 | 42 |

Average number per quadrat = $\frac{42}{5}$ = 8·4

If the pupils had used only the results of quadrat 1, then they would estimate that 4 x 100 dandelion plants (400) were in the lawn.

There is an average of 8·4 plants in one square metre.
Work out how many plants are estimated in the whole lawn? Show your working.

⚷ KEY POINT

# Graphs

## Objective:

To be able to use a line graph to complete a results table by working backwards.

**What you will need:**
Copymaster 8 as worksheets for each pupil. Pupils to work individually.

**Time:**
10 minutes

## Teaching point:

Pupils will regularly obtain results and plot an appropriate graph. This activity focuses them on the graph and allows them to work backwards to complete an empty results table.

## Activity:

Give a Copymaster worksheet to each pupil.

Ask them to look carefully at the points which have been plotted to help them complete the table.

Reinforce by questioning why repeating the investigation and taking averages of readings at each temperature would give more reliable and representative results.

Make sure that all pupils are aware that level off takes place when the room temperature has been reached.

**Answers**

| Time (min) | 0 | 5 | 10 | 15 | 20 | 25 | 30 | 35 | 40 | 45 | 50 | |
|---|---|---|---|---|---|---|---|---|---|---|---|---|
| Temperature (°C) | 75 | 65 | 58 | 50 | 41 | 32 | 25 | 24 | 24 | 24 | 24 | |

**Challenge:** Ask pupils if every point represents the average for three repeat investigations, how many readings were taken in total?

**Links to plenary:** Discuss the importance of labelling axes and including units in both tables and on graphs.

**Badger Key Stage 3 Science Starters**

# Graphs

## Graphs: let's work backwards

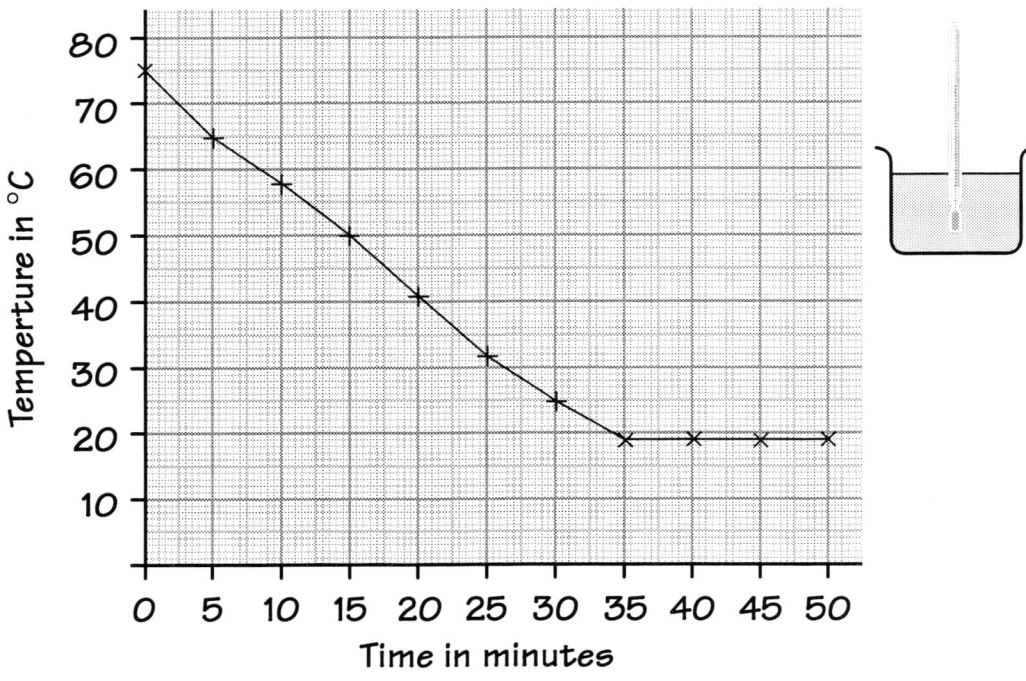

Look carefully at the graph above.

It shows the temperature change of a beaker of hot water left in a laboratory.

Use the points to help you work out the results which the pupils used to plot the graph.

Write the results in the table below:

Table

| Time (min) | 0 | | | | | | | | | | |
|---|---|---|---|---|---|---|---|---|---|---|---|
| Temperature (°C) | 75 | | | | | | | | | | |

Answer these questions:

• How many readings were taken in total during the investigation?

• What would be the advantage of repeating the investigation 3 more times and plotting average points?

• Why did the temperature level out after 35 minutes?

# What do the results mean?

### Objective:

To be able to interpret results of an investigation by analysing a graph.

### Teaching point:

Pupils need to present their results using a variety of ways. Here a graph of germinating seeds tracks the decrease then increase of their mass. You may wish to inform them that the seeds and seedlings are dried to remove water before each measurement was made. Pupils are cued by a key word list to complete the exercise.

### What you will need:
Copymaster 9 as worksheets for each pupil. Pupils to work in pairs.

### Time:
8 - 10 minutes

### Activity:

Give a Copymaster worksheet to each pupil. Allow them to work in pairs to help make the decisions.

Ask pupils to use the key words from the list to complete the passage. Inform them that it will help them to understand what happens as germination takes place.

**Answers**

The seeds started to <u>decrease</u> in mass up to day 14. During this time they used up most of their <u>food</u> reserves. After day 14 their mass began to <u>increase</u> again. This happened because shoots of the seedling pushed through the soil into the <u>light</u>. The light enabled them to make their own food by <u>photosynthesis</u>.

**Challenge:** Extra question. Using the graph, on which days was the mass of 10 seeds / seedlings 2 grams?

**Links to plenary:** Discuss the usefulness of graphs in following the pattern of relationships. Share with them the fact that pattern is shown much better by graph than by results table.

**Badger Key Stage 3 Science Starters**

# What do the results mean?

## Germinating seeds

The graph below tracks the average mass in grams of 10 seeds as they germinate and grow into seedlings.

The mass of the seeds / seedlings was measured every two days throughout the investigation.

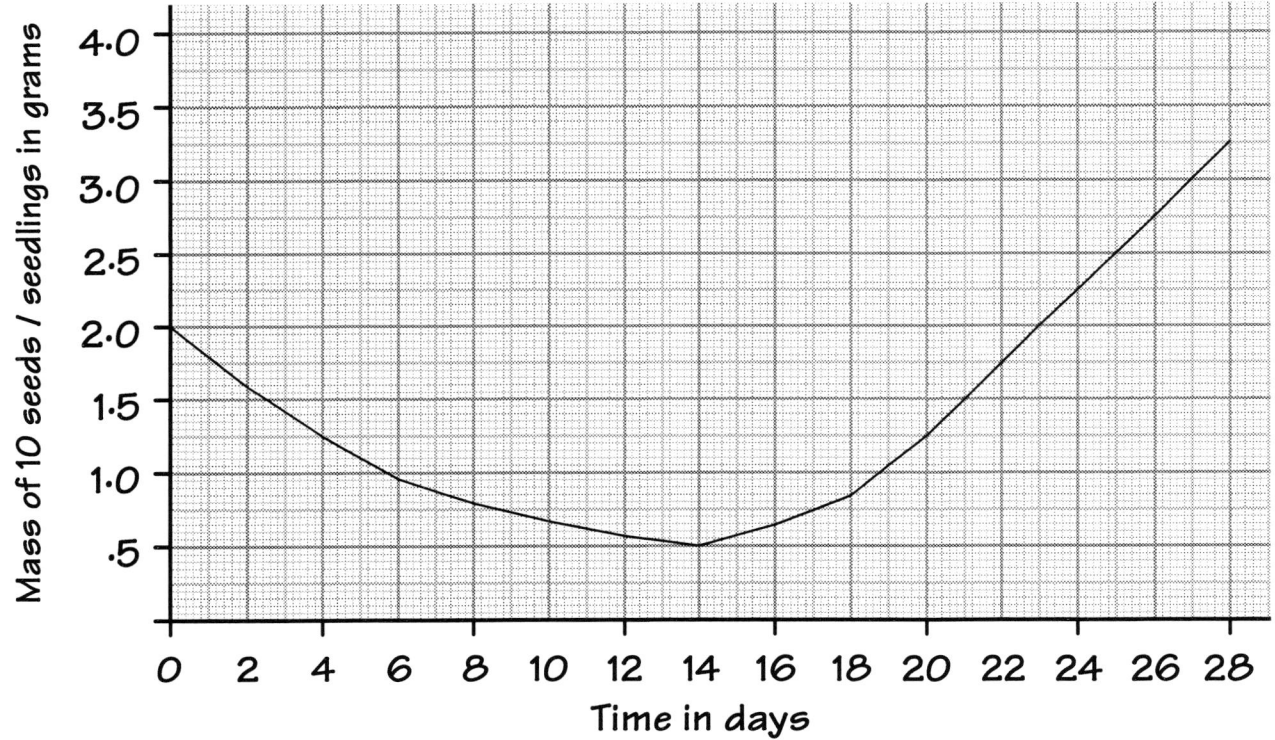

Use words from the list to complete the passage below:

light       food       increase

photosynthesis       decrease

The seeds started to . . . . . . . . . . . . . in mass up to day 14.

During this time they used up most of their . . . . . . . . . . . .

reserves. After day 14 their mass began to . . . . . . . . . . . . .

This happened because shoots of the seedling pushed through

the soil into the . . . . . . . . . . . . . The light enabled them to

make their own food by . . . . . . . . . . . . .

# Evaluation of an investigation

### Objective:

To be able to evaluate the strength of evidence obtained during an investigation; to be aware of the importance of sample size in an investigation.

### Teaching point:

The pupils need to consider the effect of sample size when planning investigations. The exercise will show the danger of not taking enough readings.

### Activity:

Project the Copymaster OHT. Cover up Scattergraph 2.

Outline the investigation, stating that 2 pupils have worked together using exactly the same technique. Wading in a pond, disturbing mud, they take pH measurements.

Henry only uses the first 10 readings whereas Sarah takes 25.

Ask the groups to discuss what Henry has found out from his scattergraph. One person from each group to write down the logical conclusion. Share group conclusions.

Now reveal Scattergraph 2.

Ask the groups to discuss what Sarah concludes from her scattergraph. One person from each group to write down the logical conclusion. Share group conclusions.

Discuss the fact that if we do not take enough readings, results may not be typical and could be very misleading.

**What you will need:**
Copymaster 10 as OHT.
Whiteboards and pens.
Pupils work in groups.

**Time:**
10 minutes

**Challenge:** Ask pupils to suggest reasons why the pH of the pond water is lower than 7.

**Links to plenary:** Discuss importance of sample size in establishing the true pattern. Inform that enough samples must be taken.

**Badger Key Stage 3 Science Starters**

# Evaluation of an investigation

## Was the sample large enough?

Sarah and Henry predicted that the pH of pond water would change from the outside to the middle. They waded into the pond and tested the pH. Henry only took 10 readings and plotted graph 1. Sarah included those readings and took a further 15.

The graphs are shown below:

## Henry's graph (Scattergraph 1)

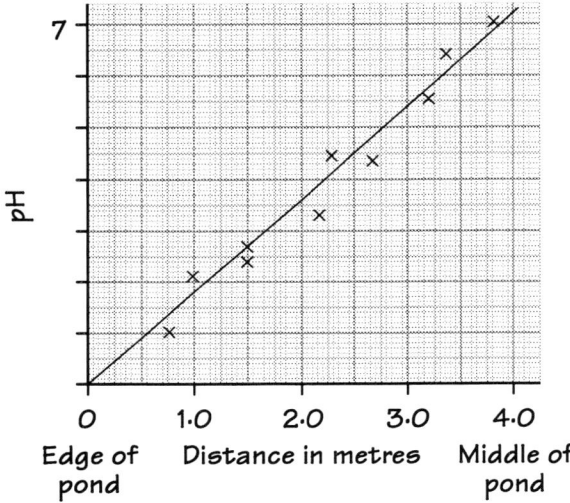

### Henry's conclusion

"I think that the pH of the pond water increases from the outside to the middle of the pond."

## Sarah's graph (Scattergraph 2)

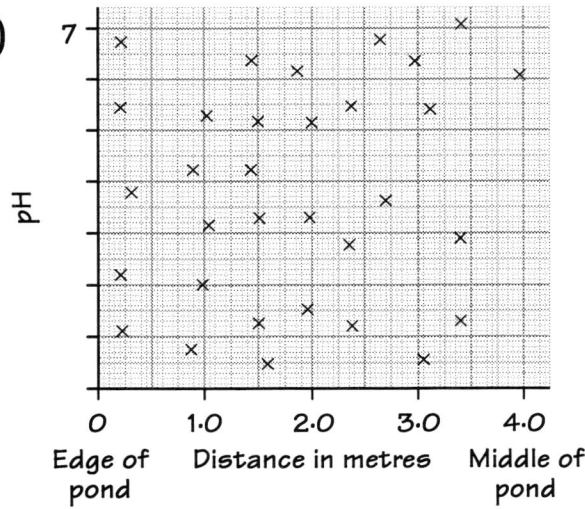

### Sarah's conclusion

"I think that there is no pattern in the pH of the pond water from the outside to the middle of the pond."

☞ **KEY POINT**

# What's in a cell?

**Objective:**

To be able to recognise the parts common to animal and plants cells as well as the differences.

**Teaching point:**

The exercise enables the pupils to focus on the parts of animal and plant cells. A table gives them clues which will help them decide how to label an animal and plant cell.

**What you will need:**
Copymaster 11 as worksheets for each pupil. Pupils to work individually.

**Time:**
8 minutes

**Key terms:** cell membrane, cell wall, chloroplast, cytoplasm, nucleus, sap vacuole

**Activity:**

Give a Copymaster worksheet to each pupil. Allow them to work individually to label the diagrams.

Explain that the table includes all the parts of animal and plant cells. They should use the information to help label the diagrams on the worksheet.

Ask pupils to underline 3 parts only found in plants.

**Answers:**

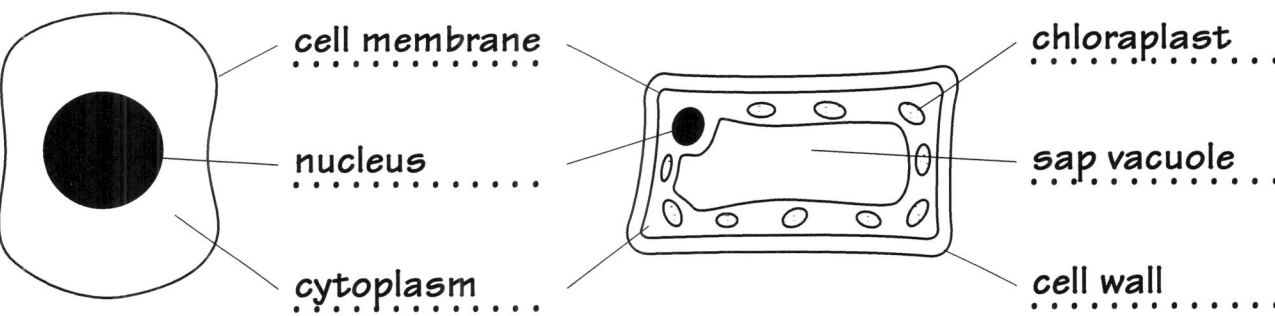

cell membrane . . . . . . . . . . . .

chloraplast . . . . .

nucleus . . . . . . . . . . . .

sap vacuole . . . . . . .

cytoplasm . . . . . .

cell wall . . . . . . . . . .

**Challenge:** Ask pupils to write down the function of each part.

**Links to plenary:** Discuss which parts are only found in plant cells and which are found in all cells. Outline their role.

**Badger Key Stage 3 Science Starters**

# What's in a cell?

| Part of cell | Animal cell | Plant cell |
| --- | --- | --- |
| cell membrane | ✓ | ✓ |
| cell wall | ✗ | ✓ |
| chloroplast | ✗ | ✓ |
| cytoplasm | ✓ | ✓ |
| nucleus | ✓ | ✓ |
| sap vacuole | ✗ | ✓ |

Use the table to help you label the diagrams below.

animal cell　　　　　　　　　　　　　plant cell

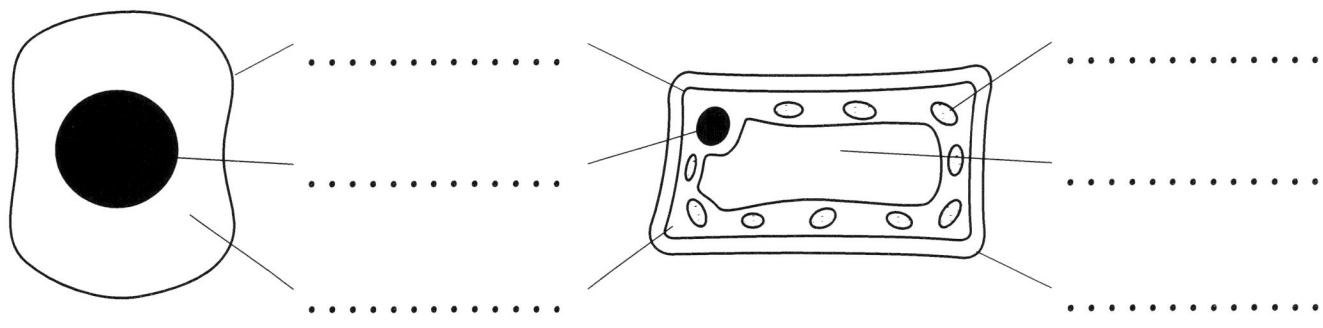

. . . . . . . . . . . . . . . . . . . . . . . . . . . . . . . . . . . . . . . . . . . . . . . . . . . . . . . . . . . . . . . . . . .

. . . . . . . . . . . . . . . . . . . . . . . . . . . . . . . . . . . . . . . . . . . . . . . . . . . . . . . . . . . . . . . . . . .

. . . . . . . . . . . . . . . . . . . . . . . . . . . . . . . . . . . . . . . . . . . . . . . . . . . . . . . . . . . . . . . . . . .

☞ **KEY POINT**

# Tissues and organs

**Objective:**

To know that a tissue is made up of a number of identical cells; to know that an organ consists of a number of different tissues.

**Teaching point:**

Pupils will be made aware that tissues consist of a number of similar cells, and that organs consist of a number of tissues.

**What you will need:**
Cards made from Copymaster 12. Pupils to work in groups.

**Time:**
5 minutes

**Activity:**

Give Copymaster cards to each group.

Explain that the cards show parts of organisms that are either tissues or organs. They need to tick or cross each box to classify them.

**Answers**

| Part of organism | Tissue | Organ |
|---|---|---|
| Muscle | ✓ | ✗ |
| Blood vessel | ✗ | ✓ |
| Cartilage | ✓ | ✗ |
| Bone | ✗ | ✓ |
| Leaf | ✗ | ✓ |

**Challenge:** Ask pupils to name 2 other organs and 2 other tissues.

**Links to plenary:** Highlight the fact that if the pupils see a number of repeated cells then this shows a tissue. Where they see a number of different tissues then they are looking at an organ.

**Badger Key Stage 3 Science Starters**

# Tissues and organs

Look at the diagrams and complete the table below by putting a tick to indicate if the part is tissue or an organ.

Remember, "Tissues make organs!"

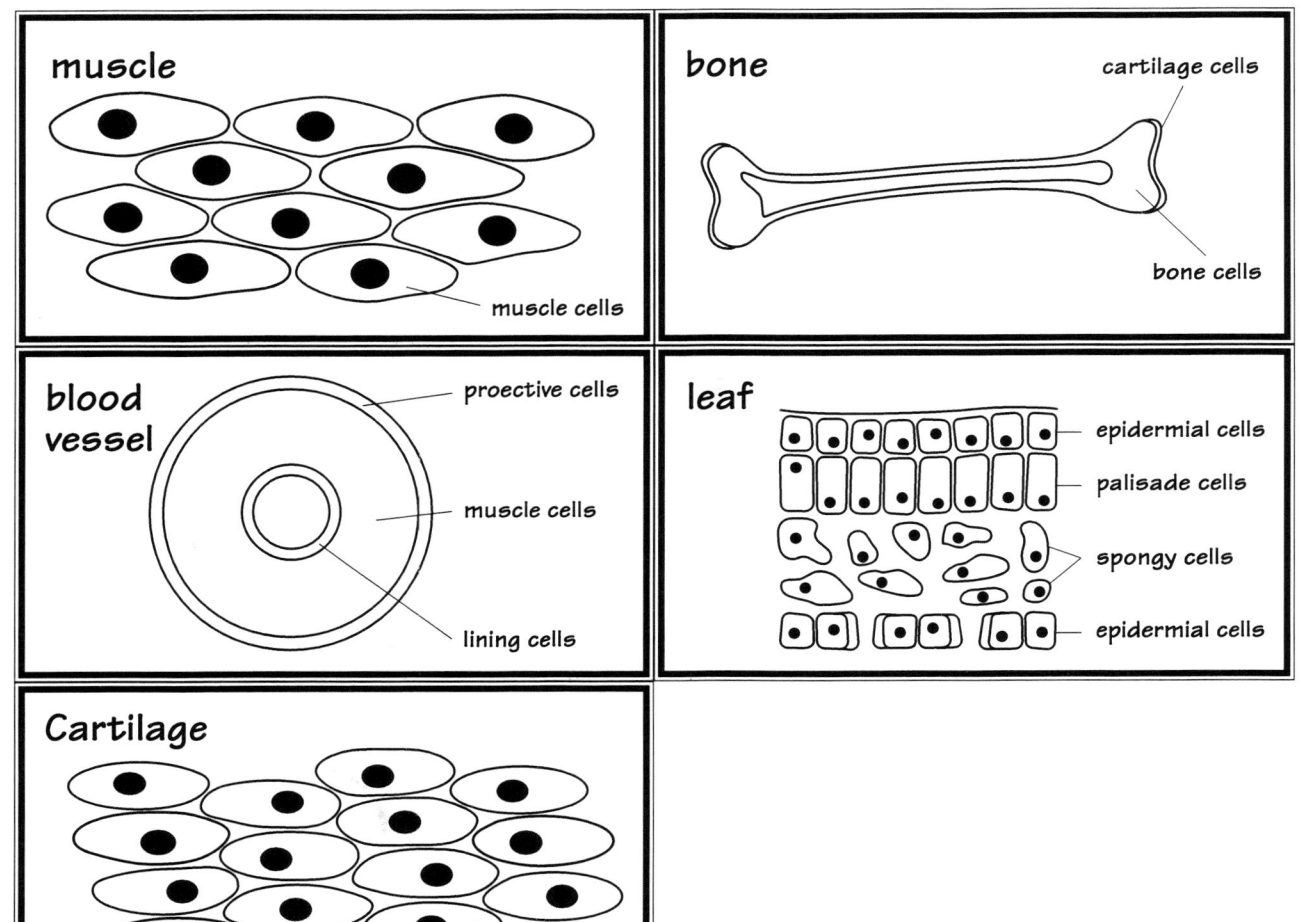

| Part of organism | Tissue | Organ |
|---|---|---|
| Muscle | | |
| Blood vessel | | |
| Cartilage | | |
| Bone | | |
| Leaf | | |

# Using a microscope

### Objective:

To be able to use a simple microscope effectively.

### Teaching point:

Most schools have a supply of "junior" microscopes. This exercise will help the pupils to remember the correct sequence of using a microscope to see a specimen. The specimen is onion epidermis, a tissue which can be successfully focused by a majority of pupils.

**What you will need:**
Statement cards from Copymaster 13a. Pupils to work in groups.

**Time:**
10 minutes

### Activity:

Give a collection of Copymaster statements to each group.

Explain that the aim is to discuss together the correct sequence of using the microscope to focus the onion cells.

After groups report back, Copymaster 13b OHT showing correct sequence can be projected.

Reinforce the fact that the adjustment knob should be rotated upwards, away from the stage to prevent the objective lens breaking the slide.

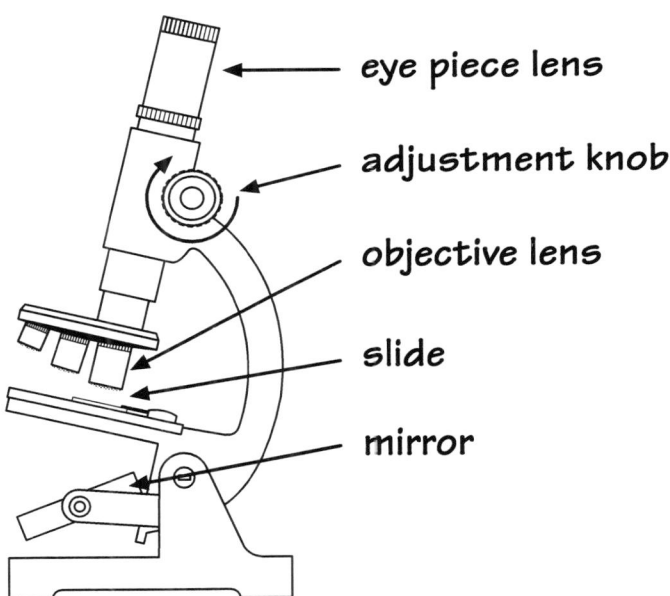

eye piece lens

adjustment knob

objective lens

slide

mirror

**Challenge:** The image is magnified by the lenses. Magnification of the image is eyepiece lens magnification x objective lens magnification. Ask pupils to work out the magnification of the onion cell image if the eyepiece lens is x10 and the objective lens is x15.

**Links to plenary:** Discuss the importance of each stage in the sequence. Explain that rotation of the objective lenses allows them to 'click into place'.

**Badger Key Stage 3 Science Starters**

# Using a microscope

How do you use a microscope to help see onion cells clearly?

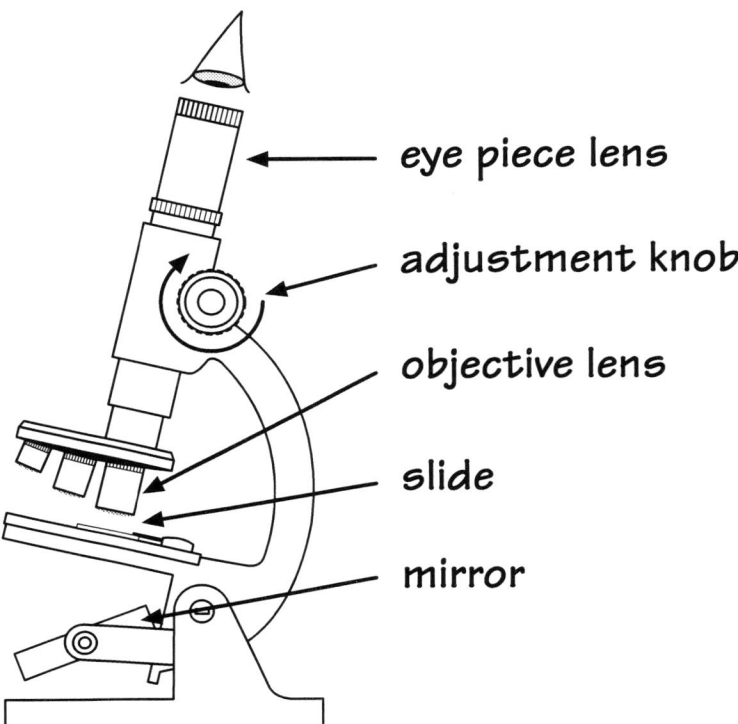

- eye piece lens
- adjustment knob
- objective lens
- slide
- mirror

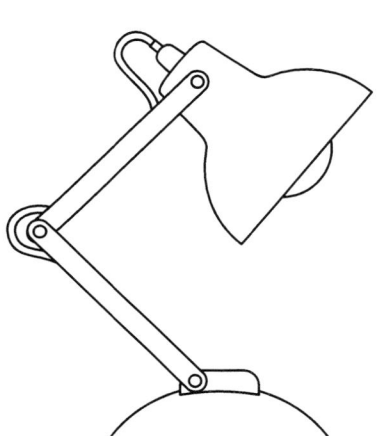

## Statement list

| | |
|---|---|
| Look down the eyepiece lens. | Turn the knob upwards to bring the onion cells into focus. |
| Put them on a clean microscope slide with a drop of water. | Put the slide onto the stage of the microscope. |
| Turn the knob so the second lens almost touches the slide. | Peel a thin layer of cells from the inner part of an onion. |
| Put them in water to stop them from drying out. | Switch on the light to illuminate the onion cells. |

# Using a microscope

## Answers:

1   Switch on the light to illuminate the onion cells.

2   Peel a thin layer of cells from the inner part of an onion.

3   Put them in water to stop them from drying out.

4   Put them on a clean microscope slide with a drop of water.

5   Put the slide onto the stage of the microscope.

6   Turn the knob so the second lens almost touches the slide.

7   Look down the eyepiece lens.

8   Turn the knob upwards to bring the onion cells into focus.

⌒ **KEY POINT**

# Different cells have different functions

## Objective:

To be aware that certain cells in multi-celled organisms are specialised to specific functions.

## Teaching point:

Given a partially completed table, the pupils fill in the blanks with diagrams or functions.

**What you will need:**
Copymaster 14 cards.
Pupils to work in pairs.

**Time:**
10 minutes

## Activity:

Cut out the Cell cards and the Fact cards prior to the lesson, and keep them in seperate decks. Shuffle the decks before handing out cards to the pupils.

Ask the pupils to look at the diagrams on the cards closely. There are clues in the structure which will help them link the correct facts.

The cells shown are typical of those expected on SAT papers at Key Stage 3.

Ask the pupils to to match each Cell card with a Fact card.

The Copymaster can be reproduced as an OHT to provide the answers.

**Challenge:** Research the structure and function of guard cells in leaves.

**Links to plenary:** Discuss the fact that there are many more types of specialised cells they will study in Science. In diagrams there are structural clues which will help with identification and will link logically to functions.

**Badger Key Stage 3 Science Starters**

# Different cells have different functions

| Diagram of cell | Facts |
|---|---|
| | This cell is produced by a man. It has a tail to swim. |
| | This cell is produced by a woman. It contains food for development. |
| | This cell is found on a plant root. It absorbs water. |
| | This cell is round to move through blood vessels. It carries oxygen. |
| | This cell can change shape. It can kill bacteria in the body. |
| | This cell can pass electrical messages. It helps muscle cells to move. |
| | This cell is found in a leaf. It can make sugar. |

# Can you describe fertilisation?

### Objective:

To be able to describe the process of fertilisation.

### Teaching point:

The Copymaster shows the process of fertilisation. Key terms are given which can be incorporated into the description.

**What you will need:**
Copymaster 15 as OHT.
Whiteboards and pens.
Pupils to work in pairs.

### Time:
10 minutes

### Activity:

Project Copymaster OHT.

Explain to class that the task is to write one or two sentences to describe what happens at each stage of fertilisation. Pupils should describe each stage in sequence on their whiteboards.

Sequence they should give:

Stage 1 - Sperm cells swim to the egg, because they are attracted to it.

Stage 2 - The head of one sperm enters the egg.

Stage 3 - The two nuclei join together and the tail falls away.

Stage 4 - A fertilised egg has been formed.

**Challenge:** Ask pupils to explain what happens to the fertilised egg after stage 4.

**Links to plenary:** Discuss the fact that genetic information is transferred via the male and female nucleus. The consequence of this being offspring take some features from male parent and some from female parent.

**Badger Key Stage 3 Science Starters**

# Can you describe fertilisation?

## Use the key terms to help you:

| | | |
|---|---|---|
| cell | egg | join |
| nucleus | fertilised egg | swim |
| tail | attracted | |

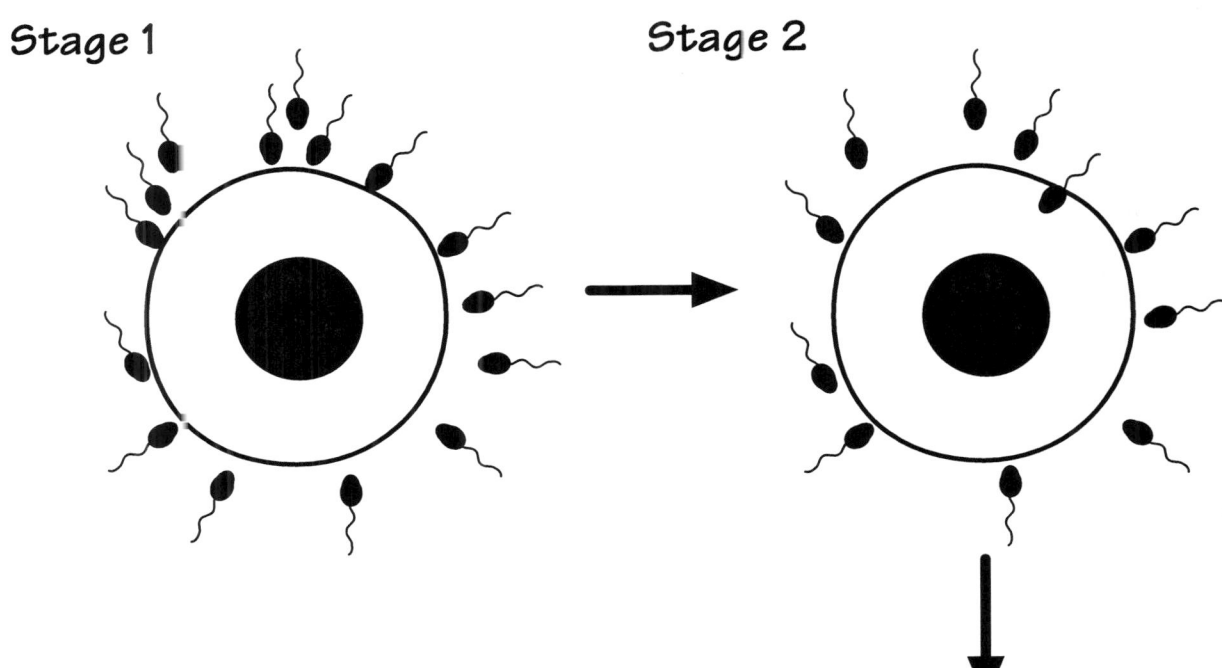

Stage 1    Stage 2

Stage 4    Stage 3

# What are the best conditions for growing pollen tubes?

### Objective:

To be aware that pollen tubes which grow down the stigma and style use sugar solution.

### Teaching point:

Certain conditions are required to stimulate pollen to germinate a tube and grow. The activity mimicks the sugar conditions on the stigma and attempts to show that a specific concentration gives better rates of pollen germination.

**What you will need:**
Copymaster 16 as OHT.
Whiteboards and pens.
Pupils to work in pairs.

**Time:**
8 minutes

### Activity:

Project Copymaster OHT.

Ask the pupils to look carefully at the bar graph. Ask the pupils the following questions; pupils to answer on whiteboards.

1.  Peter could not see the pollen grains with his naked eye. What did he use to enable him to see them?
    *Microscope*

2.  (a)  Which percentage concentration of sugar was the best for germinating the pollen grains?
    *10%*

    (b)  How many pollen grains germinated at this concentration of sugar solution?
    *16*

3.  Which percentage concentrations of sugar solution allowed no pollen to germinate?
    *0 %, 25%*

4.  Sugar can be found on the sticky stigma.
    (a)  Which percentage concentration of sugar was probably similar to the concentration found on the stigma of a lily?
    *10%*

    (b)  Why did you make this choice?
    *Largest number of pollen germinated.*

5.  Suggest ONE improvement Peter could make if he was to repeat a similar investigation.
    a.  *Take more readings.*

    b.  *Test other concentrations.*

Discuss answers given by pairs.

**Challenge:** Ask pupils to give improvements in Peter's investigation should it be repeated.

**Links to plenary:** Discuss fact that different species of plant may require different sugar concentrations to stimulate pollen tube growth. Highlight the fact that other conditions, e.g. temperature, (not shown here) may affect tube growth.

**Badger Key Stage 3 Science Starters**

# What are the best conditions for growing pollen tubes?

Peter investigated the effect of different sugar concentrations on the germination of Lily pollen grains.

Pollen grains grow down a stigma and style like this:

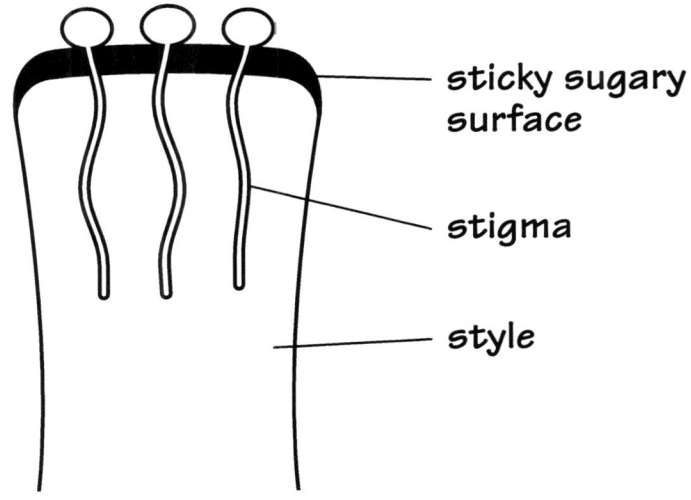

sticky sugary surface

stigma

style

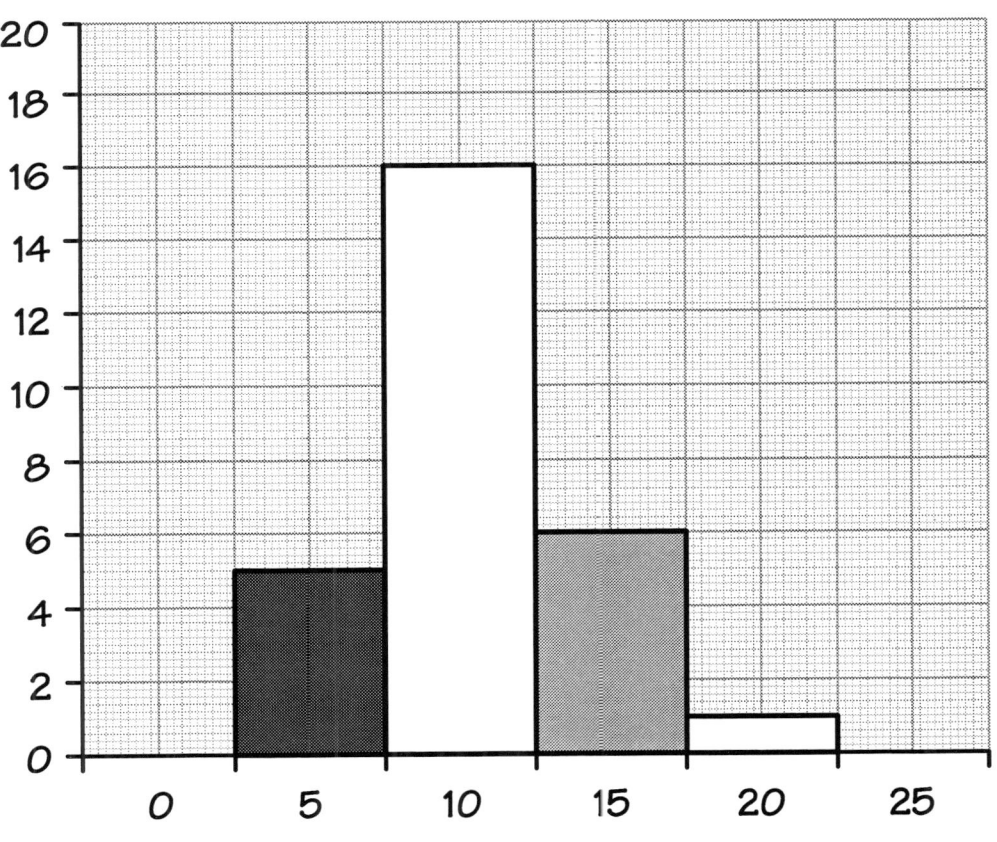

Percentage concentration of sugar

# Let's compare internal and external fertilisation

**Objective:**

To compare the features of internal and external fertilisation.

**Teaching point:**

The activity will allow pupils to classify features of organisms which reproduce by internal and external fertilisation. Additionally, four commonly known organisms can be classified as internally or externally fertilised.

**What you will need:**
Copymaster 17 statement cards. Pupils to work in groups.

**Time:**
10 minutes

**Activity:**

Cut out cards prior to lesson. Give Copymaster cards to each pupil.

Explain that internal fertilisation gives more protection to sperms and eggs.

Groups to put internal and external fertilisation as headings. Ask them to classify each statement or organism card.

**Answers**

**Internal fertilisation**

The eggs are produced in small numbers.

This method is usually used by land animals (water is not available for sperms to swim).

This method has a better chance of the offspring surviving due to improved protection.

Human, butterfly, horse.

**External fertilisation**

The eggs are produced in very large numbers.

Used by fish because water is available for sperms to swim in.

Sperms can get eaten by aquatic predators.

Fish, frog.

**Challenge:** Ask pupils to explain the success of humans rearing offspring even though they usually produce one baby at a time.

**Links to plenary:** Outline the features of both methods, leading to the advantages of internal fertilisation.

**Badger Key Stage 3 Science Starters**

# Let's compare internal and external fertilisation

| Internal fertilisation | External fertilisation |
|---|---|
| The eggs are produced in very large numbers. | The eggs are produced in small numbers. |
| This method is usually used by land animals (water is not available for sperms to swim). | Used by fish because water is available for sperms to swim in. |
| This method has a better chance of the offspring surviving due to improved protection. | Sperms can get eaten by aquatic predators. |

**human**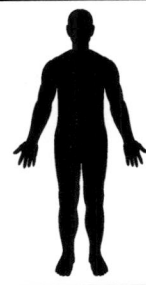

**fish**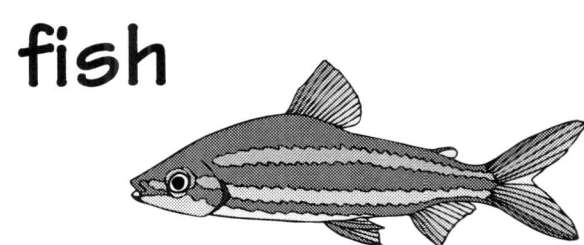

**frog**

**horse**

**butterfly**

# Identical or non-identical twins

### Objective:

To recognise how identical and non-identical twins are formed.

### Teaching point:

The sequences show fertilisation then initial development of the twins. Pupils can stick the completed worksheet into their books.

**What you will need:**
Copymaster 18 as OHT.
Whiteboards and pens.
Pupils to work in pairs.

**Time:**
5 minutes

### Activity:

Project Copymaster OHT. Ensure diagrams of twins are covered up.

Give this question, "The 2 sequences show how identical and non-identical twins are formed but can you tell which is which?"

The pupils to write down which is which on whiteboards. Reveal rest of OHT with answers.

After the exercise explain how some women ovulate twice in a month and this can lead to non-identical twins.

After ONE sperm has fertilised ONE egg the resulting ball of cells sometimes splits to form 2 identical twins.

**Challenge:** Ask pupils to consider the effect fertility drugs may have on the number of babies a woman may produce at one time.

**Links to plenary:** Outline both methods and clarify each stage.

**Badger Key Stage 3 Science Starters**

# Identical or non-identical twins

The 2 sequences show how identical and non-identical twins are formed but can you tell which is which?

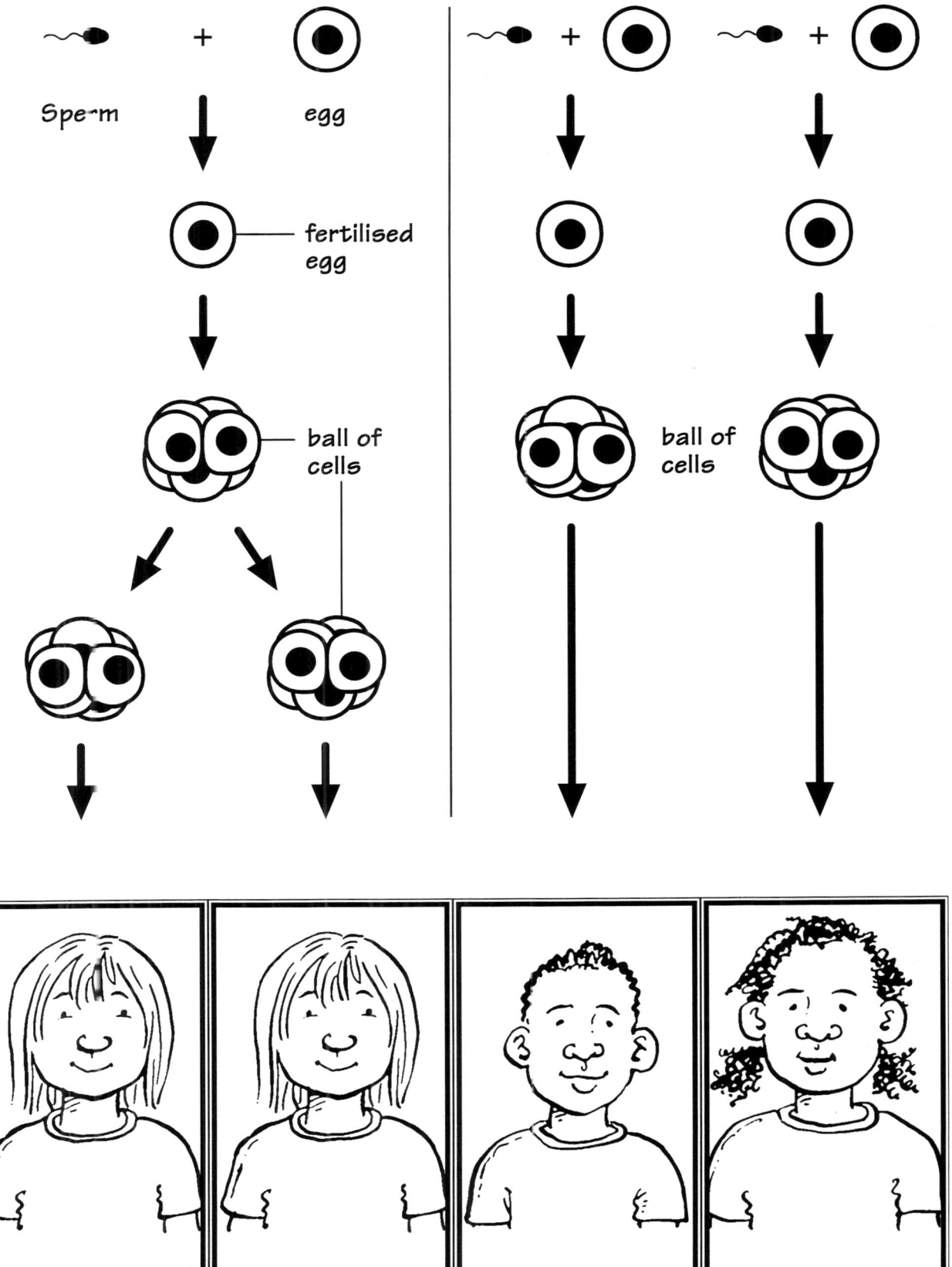

# Menstrual cycle

**Objective:**

To understand the main events of the menstrual cycle.

**Teaching point:**

The pupils will analyse the calendar showing both months. The pattern of menstruation and ovulation is not repeated during the second month. The pupils will be able to discuss the reasons for the differences.

**What you will need:**
Copymaster 19 as worksheets. Pupils to work individually.

**Time:**
10 minutes

**Activity:**

Give out a copymaster worksheet to each pupil.

Ask class to analyse the calendars and

- tick the calendar to show when menstruation takes place.

- circle when ovulation takes place.

Ask why the second month is different.

After discussion, share the fact that no ovulation or menstruation takes place when the woman becomes pregnant. On the second month she *is* pregnant!

Ask why it is important that both processes do not take place during pregnancy.

It is a good opportunity to make sure that pupils know menstruation is the monthly loss of the lining of the uterus, whereas ovulation is the production of an egg.

**Challenge:** If a sperm lives in a woman for up to 3 days, when could the woman have become pregnant.

**Links to plenary:** Clarify the differences between ovulation and menstruation to avoid confusion.

**Badger Key Stage 3 Science Starters**

# Menstrual cycle

## May

| M | T | W | T | F | S | S |
|---|---|---|---|---|---|---|
| 1 | 2 | 3 | 4 | 5 | 6 | 7 |
| 8 | 9 | 10 | 11 | 12 | 13 | 14 |
| 15 | 16 | 17 | 18 | 19 | 20 | 21 |
| 22 | 23 | 24 | 25 | 26 | 27 | 28 |
| 29 | 30 | 31 | | | | |

## June

| M | T | W | T | F | S | S |
|---|---|---|---|---|---|---|
| | | | 1 | 2 | 3 | 4 |
| 5 | 6 | 7 | 8 | 9 | 10 | 11 |
| 12 | 13 | 14 | 15 | 16 | 17 | 18 |
| 19 | 20 | 21 | 22 | 23 | 24 | 25 |
| 26 | 27 | 28 | 29 | 30 | | |

# Development 1 ~ the foetus in the uterus

### Objective:

To be able to identify key structures inside the uterus of a pregnant woman.

### Teaching point:

Pupils need to label the key structures in the uterus and their functions.

### What you will need:
Copymaster 20a as worksheets. Pupils to work in pairs.

### Time:
5 minutes

### Activity:

Give out a Copymaster worksheet to each pupil, preferably with label cards cut out in advance.

Ask pupils to correctly label the parts with the cards provided.

Inform of the correct answers. Copymaster 20b OHT is provided for this.

Once the parts are labelled correctly, highlight the functions of each part:

- amniotic membrane holds in the amniotic fluid
- amniotic fluid protects the foetus from bumps
- placenta is full of blood capillaries and helps pass substances to and from the foetus
- umbilical cord passes substances in and out of the foetus
- uterus wall is muscular, and will push out the baby at birth.

**Challenge:** Ask pupils to write down the functions of the labelled parts.

**Links to plenary:** Revisit the position of all parts. Stress the amniotic membrane which produces and holds the fluid and the amniotic fluid.

# Development 1 ~ the foetus in the uterus

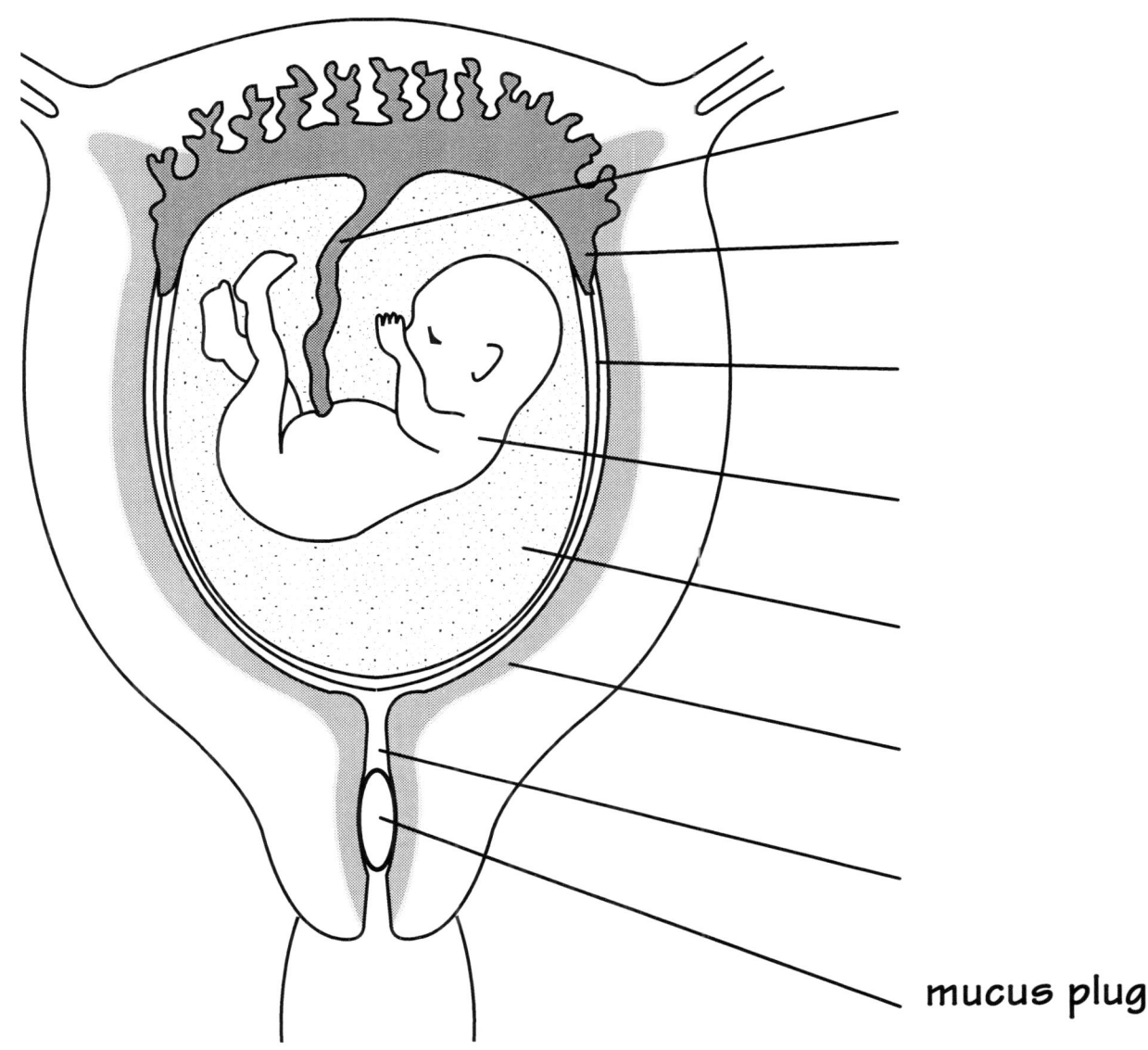

mucus plug

## List

| | |
|---|---|
| amniotic membrane | amniotic fluid |
| cervix | foetus |
| placenta | uterus wall |
| umbilical cord | |

# Development 1 ~ the foetus in the uterus

## Answers:

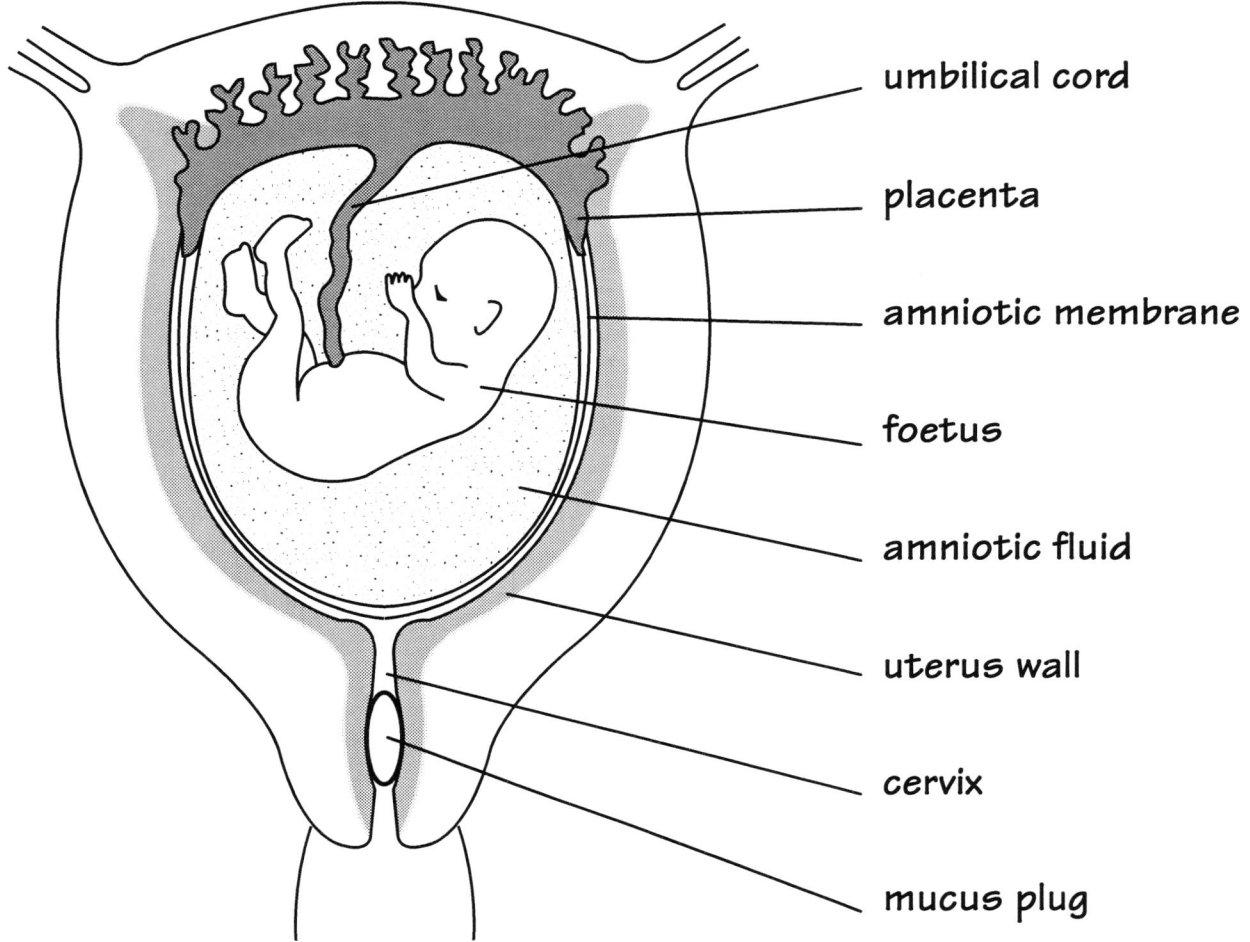

- umbilical cord
- placenta
- amniotic membrane
- foetus
- amniotic fluid
- uterus wall
- cervix
- mucus plug

# Substances across the placenta: which direction?

### Objective:

To be aware of certain useful substances which pass from mother's blood to foetal blood and waste substances which pass from the foetal blood to mother's blood.

### Teaching point:

To be aware of certain substances which cross the placenta.

**What you will need:**
Copymaster 21 as OHT.
Whole class activity.

**Time:**
8 minutes

### Activity:

Project OHT Copymaster.

Explain the task is to put each substance into the correct box.

As each suggestion is volunteered by pupils orally add the correct answers to the OHT. Question further to find out if pupils know the reason for each answer.

**Factfile**

| Mother's blood | Placenta | Foetal blood |
|---|---|---|
| Oxygen | ➡ | used for respiration of foetus |
| Calcium | ➡ | used for bones |
| Water | ➡ | used to help foetus develop / blood to flow |
| Glucose (sugar) | ⬅ | used for respiration of foetus |
| Carbon dioxide | ⬅ | waste made by foetus |
| Urea | ⬅ | waste made by foetus |

**Challenge:** Ask pupils to explain some harmful substances which can pass into the foetus from the mother, such as nicotine and drugs, and their effects (nicotine – e.g. underweight baby, drugs – e.g. addiction in baby).

**Links to plenary:** Revisit each substance in the list, outline importance. Add to list with other substances.

**Badger Key Stage 3 Science Starters**

## Substances across the placenta: which direction?

| Mother's blood | Placenta | Foetal blood |
|---|:---:|---|
|  | → |  |
|  | → |  |
|  | → |  |
|  | ← |  |
|  | ← |  |
|  | ← |  |

## List

Carbon dioxide     Oxygen

Glucose (sugar)     Calcium

Water     Urea

**Badger Key Stage 3 Science Starters**

# The needs of a premature baby: design an incubator

### Objective:

To be aware of the needs of a premature born baby.

### Teaching point:

Babies have certain needs once born. This exercise focuses on those needs. Pupils creatively supply those needs in their incubator design.

### What you will need:

No other resource. Pupils to work individually.

### Time:
12 minutes

### Activity:

Outline the following information:

- A foetus was warm inside of the uterus at 37°C and, born prematurely, may have difficulty in maintaining its temperature.
- A premature baby may have problems breathing.
- It may have difficulty fighting against harmful microbes.
- It needs nutrients.

Ask the pupils to draw a labelled diagram of an incubator to satisfy all of its needs. They should draw the baby in a comfortable position.

Allow the pupils to share designs with each other.

Effective designs will include:

- heater
- thermometer
- thermostat
- air pump / higher oxygen concentration
- air filter
- sterile conditions
- nutrients / named nutrients

**Challenge:** Pupils could research on the Internet the additional problem of jaundice (light treatment in incubator).

**Links to plenary:** Compare the needs of a foetus in the uterus and a premature baby.

**Badger Key Stage 3 Science Starters**

# The birth of a baby

### Objective:

To understand the events that take place during the birth of a baby.

### Teaching point:

The pupils need to know the sequence of events which take place during birth.

**What you will need:**
Copymaster 23 as OHT.
Whiteboards and pens.
Pupils to work in pairs.

**Time:**
5 minutes

### Activity:

Project the Copymaster OHT.

Explain that the statements give the events which take place during birth but they are in the wrong order.

Ask pupils to write the letters for the birth sequence on their whiteboards.

The process is as follows:

> The amniotic fluid bursts out through the cervix.
>
> Contractions begin.
>
> The cervix muscles relax so the cervix gets wider.
>
> The head of the foetus normally moves to the down position.
>
> The contractions become more intense and take place more often.
>
> The baby is pushed out head first.
>
> The placenta or afterbirth is pushed out.

Answer - G C D F A B E.

Note: sometimes the contractions begin before the fluid escapes.

**Challenge:** Ask pupils to research what methods are used if birth cannot take place by natural methods.

**Links to plenary:** Revisit the correct sequence. Ask what happens immediately after birth.

**Badger Key Stage 3 Science Starters**

# The birth of a baby

A - The contractions become more intense and take place more often.

B - The baby is pushed out head first.

C - The amniotic fluid bursts out through the cervix.

D - Contractions begin.

E - The placenta or afterbirth is pushed out.

F - The cervix muscles relax so the cervix gets wider.

G - The head of the foetus normally moves to the down position.

# Stages of human growth

### Objective:

To be aware of the different rates of growth in boys and girls at different stages.

### Teaching point:

By showing graphs of boys and girls, the similarites and differences in growth patterns are shown. By answering the questions the pupils will identify the patterns.

**What you will need:**
Copymaster 24 as worksheets. Pupils to work in individually.

**Time:**
8 minutes

### Activity:

Give out a Copymaster worksheet to each pupil.

Explain that they need to analyse the graphs.

Ask the pupils to answer the questions. Give the following answers:

1. 0-2 years

2. (a) girls
   (b) 12 years

3. adolescence / puberty

4. males

Stress the fact that greatest growth takes place right after birth, and that puberty is associated with a number of changes.

**Challenge:** Ask pupils to list the other changes which take place in boys and girls during puberty.

**Links to plenary:** Clarify that both sexes have a similar pattern of growth but that girls on average commence puberty much earlier than boys.

**Badger Key Stage 3 Science Starters**

# Stages of human growth

Graphs showing the height of males and females at different stages

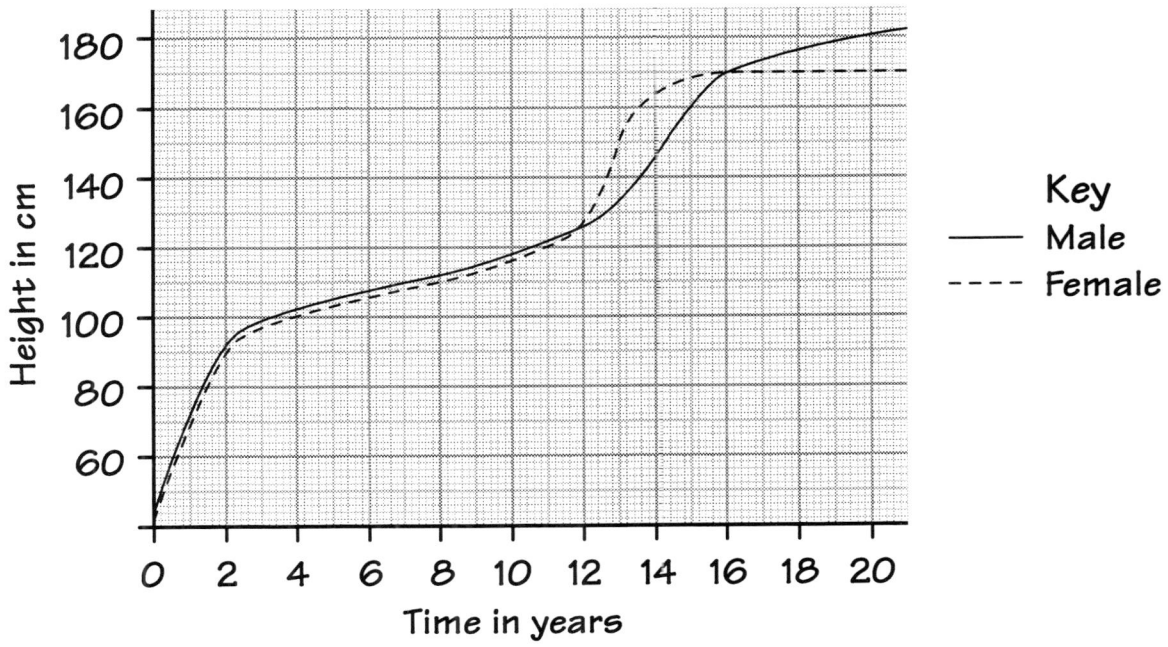

1. During which years is the rate of growth per year the greatest?

   . . . . . . . . . . . . . . . . . . . . . . . . . . . . . . . . . . . . . . . . . . . .

2. (a) Do boys or girls have a growth spurt first?

   . . . . . . . . . . . . . . . . . . . . . . . . . . . . . . . . . . . . . . . . . . . .

   (b) In which year does this take place?

   . . . . . . . . . . . . . . . . . . . . . . . . . . . . . . . . . . . . . . . . . . . .

3. What name is given to the period when major growth changes take place in boys and girls?

   . . . . . . . . . . . . . . . . . . . . . . . . . . . . . . . . . . . . . . . . . . . .

4. Which sex is, on average, bigger when maturity is reached?

   . . . . . . . . . . . . . . . . . . . . . . . . . . . . . . . . . . . . . . . . . . . .

# Changes

**Objective:**

To be aware of the changes which take place during puberty, and the common and different changes in males and females.

**What you will need:**
Copymaster 25 as worksheets. Pupils to work in individually.

**Time:**
12 minutes

**Teaching point:**

The given list of secondary sexual characteristics and associated changes to be classified into male, female, and shared changes.

**Activity:**

Give out a Copymaster worksheet to each pupil.

Explain that the statements give the changes which take place during puberty or adolescence.

The task is to put each of the items from the list into one of the 3 columns.

**Answers**

| Male | Female | Both |
|------|--------|------|
| Voice breaks | Breasts become bigger | Growth spurt |
| Increased facial hair | Hips widen | Pubic hair develops |
| Shoulders widen | Ovulation begins | Changes in hormone concentration |
| Sperm production | Menstruation begins | Changes in feelings |

Outline the reasons for selected changes. Inform of the role of hormones in *causing* the changes.

**Challenge:** Ask pupils to research important male and female hormones, i.e. testosterone, oestrogen.

**Links to plenary:** Discuss importance of the changes as teenagers become mature adults.

# Changes

| Male | Female | Both |
|------|--------|------|
|      |        |      |

Voice breaks    Breasts become bigger

Growth spurt    Pubic hair develops

Hips widen    Sperm production

Changes in hormone concentration

Changes in feelings    Ovulation begins

Shoulders widen    Menstruation begins

Increased facial hair

# Human life cycle: ages and stages

## Objective:

To be aware of the different proportions of humans through their life.

## Teaching point:

The activity will enable groups to put diagrams in the correct order to show changes in proportion through a person's life.

**What you will need:**
Copymaster 26a as worksheets. Pupils to work in groups.

**Time:**
10 minutes

## Activity:

Give out a Copymaster worksheet to each group. (As an option you can cut out the diagrams before the lesson.)

Tell the class that the diagrams each show a different stage in a person's life. The diagrams do not show the true size but they do show correct proportions.

On a sheet of paper the groups should draw a timeline as follows:

| 2 months | 4 months | newborn baby | 3 years | 12 years |
|----------|----------|--------------|---------|----------|
| foetus   | foetus   |              |         |          |

Ask groups to cut out each diagram and put it above the correct stage.

You may wish to give a clue that the growth of the head is a key factor and that they can look at each other. After all they are 12 year olds!

Discuss stages. Copymaster 26b OHT provided to project answers.

**Challenge:** The head develops more rapidly; pupils to consider the advantages of this.

**Links to plenary:** After the baby is born no more nerve cells are formed. Refer to this fact in relation to the reduced head proportion after birth to maturity.

**Badger Key Stage 3 Science Starters**

# Human life cycle: ages and stages

## Cut out each diagram.

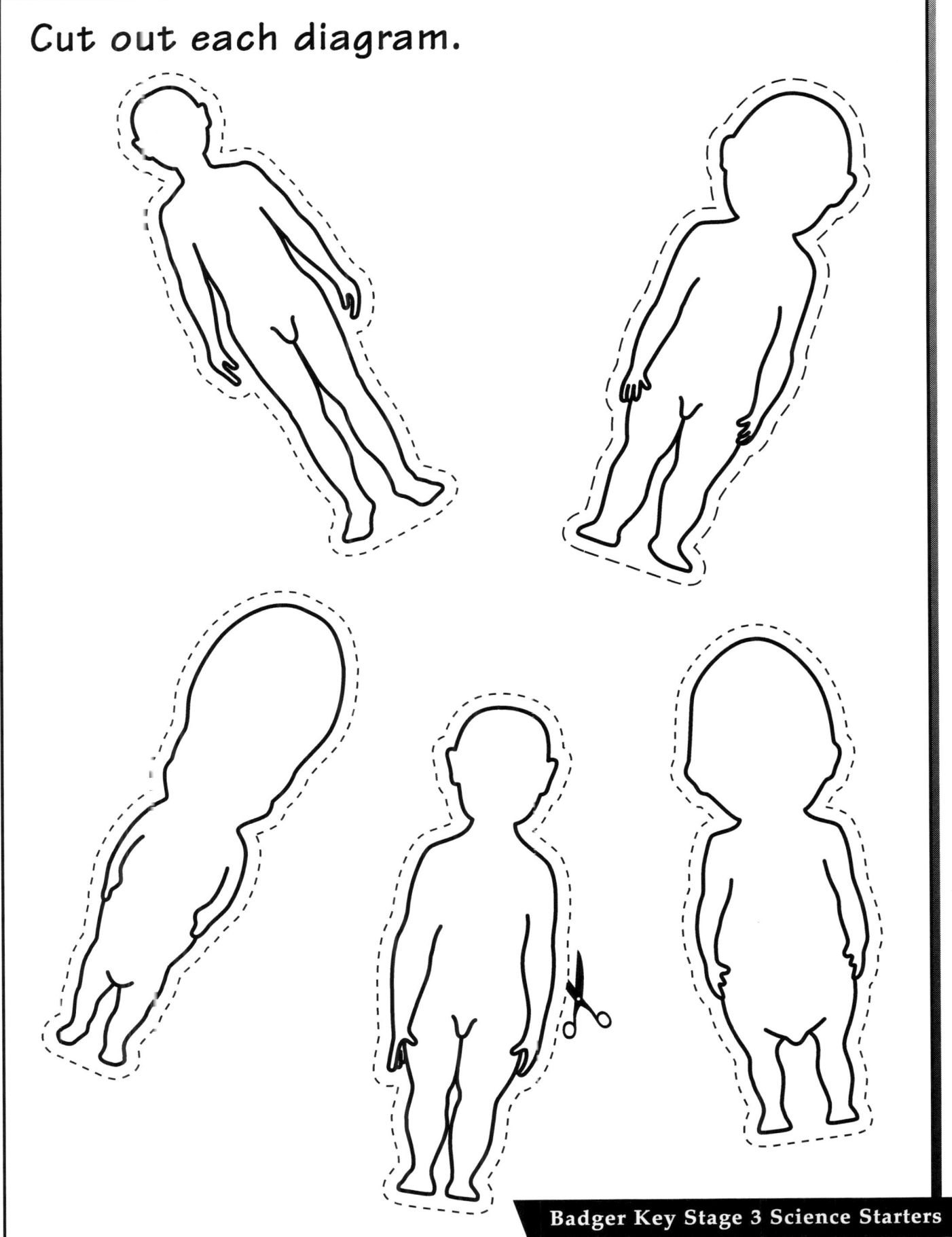

# Human life cycle: ages and stages

Answers:

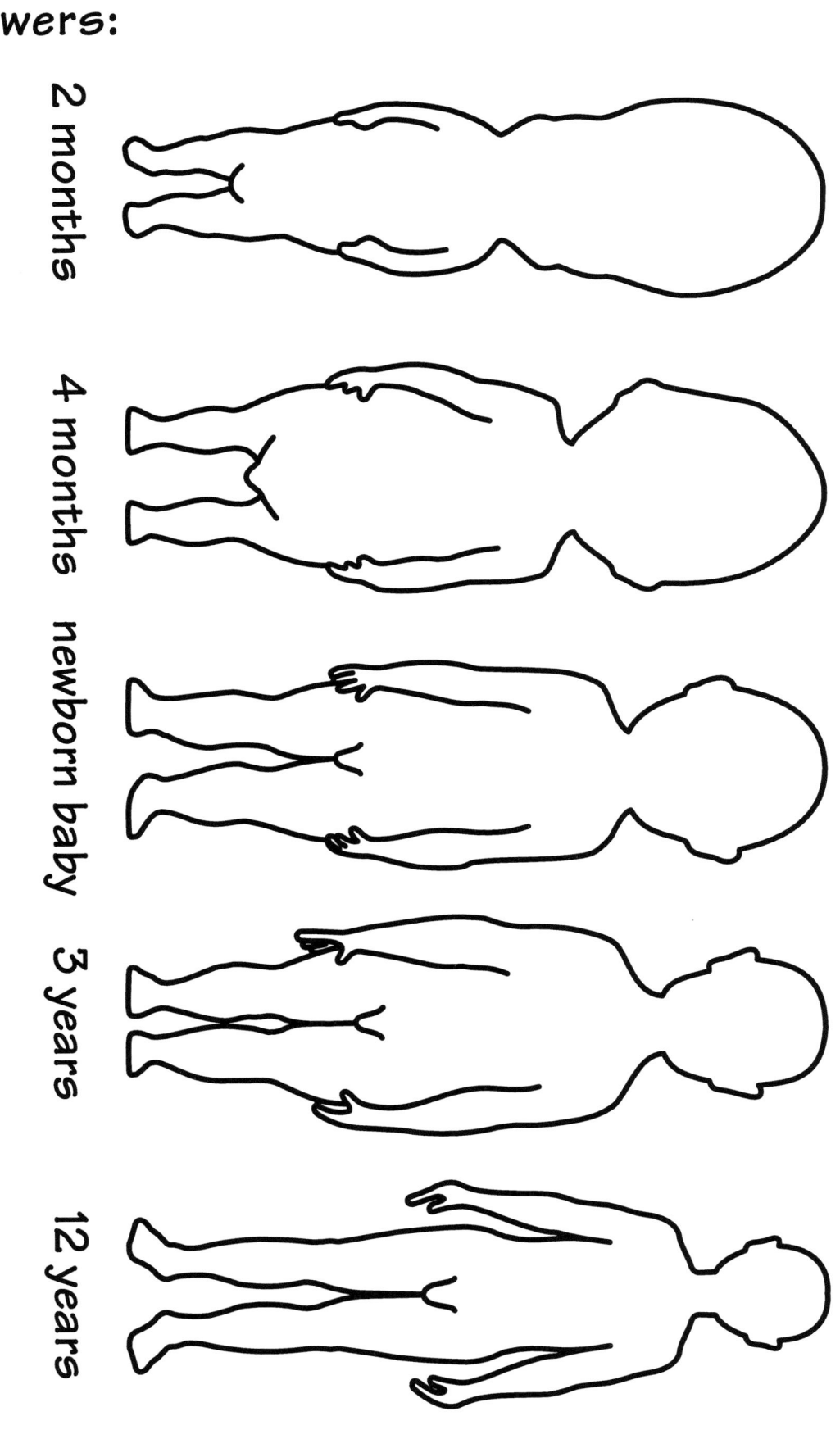

2 months

4 months

newborn baby

3 years

12 years

☞ **KEY POINT**

# Different habitats ~ different environmental factors

**Objective:**

To understand that different habitats have different environmental factors.

**What you will need:**
Copymaster 27 as worksheets. Pupils to work in groups.

**Time:**
10 minutes

**Teaching point:**

The Copymaster cards show a woodland scene and pond scene. Some groups will analyse the woodland scene and the rest will analyse the pond scene. The aim being to note all of the key environmental factors which affect the organisms of each habitat.

**Activity:**

Give out a Copymaster worksheet to each group.

Ask the groups to analyse the scene, then list all important factors in the environment which affects what lives in the habitat.

Ask groups to consider why each factor is important when considering the organisms that live in the habitat.

Groups report back orally to indicate the factors.

Possible factors they may suggest:

| **Woodland** | **Pond** |
|---|---|
| temperature of air and soil | temperature of water |
| pH of soil | pH of water |
| light | light |
| rain | depth of water |
| protection / shade | clarity / muddiness of water |
| other animals and plants which live there affect what lives there | other animals and plants which live there affect what lives there |
| | shade |

Discuss the similarities and differences between both habitats.

**Challenge:** Describe ways in which each factor could be measured.

**Links to plenary:** Discuss the fact that organisms which live in an area are **adapted** to the conditions.

**Badger Key Stage 3 Science Starters**

# Different habitats ~ different environmental factors

## Woodland

## Pond

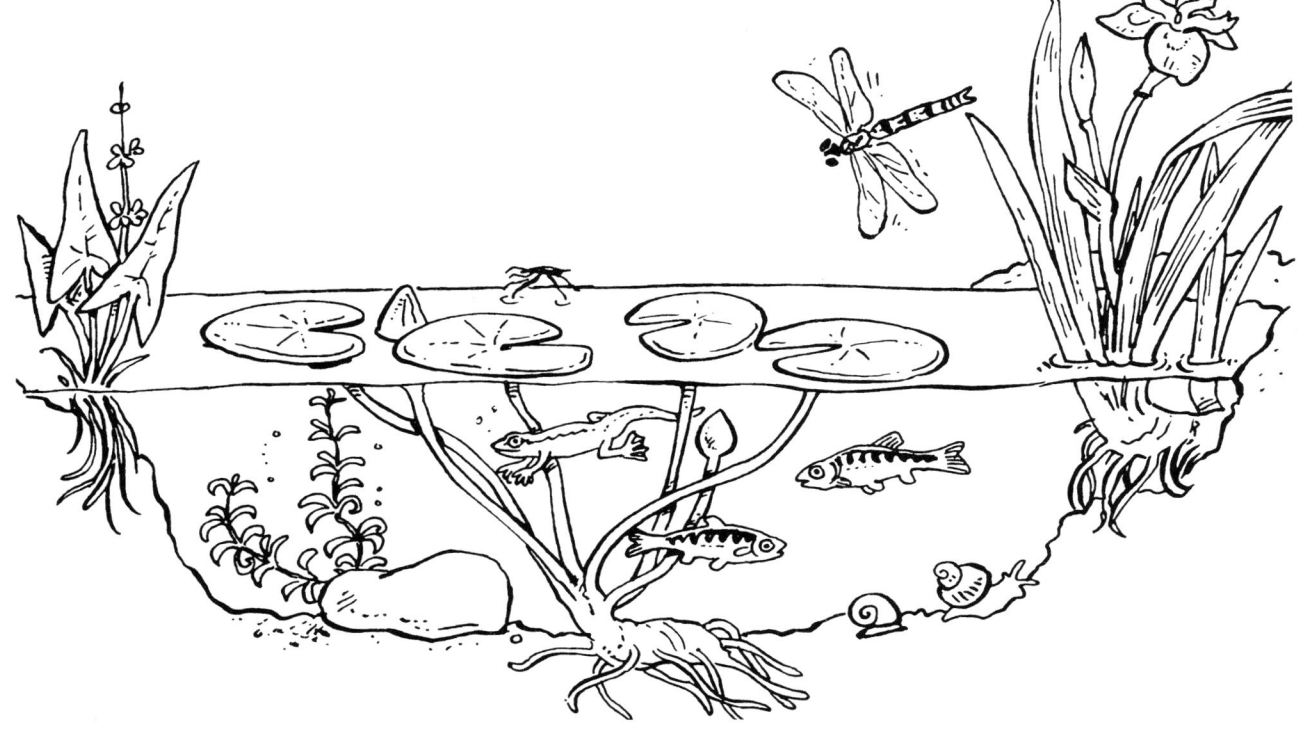

☞ KEY POINT

# How do changes in the environment affect organisms?

**Objective:**

To know that some organisms have adapted to daily changes in the environment.

**Teaching point:**

Pupils need to be aware of daily changes in behaviour of organisms in response to environmental changes.

**What you will need:**
Copymaster 28 as OHT.
Whole class activity.

**Time:**
10 minutes

**Activity:**

Project Copymaster OHT.

Outline the scenario about the organism and its environment.

- It is a small mammal which feeds on desert plant stems.
- It lives in a hot desert.
- It was monitored for presence in a burrow or outside in the environment.
- The data was sent electronically.
- The outside temperature was also measured.

Explain that the aim is to build a profile of the animal's behaviour and reasons for its behaviour at different times of the day.

Question pupils orally:

When was the mammal in its burrow? *(6am – 10pm)*

Suggest why remaining in the burrow can be an advantage. *(Avoid predators, too hot outside, too hot for its enzymes.)*

How many times did it go outside? *(5)*

Suggest reasons for it being outside the burrow. *(Feeding, mating, getting rid of waste.)*

Why should it be outside at night, rather than the day?
*(Cooler, less predators, less likely to be seen.)*

**Challenge:** The temperature was only taken once each hour. Can pupils suggest a better method of measuring temperature change throughout a day?

**Links to plenary:** Discuss this daily change and refer to seasonal changes.

**Badger Key Stage 3 Science Starters**

# How do changes in the environment affect organisms?

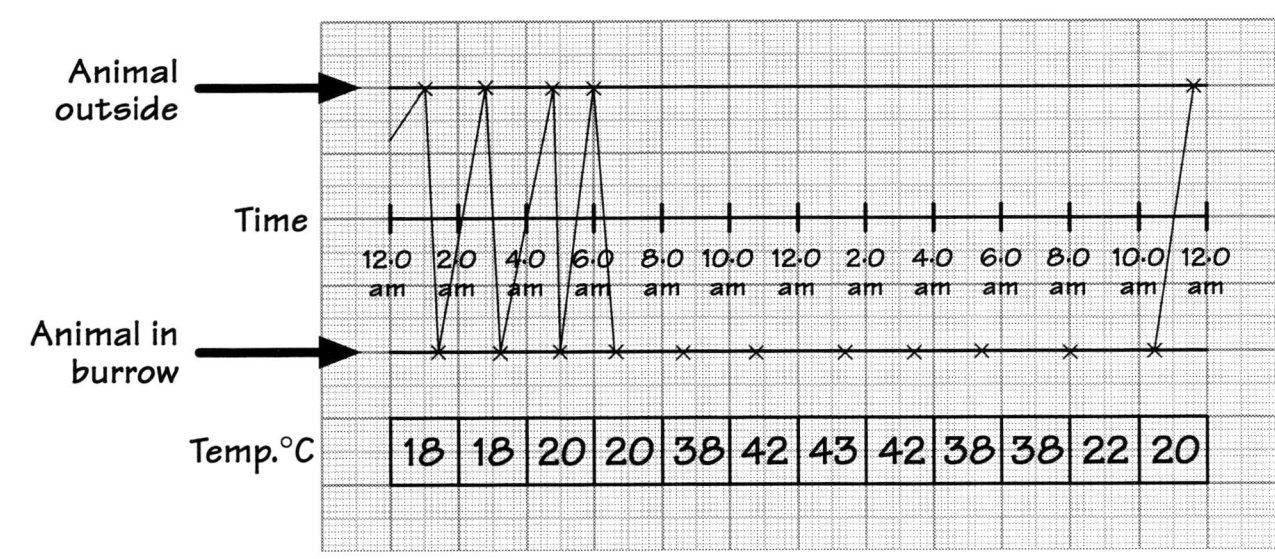

Animal outside →

Time

| | 12.0 am | 2.0 am | 4.0 am | 6.0 am | 8.0 am | 10.0 am | 12.0 am | 2.0 am | 4.0 am | 6.0 am | 8.0 am | 10.0 am | 12.0 am |

Animal in burrow →

| Temp.°C | 18 | 18 | 20 | 20 | 38 | 42 | 43 | 42 | 38 | 38 | 22 | 20 |

# Measurement and recording of environmental factors

### Objective:

To be aware of uses of environmental probes and data logging techniques.

### Teaching point:

The pupils may be aware of a range of different methods of measuring environmental factors. Additionally they need to know that the same factor, e.g. light, may vary through the environment.

**What you will need:**
Copymaster 29 as OHT.
Whole class activity.

**Time:**
5 minutes

### Activity:

Project Copymaster OHT.

Explain that the diagram shows sensors / probes measuring light levels in a pond.

Ask:

Why are light probes used at different depths?
*(Different levels may receive different amounts of light.)*

Why is light important to pond organisms?
*(Photosynthesis needs light so less light means less food for animals.)*

Pupils to answer orally.

Remind pupils that factors vary through each day, and through the seasons, and that there are many other factors which could be measured.

**Challenge:** List other factors which could be measured by environmental probes.

**Links to plenary:** Discuss importance of measuring the same factor at different parts of a habitat as well as across days, weeks, seasons.

**Badger Key Stage 3 Science Starters**

# Measurement and recording of environmental factors

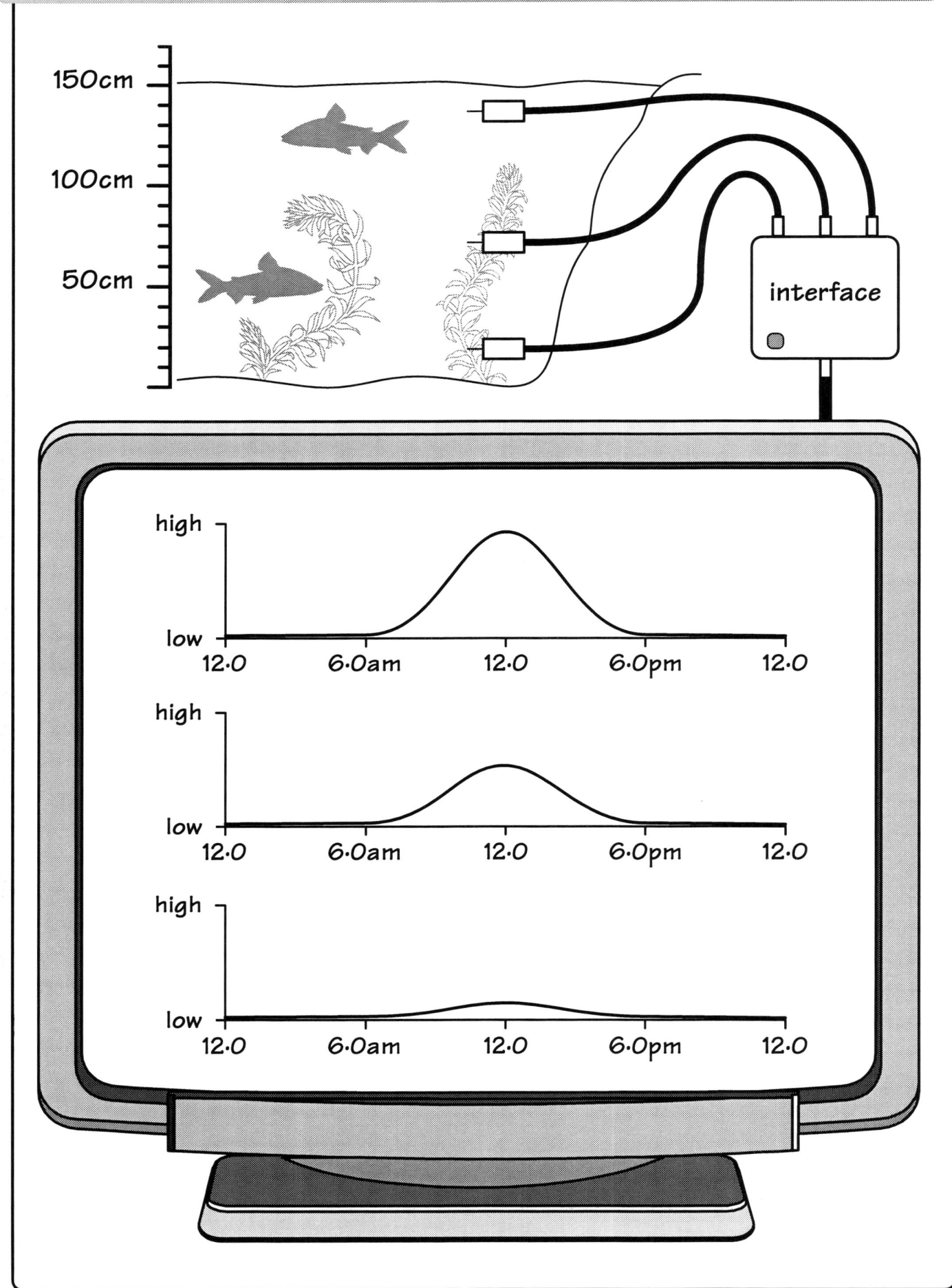

☞ **KEY POINT**

# Adaptations

## Objective:

To be able to make accurate observations of organisms and determine adaptations which help an organism to fit into its habitat.

## Teaching point:

Activity is centred on observation and analysis on the profile of organisms.

**What you will need:**
Copymaster 30 as worksheets. Whiteboards and pens. Pupils to work in groups.

**Time:**
10 minutes

## Activity:

Give out a Copymaster worksheet to each group.

Explain the following information to the class.

- Caddis-fly larvae live in water.

- The caddis-fly larvae in this activity make tubes to live in.

- They make the tubes from materials they find in their environment and stick it together with silk.

- Each species of caddis-fly makes tubes out of specific materials.

Ask the groups to analyse the diagrams and features, then to write a list of all the important factors in the environment which affect what lives in the habitat, on their whiteboards.

Ask them to work out which one lives in a pond and which lives in a fast moving stream. They should give evidence for their choice.

Species 1  makes a green tube to live in to be good camouflage and protection from predators.

Species 2  makes a pebble tube to give good camouflage from predators, on stream bottom. This also anchors it to the bottom to prevent it being moved away with the current.

**Challenge:** Ask pupils: if species 2 was put into water with pebbles and plant material, what would it look like? (It would look just the same! It would make a pebble tube and ignore the plant material.)

**Links to plenary:** Discuss importance of making good observations and relating them to function.

**Badger Key Stage 3 Science Starters**

# Adaptations

## Caddis-fly larvae

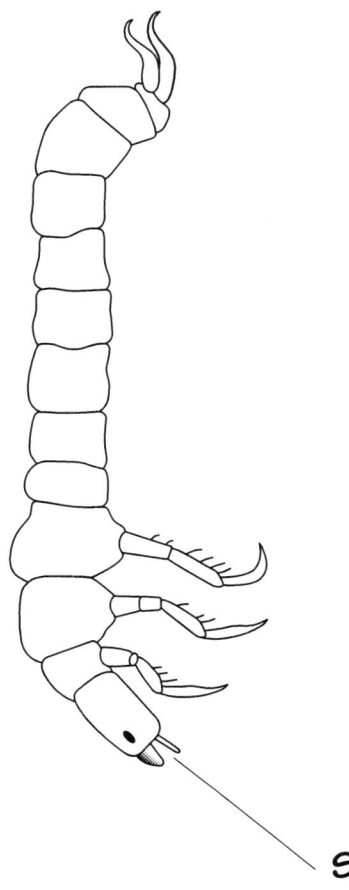
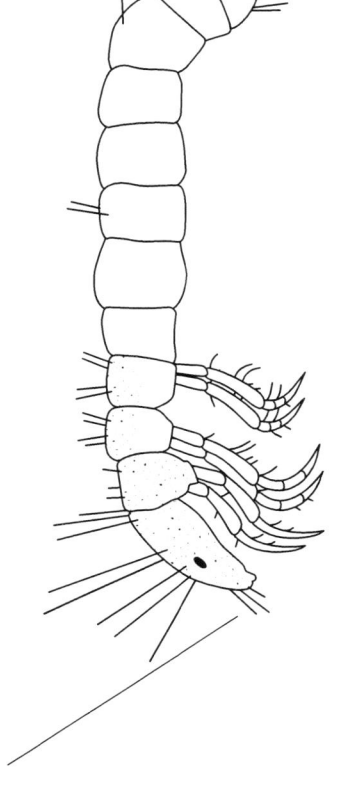

Silk producing glands

| Caddis-fly species 1 |
| --- |
| Features |
| eats plants |
| produces silk |
| picks up plant material |

| Caddis-fly species 2 |
| --- |
| Features |
| eats insects |
| produces silk |
| picks up tiny pebbles |

☞ KEY POINT

# The seasons in Bluebell Wood

### Objective:

To understand that some plants are adapted to seasonal change in their habitat.

### Teaching point:

Seasonally, there are different conditions in a deciduous woodland. The activity will help the pupils to know the sequence of events throughout the year.

**What you will need:**
Copymaster 31 as statement cards. Pupils to work in groups.

**Time:**
10 minutes

### Activity:

Give out Copymaster statement cards in random order.

Explain that the activity is to classify the statements into each of the 4 seasons beginning with winter. Ask pupils to write the correct season next to each statment.

Question the groups.

Correct classification:

**Winter**
> The trees are bare and light can stream to the ground level.
> It is really cold.
> It is too cold for most plants to grow.

**Spring**
> The temperature begins to increase and the bluebells begin to grow.
> They produce leaves, flowers, then seeds.

**Summer**
> The leaves of the tree canopy begin to grow, cutting out light to the plants below.
> The bluebells spread their seeds then die down, leaving bulbs under the soil.

**Autumn**
> The leaves on the trees gradually die then fall off the trees.
> The leaves begin to rot down, releasing fertiliser into the soil.

Link the growth of the bluebells to light availability plus suitable temperature (Spring). Once the canopy has formed then there is no photosynthesis of plants below (Summer).

**Challenge:** Ask pupils to explain what may happen in a coniferous forest where leaves are not shed in Autumn.

**Links to plenary:** Revisit the sequence and reasons.

**Badger Key Stage 3 Science Starters**

# The seasons in Bluebell Wood

The trees are bare and light can reach ground level.

It is really cold.

The leaves on the trees gradually die then fall off the trees.

The leaves begin to rot down, releasing fertiliser into the soil.

It is too cold for most plants to grow.

The temperature begins to increase and the bluebells begin to grow.

They produce leaves, flowers, then seeds.

The leaves of the tree canopy begin to grow, cutting out light to the plants below.

The bluebells spread their seeds then die down, leaving bulbs under the soil.

# Avoiding the cold

### Objective:

To recognise a number of different ways which organisms overwinter, before warmer conditions return.

### What you will need:

No other resource. Pupils work individually.

**Time:**
5 - 10 minutes

### Teaching point:

A passage is be read out which includes a number of ways of avoiding the effects of cold weather.

### Activity:

Explain that a passage will be read out during which pupils do not write.

After reading the passage, ask the pupils to bullet point the main ways of avoiding or surviving the cold season, and reasons for the behaviour.

Read this passage:

Cold weather is a problem to many plants and animals. In the UK animals which feed on insects alone may die if they stayed. For this reason, **swallows** leave and fly to South Africa where it is warmer.
Adult **butterflies** could not survive through the winter. Their life cycle includes pupae which need no food and can survive low temperatures.
**Fat hen** is a weed. Frost kills the plants but the species can overwinter as a seed. The seeds survive freezing conditions and only germinate in warm conditions.
**Bears** have an excellent technique of surviving winter. They build up a fat store in their bodies before hibernating.

You should re-read each paragraph to highlight the organisms individually. Then ask pupils to write down the main points for each organism:

**swallows**        **butterflies**        **fat hen**        **bears**

**Challenge:** Some plants need the cold. Holly seeds will not germinate unless they have been subjected to cold. Investigate with fresh berries and a freezer!

**Links to plenary:** Discuss the main points of overwintering techniques. Compare with organisms which can survive actively, e.g. Holly can photosynthesize in winter!

**Badger Key Stage 3 Science Starters**

# Investigating soil organisms

**Objective:**

To understand how the motile organisms in soil samples can be counted.

**Teaching point:**

By supplying a diagram of the Tullgren funnel, pupils can work out how the animals are forced from soil samples and how the soil may be suitably sampled.

**What you will need:**
Copymaster 33 as OHT.
Whole class activity.

**Time:**
10 minutes

**Activity:**

Project Copymaster OHT.

Explain that the method is used to compare organisms such as insects in soil samples.

Ask pupils:

How does the method work?
*(Heat and light force out the motile (moving) organisms. Only those small enough to pass through the grid reach the collection beaker. Water traps the insects.)*

How would you make sure that taking soil samples was done with fair test principles?
*(Same size of soil sample, at the same time.)*

What effect may taking soil from different depths have?
*(Different results at different depths likely.)*

**Challenge:** Millions of bacteria are found in all soil. Can pupils describe an appropriate method to investigate them.

**Links to plenary:** Remind pupils that the method is effective for some insects but other large ones are excluded as they cannot pass through the grid. Some insects may die due to desiccation.

**Badger Key Stage 3 Science Starters**

# Investigating soil organisms

## The Tullgren funnel

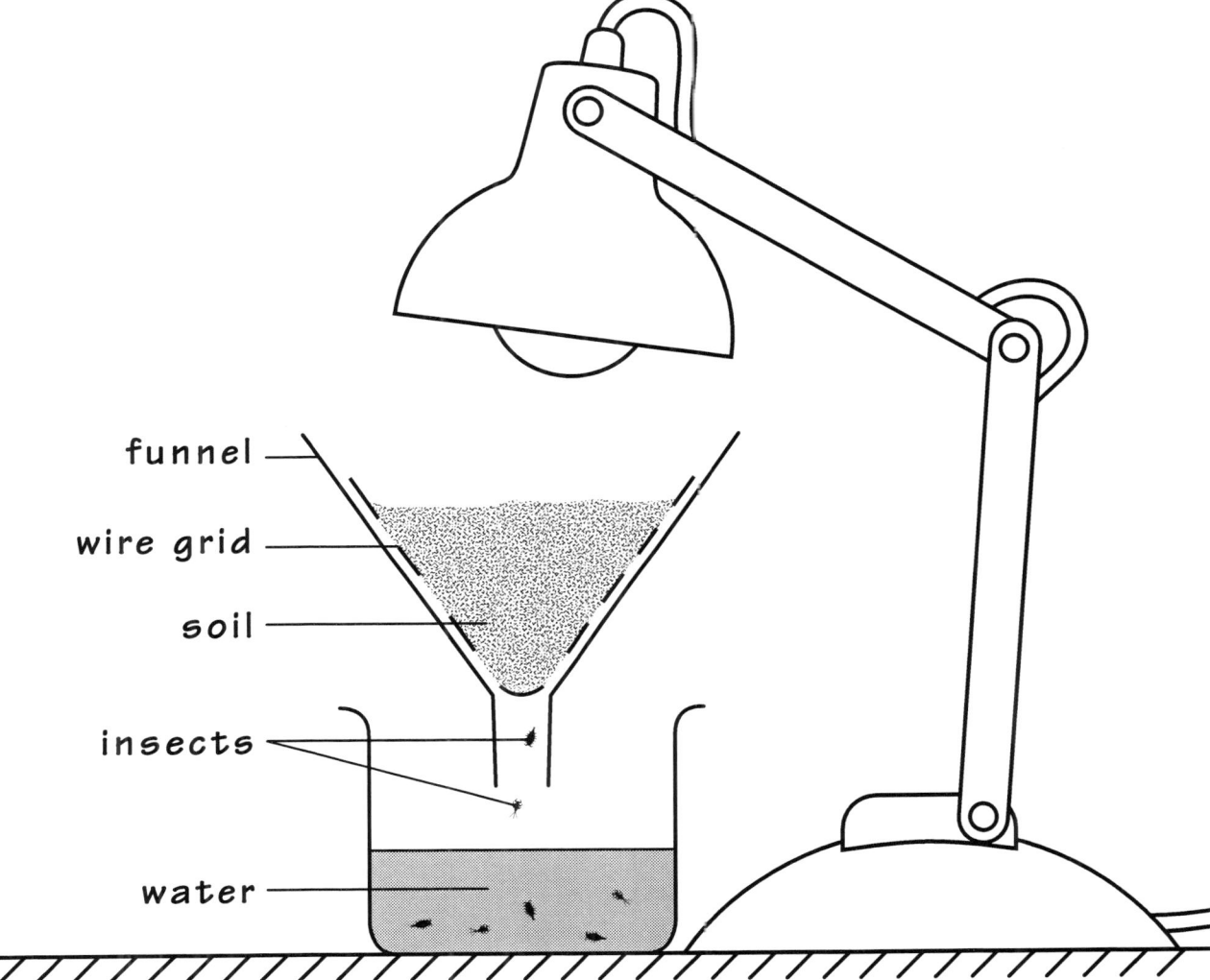

funnel

wire grid

soil

insects

water

☞ KEY POINT

# Adaptations: predator or prey? (1)

## Objective:

To recognise features in prey which are adaptations against predators; recognise features in predators that are adaptations to their food source.

## Teaching point:

The activity will enable pupils to construct a table of general features of both predators and their prey.

**What you will need:**
Copymaster 34 as statement cards. Pupils to work in groups.

**Time:**
10 minutes

## Activity:

Give out Copymaster statement cards in random order.
Explain that the activity is to classify the statements into each of predator, prey, or both.

Groups to report back once complete.

Ask if pupils can give other features not in their statements.

Correct classification:

| Predator | Prey | Both |
|---|---|---|
| eyes in a forward position on the head | eyes at side of head | camouflaged |
| excellent vision | easily startled | excellent sense of smell |
| sharp curved claws | | |
| sharp curved beak | | |

**Challenge:** Ask pupils to explain how a cat is adapted as a predator.

**Links to plenary:** Explore by questions the use of each feature, especially those features shared by both, e.g. camouflage of predator to creep up on prey, and camouflage from predator by prey.

**Badger Key Stage 3 Science Starters**

# Adaptations: predator or prey? (1)

| | |
|---|---|
| eyes in a forward position on the head | eyes at side of head |
| excellent vision | excellent sense of smell |
| sharp curved claws | sharp curved beak |
| easily startled | camouflaged |

 **KEY POINT**

# Adaptations: predator or prey? (2)

### Objective:

To recognise features in predators that are adaptations to their food source.

### Teaching point:

Given a diagram of an organism, the pupils should be able to identify features of predators or prey.

**What you will need:**
Copymaster 35 as OHT.
Whole class activity.

**Time:**
5 minutes

### Activity:

Project Copymaster OHT.

Ask the pupils to look carefully at the diagram. The aim is to identify the bird as a herbivore or carnivore.

Pupils to volunteer their ideas, giving evidence only from what they can see in the diagram. The teacher can list the evidence.

- sharp talons / claws
- hooked sharp beak
- eyes at the front

**Challenge:** Research a named aquatic predator and describe its features.

**Links to plenary:** Inform of fact that many questions in SATs ask pupil to use what they see in the diagram. Ask what features prey may have to avoid the predator in this activity.

**Badger Key Stage 3 Science Starters**

# Adaptations: predator or prey? (2)

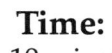 KEY POINT

# Food chains

### Objective:

To understand energy transfer through a food chain.

### Teaching point:

(i) The exercise stimulates recall so that the pupils will understand the types of organism along a food chain.

(ii) From one food chain, pupils will build to an understanding of inter-linked food chains; the food web.

**What you will need:**
Copymaster 36 as jigsaw pieces for each pupil.

**Time:**
5 - 10 minutes

### Activity:

Give background information that no food chain would be possible without the INPUT of light energy. Question pupils to find the major source of this light energy, the sun!

Give out set 1 of jigsaw pieces, i.e. lettuce, slug, thrush, hawk, and three arrows, kept in a Petri dish *randomly*. The pupil has to fit them together in the sequence below.

The correct sequence is:

lettuce ➔ slug ➔ thrush ➔ hawk.

Give out set 2 of jigsaw pieces, i.e. producer, herbivore, carnivore 1, carnivore 2 and three arrows, kept in a Petri dish *randomly*. The pupil has to fit them together in the sequence below.

The correct sequence is:

producer ➔ herbivore ➔ carnivore 1 ➔ carnivore 2.

Once this correct sequence is shown, the pupils align the two versions of the same food chain:

lettuce ➔ slug ➔ thrush ➔ hawk

producer ➔ herbivore ➔ carnivore 1 ➔ carnivore 2

When the correct sequence is shown the pupil can stick pieces in their book or write in sequence.

Tell pupils that arrows in the wrong direction is a common mistake! Another mistake is to start with the sun.

**Challenge:** Ask what would happen to a food chain if light energy was not available. Give another food chain with 5 types of organism.

**Links to plenary:** Discuss the ideas of what can happen if two or more types of organism eat a plant, e.g. lettuce. The idea of interlinked food chains forming a food web will develop.

**Badger Key Stage 3 Science Starters**

# Food chains

## Food Chain Jigsaws

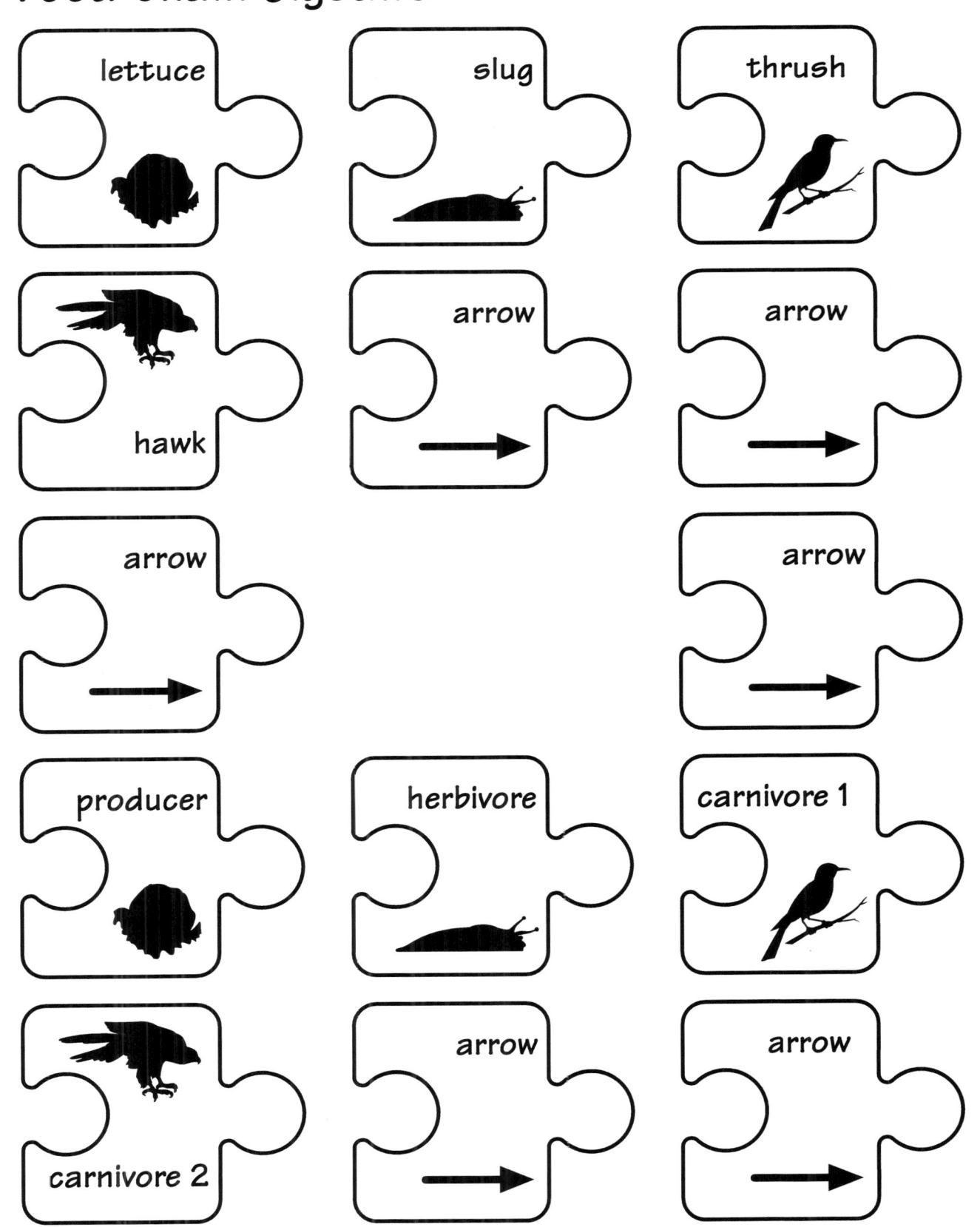

lettuce

slug

thrush

hawk

arrow

arrow

arrow

arrow

producer

herbivore

carnivore 1

carnivore 2

arrow

arrow

# Food web

**Objective:**

To understand that food chains link together in food webs; show the food relationships of a number of different organisms.

**Teaching point:**

Food chains interlink to form food webs. The activity will highlight the consequences of a species which dies out in the food web.

**What you will need:**
Copymaster 37 as worksheets. Pupils to work in groups.

**Time:**
10 minutes

**Activity:**

Give out a Copymaster worksheet to each group.

Give the tasks orally.

Name a producer in the food web. *(Wheat)*

What do the arrow heads on the lines show?
*(Direction of energy flow – the one which arrow points to eats the other.)*

How many food chains are shown? *(7)*

Explain what would happen if slugs died out due to a disease.
*(Wheat grows better - less wheat eaten / song thrushes eat more snails - song thrushes have less food.)*

Highlight fact that when an organism dies out,

- some species may benefit.

- some species may die out or have to use an alternative food source.

**Challenge:** Explain TWO ways that energy from a field mouse can reach a fox.

**Links to plenary:** Link relationships shown on food web to agricultural use of pesticides. Consider effects.

**Badger Key Stage 3 Science Starters**

# Food web

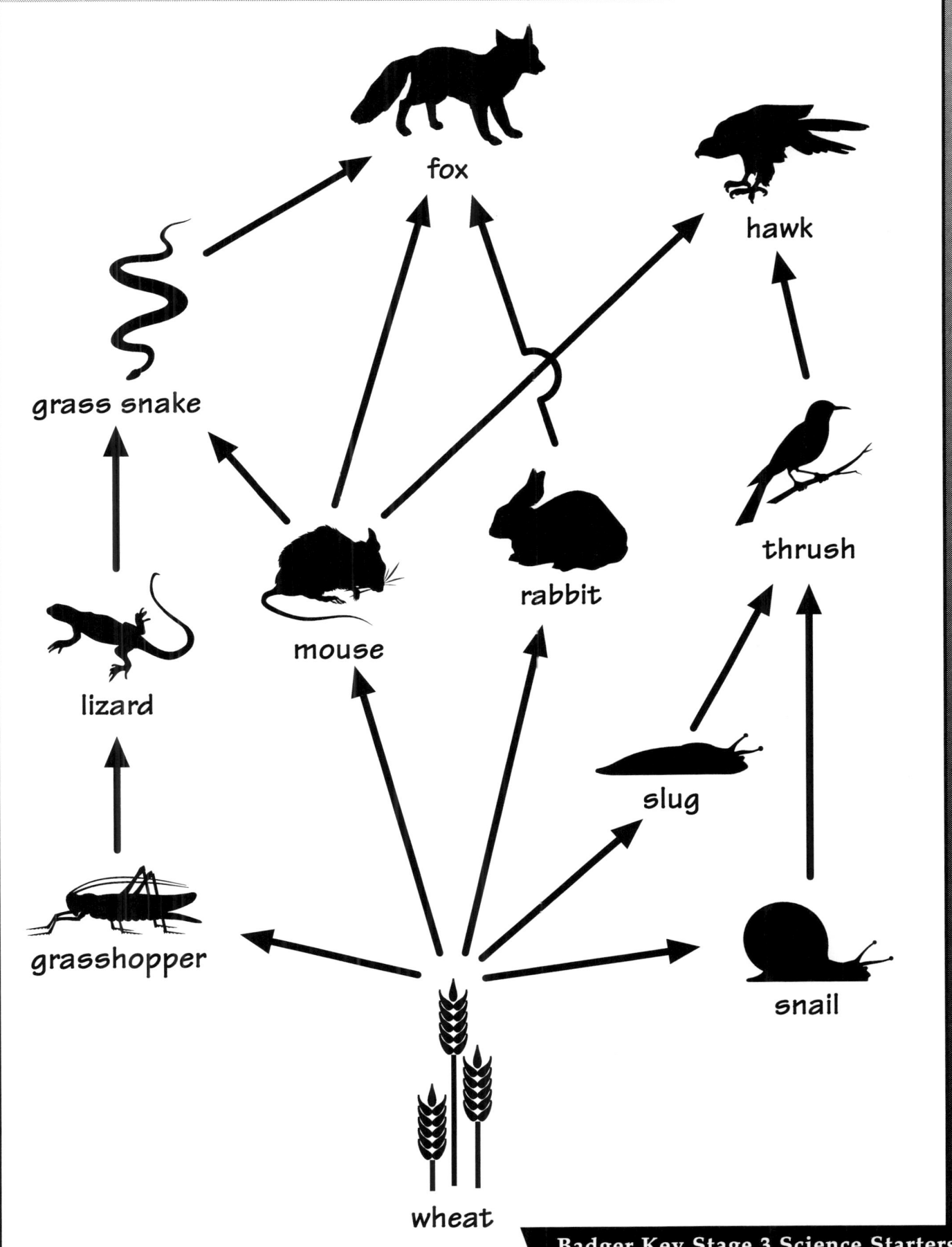

⊙━ KEY POINT

# Predator and prey patterns

### Objective:

Be aware the pattern of a predator-prey relationship.

### Teaching point:

Pupils should be aware that all predator-prey relationships have a similar pattern. A population increase of prey is followed by an increase in predators, then a decrease in the prey.

**What you will need:**
Copymaster 38 as OHT.
Pupils to work in pairs.

**Time:**
10 minutes

### Activity:

Project Copymaster OHT.

Explain that the graph shows the changing numbers of a species of predator and a species of prey. They are identified as species A and B.

Ask the pupils to analyse the changes in numbers, then write each letter on the whiteboard to show which is prey and which is a predator.

Then ask:

Which species is the predator? *(B)*

Which species is the prey? *(A)*

What is the evidence for each choice?

- *Prey always increase in numbers first;*
- *are an increased amount of food, for the predators;*
- *so predators increase in number.*

**Challenge:** Ask pupils to suggest why prey would increase in the first instance (increased food for them).

**Links to plenary:** Discuss the pattern and inform that it is repeated for many different predator–prey relationships, e.g. ladybird-greenfly.

**Badger Key Stage 3 Science Starters**

# Predator and prey patterns

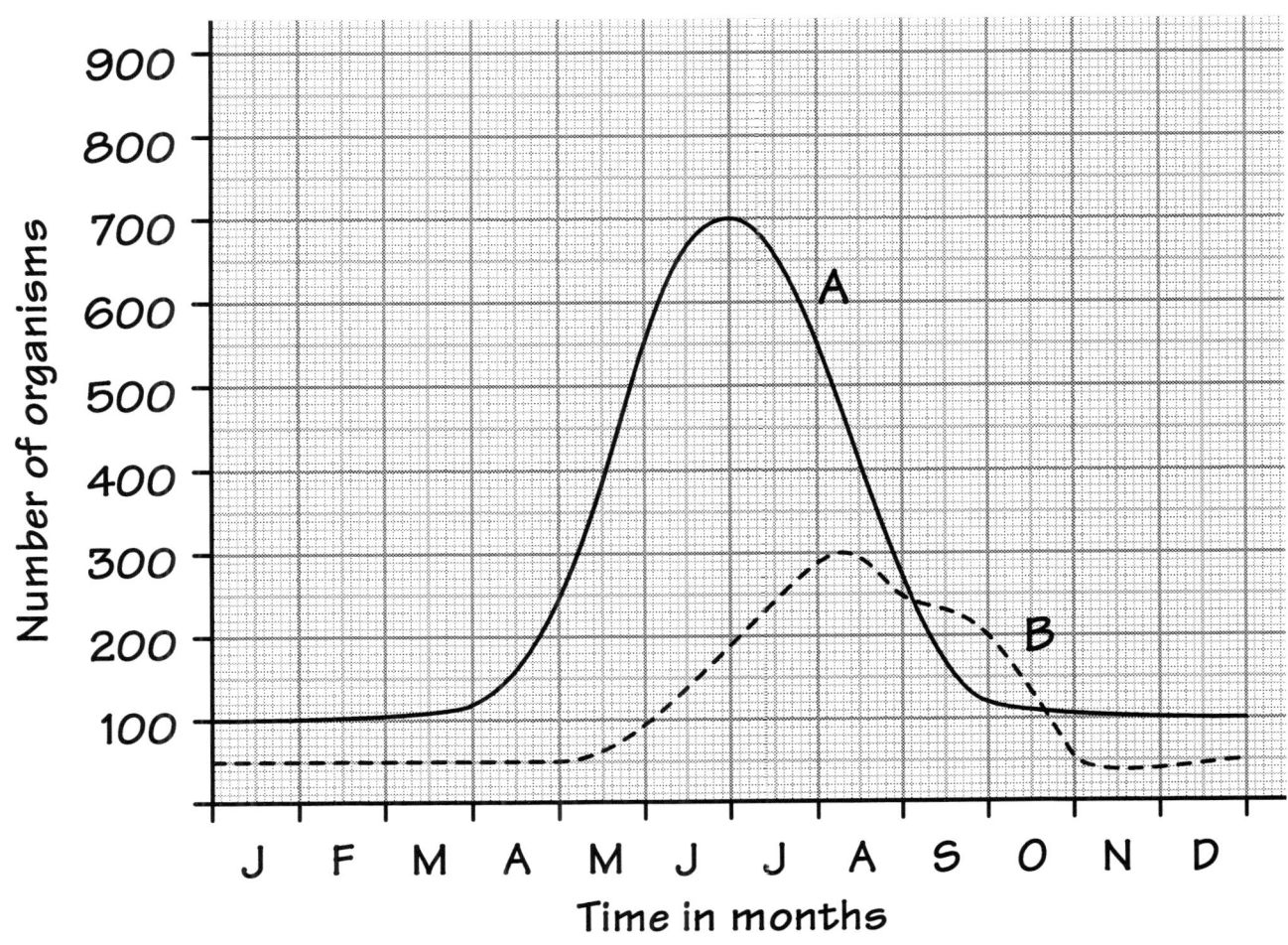

⚲ KEY POINT

# Competing for resources

### Objective:

To recognise that organisms compete for resources from the environment.

### Teaching point:

The class will be given an aquatic scenario. They will interpret the diagram and make a prediction based on information given and scientific knowledge.

**What you will need:**
Copymaster 39 as OHT.
Whiteboards and pens.
Pupils to work in pairs.

**Time:**
8 minutes

### Activity:

Project Copymaster OHT.

Give background information:

Duckweed grows on the surface.

Canadian pondweed grows under the water.

Nitrates enter the water, which are a useful fertiliser for both.

Ask pupils to predict what may happen over the coming months on their whiteboards. Finally ask which is the best competitor.

**Sequence**

Both use nitrates and light so they grow in size and number.

Duckweed covers the surface.

Less light reaches the Canadian pondweed.

It cannot photosynthesise.

So the Canadian pondweed dies off.

**Challenge:** Ask what may happen to the remains of the dead Canadian pondweed.

**Links to plenary:** Discuss the ways in which the duckweed is a better competitor.

**Badger Key Stage 3 Science Starters**

# Competing for resources

## Sunlight

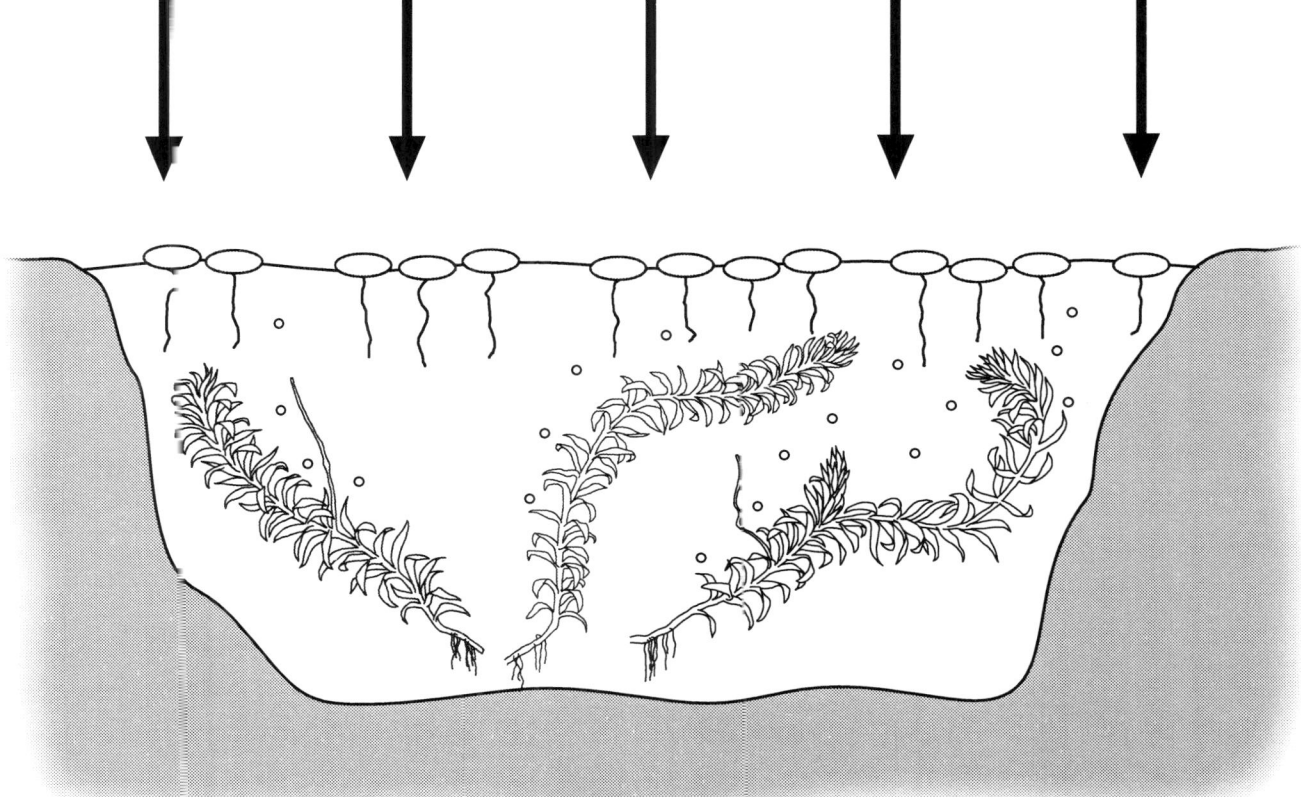

## Clearlake pond

# Can you tongue roll?

### Objective:

To know that members of the same species display variation.

### Teaching point:

Many features vary within the human species. For this activity, tongue rolling will be checked out throughout the class. Pupils can either tongue roll or they cannot. Data can be displayed in a pie-chart.

### What you will need:

Copymaster 40a as OHT. Copymaster 40b as a worksheet for each pupil. Whole class activity.

### Time:
10 minutes

### Activity:

Project Copymaster OHT.

Give background information:
All people can either roll their tongue or they cannot. This is genetically controlled.

Predict that more pupils will be able to tongue roll than cannot.

Ask pupils to demonstrate if they can do it. Put the collected data into % tongue-roller and % non-roller, and ask pupils to complete the pie-chart.

The data will show clear differences.

**Challenge:** Pupils could increase the sample by extending to more classes in the school. Collect tongue-roll database and use a spreadsheet.

**Links to plenary:** Discuss fact that many other features vary within all species. We are just one example! Give eye colour as another feature which varies.

**Badger Key Stage 3 Science Starters**

# Can you tongue roll?

Non-tongue rolling          Tongue rolling

# Can you tongue roll?

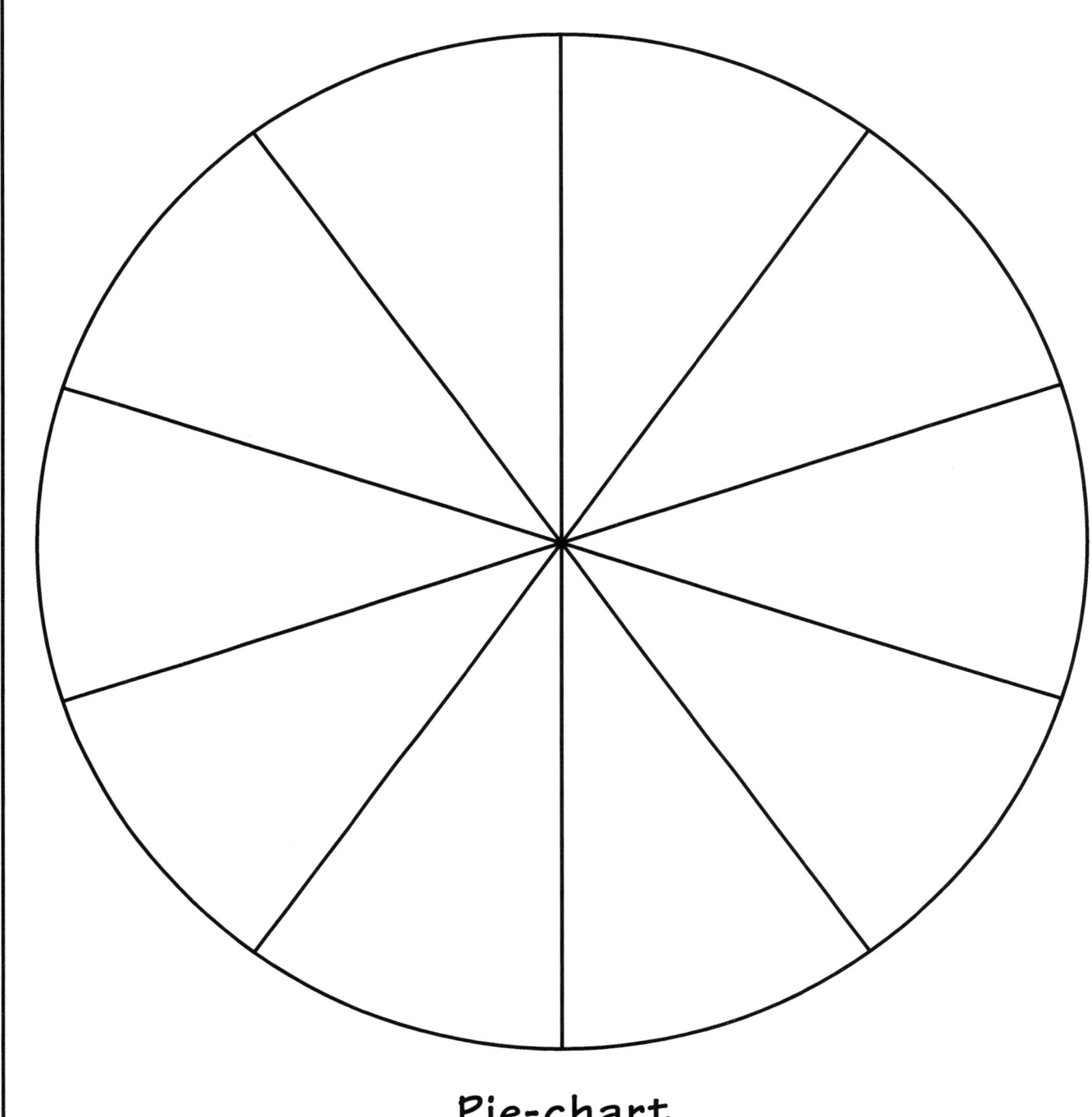

Pie-chart

# What causes variation? (1)

### Objective:

To know that organisms are influenced by the environment.

### Teaching point:

It is difficult to determine which variations are controlled by genetics and which are caused by the environment. Here genetic variation is controlled because all grass plants shown are genetically identical (a clone!). Pupils are likely to conclude that the environment is responsible for differences in the grasses.

**What you will need:**
Copymaster 41 as OHT.
Whiteboards and pens.
Pupils to work in groups.

**Time:**
10 minutes

### Activity:

Project Copymaster OHT.

Give background information:
The grasses are from one parent, so have inherited exactly the same characteristics.

Explain that groups should give details of why the grass plants look different, even though they are clones. They should write down the reasons for why the grass plants are different on their whiteboards.

Groups to report back. (Remind pupils to give details of their theory, and use evidence from the diagram.)

Possible conclusion:

- Cold wind came from north to south.
- Grasses have been windswept so dried out.
- Exposed grasses are smaller.
- The taller grasses have more protection.
- Taller grasses are further away from tree roots.
- So get more water from soil.

Share the range of conclusions with the groups.

**Challenge:** Find out how to take cuttings from a plant, then root them. Each will be identical to the parent.

**Links to plenary:** Discuss the protection given by the tree as well as the competition it has with the grass plants.

**Badger Key Stage 3 Science Starters**

NORTH　　　　　　　　　　　　　　　　　　　SOUTH

## A windy garden!

# What causes variation? (2)

### Objective:

To show that organisms are influenced by parents.

### Teaching point:

It is difficult to determine which variations are controlled by genetics and which are caused by the environment. Here environmental variation is controlled because all compost, water, and air conditions are identical. Pupils are likely to conclude that the parental genetics, passed on to offspring, are responsible for differences in flower colour.

**What you will need:**
Copymaster 42 as OHT.
Pupils to work in groups.

**Time:**
10 minutes

### Activity:

Project Copymaster OHT.

Give background information:
The seeds were collected from plants then sown in these conditions:

- the same amount of compost.

- the same amount of water.

- the same temperature.

- the same light.

- the same air conditions.

Ask groups to report on their conclusions. They should conclude that given there were identical environmental conditions the differences must be genetic.

Some flowers displayed RED, some flowers displayed WHITE and some PINK, which was not shown by either parent.

**Challenge:** Ask pupils how they would breed a red flowered plant with a white flowered plant.

**Links to plenary:** Discuss the fact that organisms are inflenced by factors passed on by parents and factors in the environment.

# What causes variation? (2)

A red Campion flower pollinated a white Campion flower

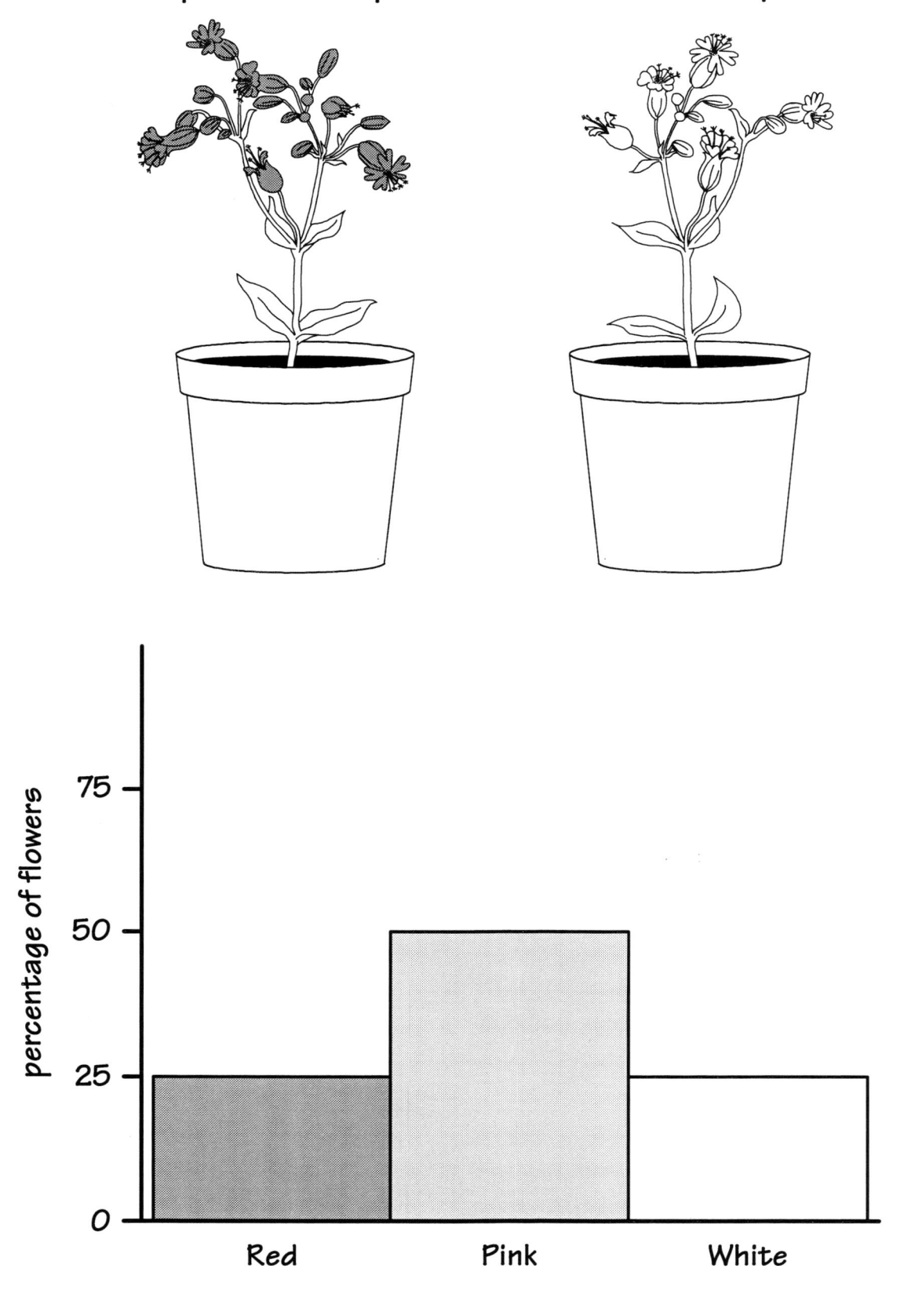

# Is it living?

### Objective:

To recognise processes common to living things.

### Teaching point:

The diagrams are of a variety of items. Groups will apply the criteria of living things to the organisms on the cards.

**What you will need:**
Copymaster 43a + b cards. Pupils to work in groups.

**Time:**
10 minutes

### Activity:

Each group to get:

- the cards which outline the processes common to living things.

- the pictures of a variety of life plus robot.

Explain that to state something is a living organism, it must be capable of all of the processes. Each group should discuss each picture and apply the living criteria.

Groups should report back after making their decisions. Note that not all living things die. Bacteria which divide repeatedly never appear to die of "old age".

Explain that all living things do respond to a stimulus, but the type of stimulus to which an organism responds varies.

**Challenge:** Research the characteristics of viruses. In some ways they appear to live (reproduction, response to stimulus) but for others they do not.

**Links to plenary:** Ask pupils to orally explain each process, to establish the list and detail to long term memory.

**Badger Key Stage 3 Science Starters**

# Is it living?

Frog

Rabbit

Tree

Grass

Fish

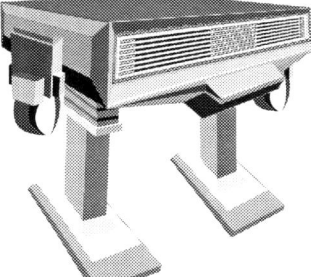

Robot

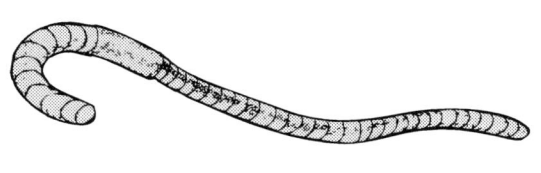

Worm

Limpet

# Is it living?

## Can it feed? 1

This is nutrition.

## Does it respire? 2

Respiration is the release of energy inside the organism.

## Does it grow? 3

This is getting bigger, when cells increase in number and size.

## Does it move? 4

From place to place, or even a bud / flower opening shows this.

## Does it get rid of waste? 5

This is excretion; includes urinating and breathing out.

## Does it reproduce? 6

This is making more of the species.

## Does it respond to a stimulus? 7

This is like a plant growing towards light, or a person crying when peeling an onion.

# Sorting things into groups: fingerprints

### Objective:

To be able to classify fingerprints into groups.

### Teaching point:

The activity is to classify fingerprints. Different types of fingerprint are supplied on Copymaster 44a. Specimens' fingerprints are supplied on Copymaster 44b.

### What you will need:
Copymaster 44 as worksheets. Pupils to work in groups.

### Time:
10 minutes

### Activity:

Give out Copymaster worksheets 44a and b.

Explain that the task is to classify the 20 fingerprints into each of the 4 categories, arch, loop, whorl, and compound. Copymaster 44a illustrates the characteristic of each type of fingerprint. Compound is a mixture of the characteristics.

Pupils could put data into a bar-graph.

Help groups to compare their classification with the correct numbers in each category:

| 5 | 5 | 5 | 5 |
|------|------|-------|----------|
| arch | loop | whorl | compound |

**Challenge:** Individual pupils could classify their own fingerprints with the use of a magnifying lens.

**Links to plenary:** Discuss the fact that within a species such as human, there are both similarities and differences. Across the "living world" these similarities and differences are the key to classification.

**Badger Key Stage 3 Science Starters**

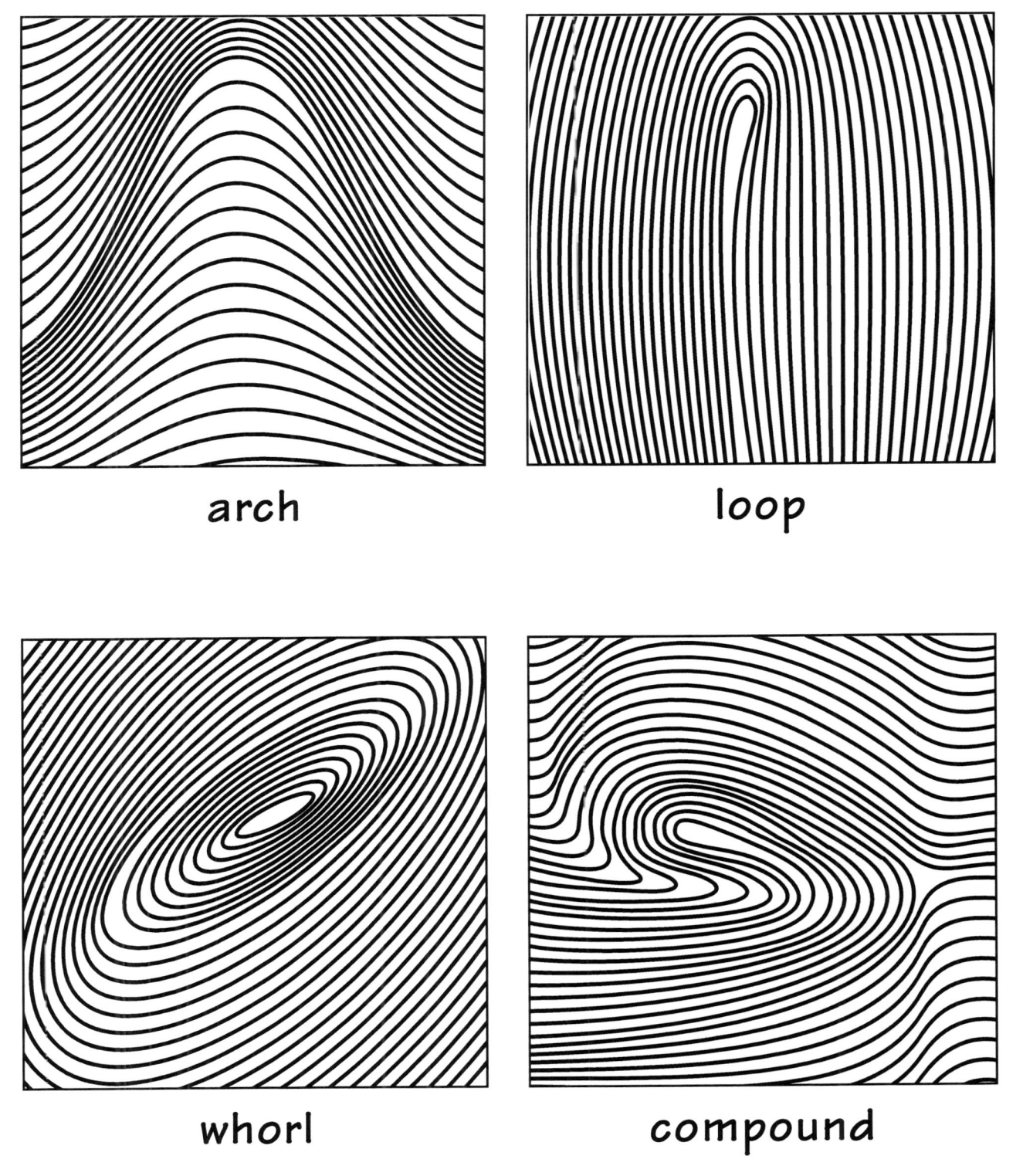

arch

loop

whorl

compound

## Sorting things into groups: Fingerprints

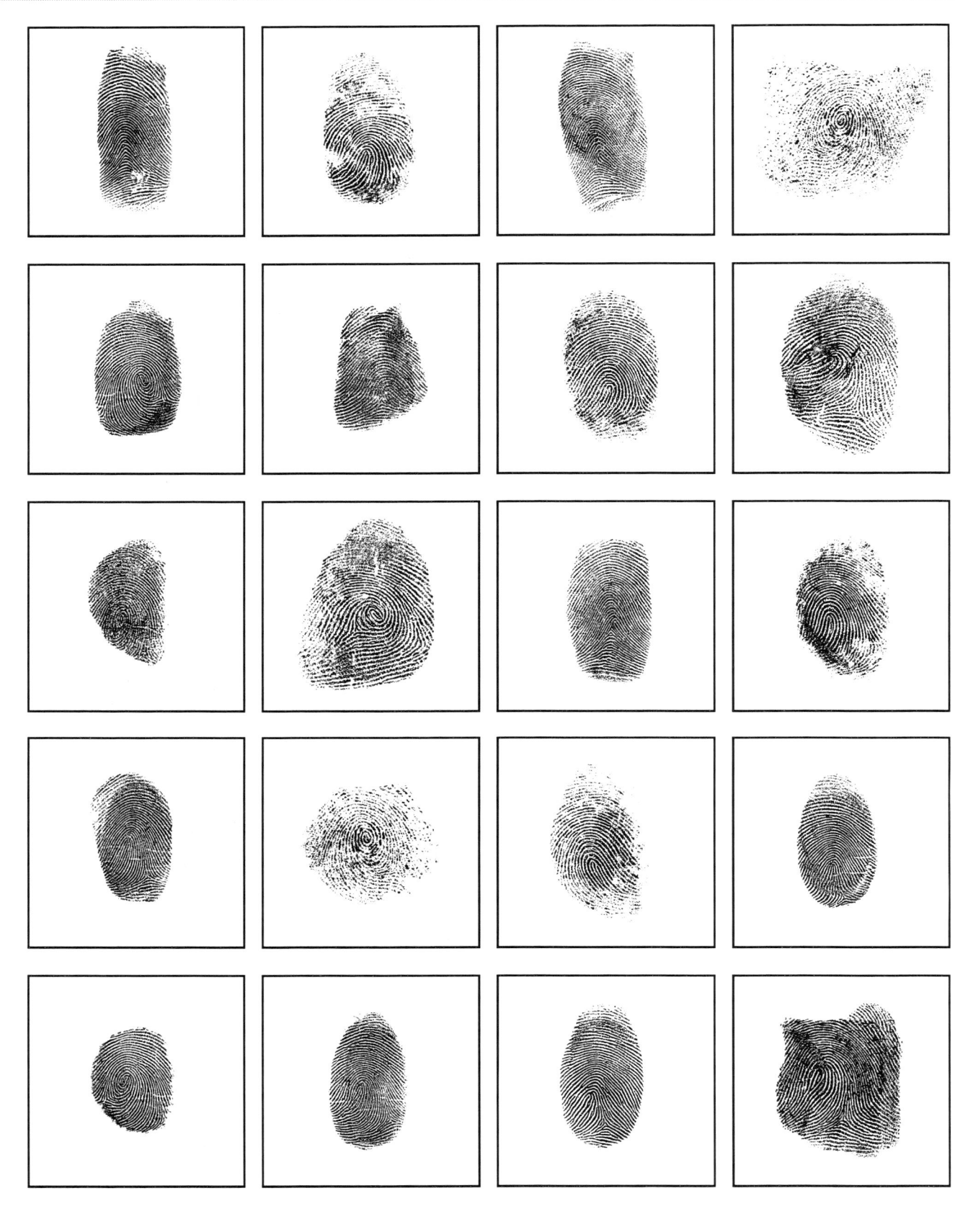

# Animal or plant?

### Objective:

To be able to sort organisms into groups according to key features.

### Teaching point:

The activity will enable pupils to look more closely at common and different characteristics of three different groups. Some will be easily classified but others will make the pupils think.

**What you will need:**
Copymaster 45 as OHT.
Whole class activity.

**Time:**
5 minutes

### Activity:

Project Copymaster OHT.

Explain that each of the list of characteristics is shown by one, two or all three of the organisms. Question the class so that using their guidance the correct letters **S, M, O** are written next to each statement.

**Answers**

Snail                          Mouse                          Oak

Has a hard shell **S**
Has chloroplasts **O**
Can move from place to place **SM**
Can produce flowers **O**
Is made of cells **SMO**
Has nerves **SM**
Gives off carbon dioxide **SMO**
Is a vertebrate **M**
Is an invertebrate **S**
Can digest food **SM**
Can make food by photosynthesis **O**
Takes in oxygen for respiration **SMO**
Gives off oxygen as waste **O**
Has muscles and bones **M**

Inform of the confusion they may have with plants and oxygen. It is given off in the day due to photosynthesis and used at night for respiration.

**Challenge:** Research differences in the vertebrates; mammals, birds, fish, reptiles, amphibians.

**Links to plenary:** Discuss fact that not all features are needed to classify an organism. The same group, e.g. snails, have many sub-groups across the world which display a range of differences.

**Badger Key Stage 3 Science Starters**

# Animal or plant?

## Snail          Mouse          Oak

Has a hard shell

Has chloroplasts

Can move from place to place

Can produce flowers

Is made of cells

Has nerves

Gives off carbon dioxide

Is a vertebrate

Is an invertebrate

Can digest food

Can make food by photosynthesis

Takes in oxygen for respiration

Gives off oxygen as waste

Has muscles and bones

# Acid or alkali?

### Objective:

To recognise a number of everyday household chemicals as acid, alkali or neutral.

### Teaching point:

The activity involves the completion of a table aided by ideas of the pupils. One property for each substance gives a clue on which to base selection. Only mild acids and alkalis are included to give the idea that not all acids and alkalis are strong and dangerous!

**What you will need:**
Copymaster 46 as OHT.
Whole class activity.

**Time:**
5 minutes

### Activity:

Project Copymaster OHT.

Explain that the table is not complete.

Ask for pupil suggestions to help teacher to classify as acid, alkali or neutral.

Discuss the facts that:

- Alkalis feel soapy because they react with oils on your skin.

- Acids give a sour taste.

- Water can weaken the strength of both acids and alkalis.

**Answers**

| | |
|---|---|
| Toothpaste | alkali |
| Lemon juice | acid |
| Washing up liquid | alkali |
| Vinegar | acid |
| Water | neutral |

**Challenge:** Ask pupils to list other chemicals in the home which may be acid or alkaline.

**Links to plenary:** Discuss the fact that the activity included weaker acids and alkalis, but there are others in home and industry which are stronger and hazardous.

**Badger Key Stage 3 Science Starters**

# Acid or alkali?

| Substance used in the home | Property | Acid, alkali or neutral |
|---|---|---|
| Toothpaste | neutralises acid in the mouth | |
| Lemon juice | tastes sour | |
| Washing up liquid | feels soapy | |
| Vinegar | tastes sour | |
| Water | can be used to dilute an acid or alkali | |

# Hazard signs: Danger!

### Objective:

To recognise and interpret common hazard signs.

### Teaching point:

The pupils will be given Copymaster worksheet to identify the types of hazard signs which label substances used in the home. It should be stressed that alongside each hazard symbol is additional information to give further help.

**What you will need:**
Copymaster 47 as worksheets. Whiteboards and pens. Pupils to work in groups.

**Time:**
10 minutes

### Activity:

Give out Copymaster worksheets.

The groups should discuss each hazard symbol. Explain that dangerous substances must all be clearly marked with the symbols.

Ask groups to answer the following on their whiteboards:

What does each symbol mean?

Why are the safety precautions given alongside the symbol important?

Further prompts:

Why are there two hazard symbols for one of the diagrams shown?

Why does the symbol from the back of a tanker have a telephone number?

Tankers also name the chemical they are transporting. Why is this important information?

**Challenge:** Research other hazard symbols in the home and industry.

**Links to plenary:** Discuss the importance of warning people about hazardous substances and the need to read additional information next to every hazard sign. Inform of the Hazard symbols from chemicals they use in the laboratory.

**Badger Key Stage 3 Science Starters**

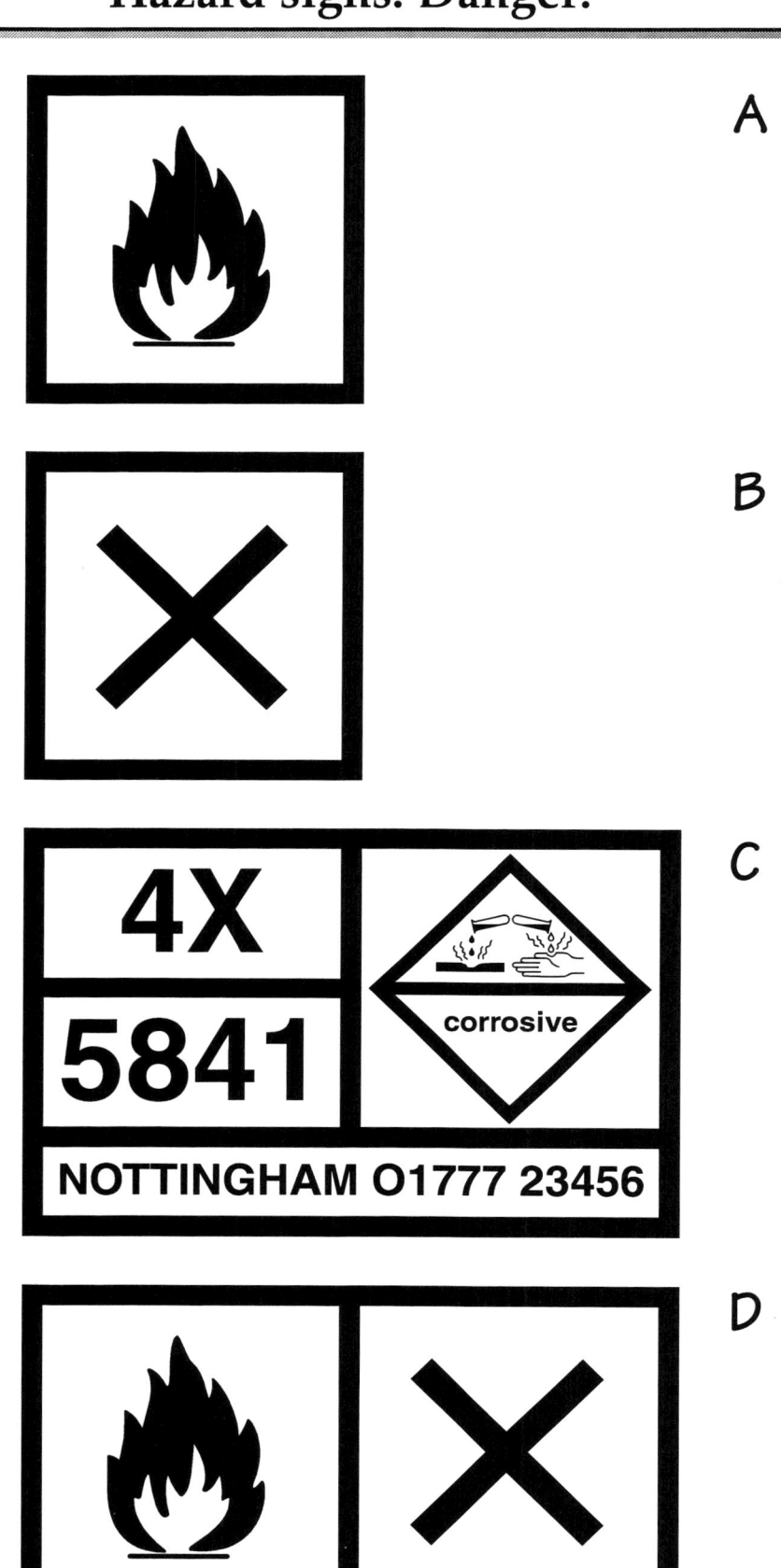

A

B

C

D

# Indicators

**Objective:**

To be able to classify substances as acid or alkali using indicators.

**Teaching point:**

Dyes for indicators come from a variety of sources. The activity involves results of an incomplete investigation. Only blue litmus is used in this test for the suitability of red cabbage as an indicator. Further discussion should reveal that the pupils omitted to find out if red cabbage changes colour in alkaline conditions.

**What you will need:**
Copymaster 48 as worksheets. Pupils to work in groups.

**Time:**
10 minutes

**Activity:**

Give out Copymaster worksheets.

Explain that Anna and Jake carried out an investigation to find out if the juice of red cabbage is a useful indicator. Inform them that blue litmus changes to red in acid.

They tested lemon juice with litmus paper and with red cabbage juice then tested vinegar.

This is what Anna and Jake wrote:

"We decided to use blue litmus paper, a known indicator, as well as red cabbage juice. Lemon juice and vinegar were tested to find out if they were acids or not.

We observed:

- red cabbage juice was purple at the start
- with lemon juice the litmus changed to red
- with lemon juice the cabbage juice changed to yellow
- with vinegar the litmus changed to red
- with vinegar the cabbage juice changed to yellow."

Ask the pupils to write the four missing colours in the table then to write down if each substance is acid or alkali.

**Challenge:** Ask pupils to research other indicators used in the laboratory, especially universal indicators.

**Links to plenary:** Ask groups if the investigation confirmed that red cabbage is a suitable indicator.

**Badger Key Stage 3 Science Starters**

# Indicators

Complete the table of results.

| Substance tested | Litmus | | Red cabbage | | Acid or alkali |
|---|---|---|---|---|---|
| | colour before test | colour after test | colour before test | colour after test | |
| Lemon juice | blue | | purple | | |
| Vinegar | blue | | purple | | |

Do the results show that red cabbage juice is a suitable indicator?

Yes or No? . . . . . . . . . . . . . . . . . . . . . . . . . . . . . . . . . . . . . . . .

Give a reason . . . . . . . . . . . . . . . . . . . . . . . . . . . . . . . . . . . . . .

. . . . . . . . . . . . . . . . . . . . . . . . . . . . . . . . . . . . . . . . . . . . .

# The pH scale

## Objective:

To recognise that pH numbers indicate how acid or alkaline a substance is; recognise that neutral solutions are pH 7, acidic solutions are below pH 7 and alkaline solutions are above pH 7.

## Teaching point:

The Copymaster gives a pH scale. It is advisable to enlarge the Copymaster to A3 size. Groups will be able to stick the arrowed substances along the pH scale. The activity will help commit common substances to long term memory.

## Activity:

Give out Copymaster worksheets.

Explain that the activity will involve cutting and pasting. The pH scale should be cut out and so should the substance labels. The pupils should stick the labels onto the correct part of the scale.

If supplied with a universal indicator colour table then their scale can also be coloured appropriately.

Discuss the different pH values of the common substances printed on the labels.
Tell the pupils that rain water is a dilute solution of carbonic acid.

**What you will need:**
Copymaster 49 as worksheets. Pupils to work in pairs.

**Time:**
12 minutes

**Challenge:** Ask pupils to explain the advantages of using data logging equipment to measure changes in pH.

**Links to plenary:** Discuss the fact that acids are below pH 7 and alkalis are above. State that universal indicator is a mixture of dyes which can, together, cover the complete pH range.

**Badger Key Stage 3 Science Starters**

# The pH scale

| | | pH |
|---|---|---|
| ACID | | 1 |
| | | 2 |
| | | 3 |
| | | 4 |
| | | 5 |
| | | 6 |
| NEUTRAL | | 7 |
| ALKALI | | 8 |
| | | 9 |
| | | 10 |
| | | 11 |
| | | 12 |
| | | 13 |
| | | 14 |

rain water  pH 6

water  pH 7

car battery acid  pH 1

oven cleaner  pH 12

lemon juice  pH 4

vinegar  pH 4

sodium hydroxide  pH 13

ammonium hydroxide  pH 13

cola drink  pH 6

washing up liquid  pH 8

salt  pH 7

citric acid  pH 6

# Neutralisation (1)

## Objective:

To recognise that a neutral solution can be obtained when an acid is added to an alkali.

## Teaching point:

The neutralisation process is fundamental to knowledge of chemistry. The activity involves pupils putting together two sets of cards to show neutralisation. The activity is simple but important to enter long term memory.

**What you will need:**
Copymaster 50 cards.
Whole class activity.

**Time:**
5 minutes

## Activity:

Give out cards prepared from Copymaster.

Explain that the pupils should cut out the cards and put together 2 equations.

Give information:

equation 1 is in the form A + B = C + D

equation 2 is in the form A + B = C

For both equations volumes and concentrations are assumed equal.

Ask pupils to arrange each equation with their cards. Ask for 1 volunteer to come to the front to display their correct equations.

Correct equations:

acid + alkali = salt + water

pH 6 + pH 8 = pH 7

**Challenge:** Ask pupils to explain how neutralisation can be used to counteract dangers from strong acids and alkalis.

**Links to plenary:** Discuss importance of the neutralisation reactions, relate to potential uses.

(equation 1)

| Acid | + |
|------|---|
| Salt | + |
| Alkali | = |
| Water | |

(equation 2)

| | pH 7 |
|---|------|
| + | pH6 |
| = | pH 8 |

# Neutralisation (2)

### Objective:

To know that acids and alkalis are used in a range of everyday situations.

**What you will need:**
Copymaster 51 as OHT.
Whole class activity.

**Time:**
10 minutes

### Teaching point:

Class will be given two images, a bee sting and a wasp sting. Pupils will be asked to produce an imaginary cream to counteract an insect sting. The teacher will collate ideas which should be centred around neutralisation.

### Activity:

Project Copymaster OHTs.

Explain diagram 1; a bee is stinging a person and it is known to be acidic. Get ideas from class and add a suitable ingredient to the bee sting cream.
*(alkali, to neutralise the acid)*

Explain diagram 2; a wasp is stinging a person and it is known to be alkaline. Get ideas from class and add a suitable ingredient to the wasp sting cream.
*(acid, to neutralise the alkali)*

**Challenge:** Ask pupils to design soothing creams to counteract nettles (acid sting) and ants (acid attack).

**Links to plenary:** Discuss the neutralisation strategy of counteracting a number of different stings.

## Bee sting

## Wasp sting

# Too much acid!

### Objective:

To know that preliminary work could lead to a remedy to counteract tooth decay.

### Teaching point:

The activity is based on analysis of a graph. This shows the build up of acid after consuming food.

**What you will need:**
Copymaster 52 as OHT.
Whiteboards and pens.
Pupils to work in pairs.

**Time:**
10 minutes

### Activity:

Project Copymaster OHT.

Explain that the graph shows the changes in pH of the conditions in a person's mouth. A person was given some food and the pH was measured over the next 60 minutes.

Inform pupils that bacteria convert sugar in the mouth into acid which can decay the teeth.

Ask the following questions in sequence and give time for responses. Pupils should answer the questions on their whiteboards:

1.  What was the lowest pH produced after eating the food?
    *(4·5)*

2.  For how many minutes was there acid in the mouth strong enough to decay the teeth?
    *(36-37 minutes)*

3.  If the person had washed out the mouth with water, what effect would this have had on the acid in the mouth?
    *(It would be diluted.)*

4.  Suggest an effective way of reducing the acid level of the mouth after eating.
    *(Use alkali; alkaline toothpaste, alkaline mouthwash, alkaline chewing gum.)*

**Challenge:** Research other applications of the process of neutralisation.

**Links to plenary:** Discuss the use of neutralisation to avoid tooth decay.

**Badger Key Stage 3 Science Starters**

# Too much acid!

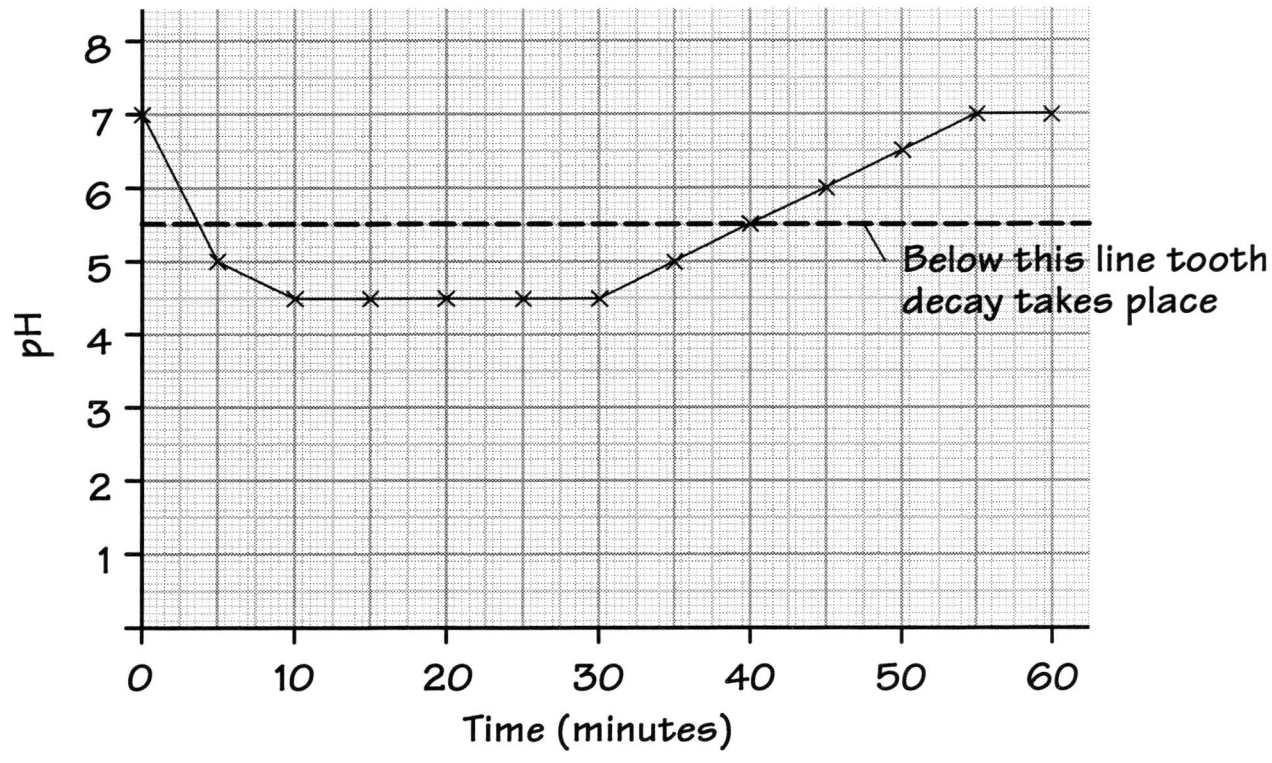

Below this line tooth decay takes place

# Questions:

1. What was the lowest pH produced after eating the food?


2. For how many minutes was there acid in the mouth strong enough to decay the teeth?


3. If the person had washed out the mouth with water, what effect would this have had on the acid in the mouth?


4. Suggest an effective way of reducing the acid level of the mouth after eating.

# Reversible or irreversible?

### Objective:

To interpret observations and classify irreversible reactions as chemical reactions.

**What you will need:**
Copymaster 53 as OHT.
Whole class activity.

**Time:**
8 minutes

### Teaching point:

At Key Stage 2 pupils experienced reversible and irreversible reactions. Here they are given a variety to classify. By the end of the exercise, pupils should also recognise irreversible reactions as chemical reactions.

### Activity:

Project Copymaster OHT.

Explain that the activity is to divide the list into reversible and irreversible reactions.
Remind pupils that the reversible reactions allow the easy return of origin reactants whereas the irreversible reactions are one way.

Pupils should help to classify the reactions.

Adding salt to water  R
Burning a candle  I
Frying an egg  I
Making an ice-lolly  R
Burning coal in a fire  I
Burning a sparkler  I
Making wine  I
Adding sugar to water  R
Making concrete  I
Releasing superglue from its tube to harden  I
Burning natural gas  I
Adding water to "cuppa-soup"  R
Fungi rotting an orange  I

**Challenge:** Ask pupils to consider if they could return to pure water and salt crystals after mixing the two.

**Links to plenary:** Point out that all of the irreversible reactions are also called chemical reactions.

# Reversible or irreversible?

Adding salt to water

Burning a candle

Frying an egg

Making an ice-lolly

Burning coal in a fire

Burning a sparkler

Making wine

Adding sugar to water

Making concrete

Releasing superglue from its tube to harden

Burning natural gas

Adding water to "cuppa-soup"

Fungi rotting an orange

# Which gas?

## Objective:

To know the tests for carbon dioxide and hydrogen; to know that oxygen supports burning.

## Teaching point:

This Starter should be used after the pupils have been introduced to burning and the tests for hydrogen and carbon dioxide.

The given table shows responses to tests for carbon dioxide and hydrogen. Additionally the reaction of a lighted splint to oxygen is included. The tests plus oxygen reaction will support further work.

## Activity:

Give out Copymaster worksheets.

Explain that the table shows what happened when a lighted splint was put into each of three gases A, B and C.

The same gases were tested by being bubbled through limewater. On the basis of the results in the table, ask the pupils to identify the three gases.
*(A = hydrogen, B = oxygen, C = carbon dioxide)*

**What you will need:**
Copymaster 54 as worksheets. Pupils to work in pairs.

**Time:**
5 minutes

**Challenge:** Research how oxygen reacts with a number of other substances.

**Links to plenary:** Discuss the results which help identify the gases. The negative results are equally as important as the positive reactions in identification.

**Badger Key Stage 3 Science Starters**

# Which gas?

| Test for gas | Gas | | |
|---|---|---|---|
| | A | B | C |
| Gas bubbled through lime water | no reaction | no reaction | became cloudy |
| Lighted splint put into gas | produced a squeaky pop | flame flared up | flame went out |

A =

B =

C =

# How do acids react with metals?

### Objective:

To be aware that acids react with metals to form new substances plus hydrogen.

### Teaching point:

The pupils need to know that metals react with acids to form hydrogen plus another compound. Here the apparatus is shown as a clue to help them sequence a word equation.

### What you will need:
Copymaster 55a as OHT and 55b as worksheets. Pupils to work in pairs.

### Time:
10 minutes

### Activity:

Project Copymaster OHT 55a.

Give out Copymaster 55b worksheets. Pupils need to cut out the word and symbol cards.

Explain that the diagram will help the completion of the equation using the word / symbol cards.

Correct equation:

Zinc + hydrochloric acid ➔ zinc chloride + hydrogen

Ask why an inverted measuring cylinder is

(a) filled with water at the start *(water is displaced by gas)*

(b) upside down *(to collect the gas)*

Ask pupils how they could test the gas to make sure that it is hydrogen.

**Challenge:** Ask pupils to plan an investigation to compare the reaction of hydrochloric acid with different metals.

**Links to plenary:** Discuss the role of each component of the apparatus. Ask where in the apparatus zinc chloride would be produced. Inform that metals plus acids follow the pattern of hydrogen production.

**Badger Key Stage 3 Science Starters**

# How do acids react with metals?

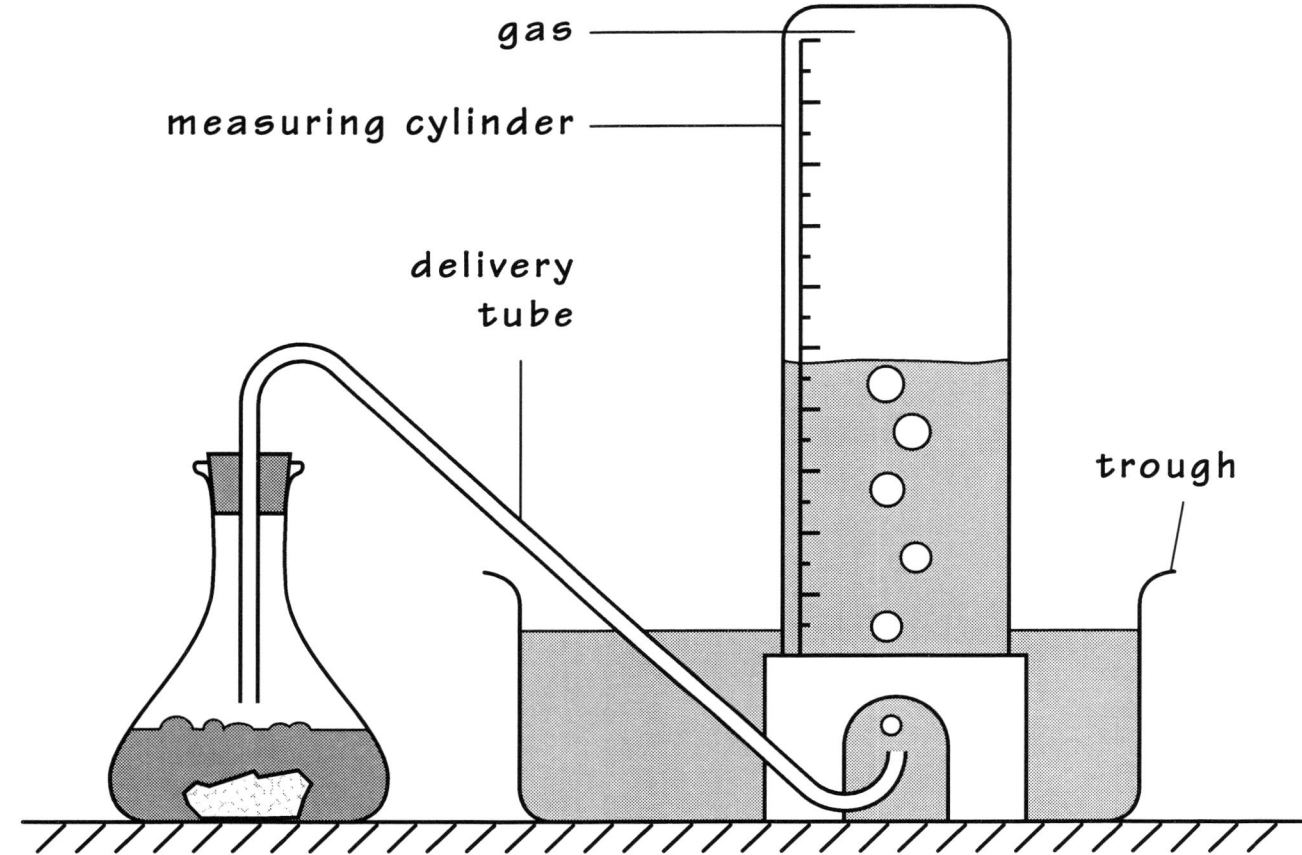

gas

measuring cylinder

delivery tube

trough

# How do acids react with metals?

| | |
|---|---|
| zinc chloride | zinc |
| hydrogen | hydrochloric acid |
| ➡ | + |
| + | |

# How do acids react with carbonates?

## Objective:

To be aware that acids react with carbonates to form new substances plus carbon dioxide; to be able to interpret data from a graph.

## Teaching point:

The Copymaster worksheets show the apparatus used to produce the data in the table. The data should be used to plot on graph paper. The graph should be used to help the pupils answer the questions.

**What you will need:**
Copymaster 56a as worksheets. Pupils to work individually.

**Time:**
12 minutes

## Activity:

Give out Copymaster worksheets.

Explain that Tanya investigated the effect of hydrochloric acid on calcium carbonate (marble chips). The results are shown on the worksheet.

Tanya used $25cm^3$ dilute hydrochloric acid for every reading she took. She increased the mass of marble chips by 5g each time then measured the volume of gas given off in a minute.

Ask the pupils to draw suitable axes and plot the points. They should plot mass of marble chips on the $y$ axis and volume of carbon dioxide on the $x$.

Once plotted, the pupils should be able to answer this question:

How much gas would be produced with 12·5g of marble chips?
$(50cm^3)$

A correctly plotted graph can be found on Copymaster 56b OHT.

**Challenge:** Ask pupils to suggest how Tanya may have collected her data.

**Links to plenary:** Discuss the fact that graphs must always be labelled, showing units, and importance of repeated readings.

**Badger Key Stage 3 Science Starters**

# How do acids react with carbonates?

| Mass of marble chips (g) | 5 | 10 | 15 | 20 | 25 | 30 | 35 |
|---|---|---|---|---|---|---|---|
| Volume of carbon dioxide (cm$^3$) | 20 | 42 | 58 | 83 | 95 | 124 | 130 |

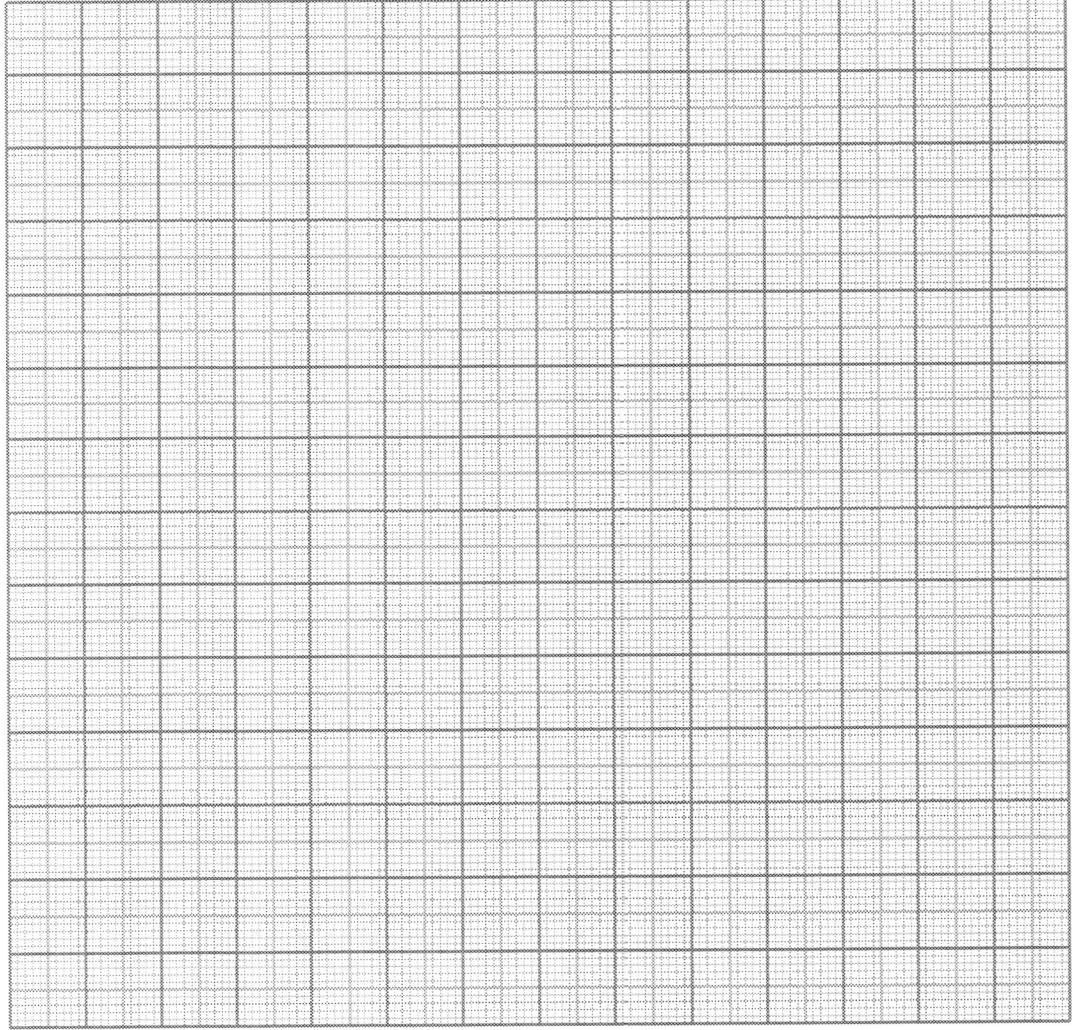

# How do acids react with carbonates?

## Answers:

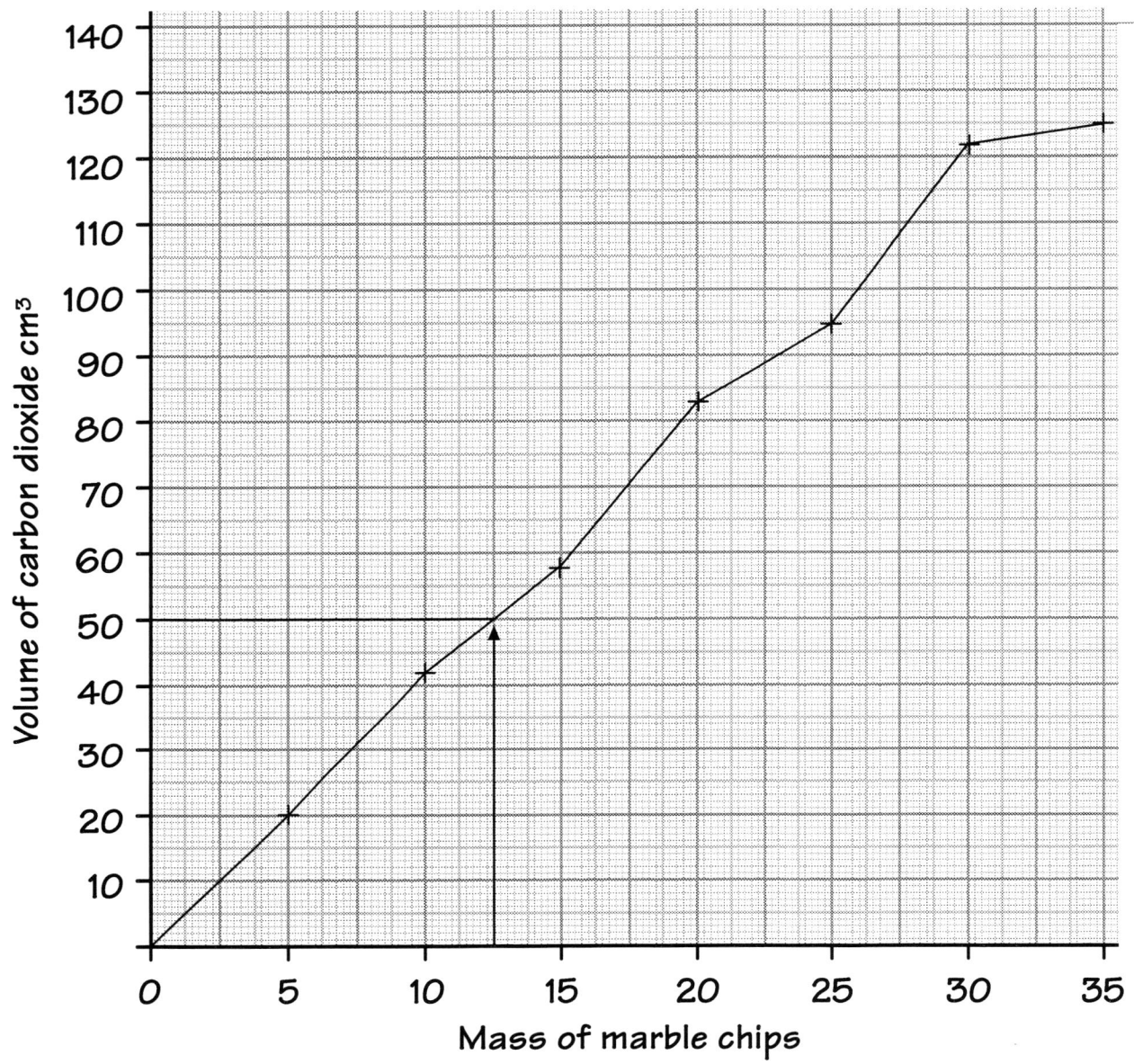

# A burning candle

## Objective:

To be aware that burning uses oxygen.

## Teaching point:

The "before and after" diagrams show what happens to a floating candle in a gas jar of air. The pupils should be asked to interpret what happens.

**What you will need:**
Copymaster 57 as OHT.
Whole class activity.

**Time:**
8 minutes

## Activity:

Project Copymaster OHT.

Explain: A lit candle in a dish was put in a gas jar as shown. It floated on the water level.

Ask pupils to explain the details of what happened and why.

Point out both the rise of water in the measuring cylinder and the fall in the trough. Refer to pressure change in the measuring cylinder which results in the rise of the water level.

At the end of the experiment the candle went out and the water level rose.

**Challenge:** Ask pupils to explain how the gases produced by burning the candle could have been tested.

**Links to plenary:** Discuss combustion, use of oxygen in the process , the pressure reduction in the gas jar, change in water levels.

**Badger Key Stage 3 Science Starters**

# A burning candle

water

water

# Reactions: before and after

**What you will need:**
Copymaster 58 as
worksheets. Pupils to
work in pairs.

**Objective:**

To be aware that products can be deduced from reactants and
vice versa.

**Time:**
8 minutes

**Teaching point:**

The activity will develop an ability in pupils to predict products
from given reactants. Additionally pupils may become aware of
patterns in acid + metal, acid + carbonate and combustion.

**Activity:**

Give out Copymaster worksheets. They need to cut out the equation cards.

Explain that the equations are not complete. The activity is to match the correct equation front
with the back of the equation.

Correct word equations:

calcium carbonate + hydrochloric acid = calcium hydroxide + carbon dioxide

sodium carbonate + hydrochloric acid = sodium hydroxide + carbon dioxide

hydrochloric acid + magnesium = magnesium chloride + hydrogen

hydrochloric acid + calcium = calcium chloride + hydrogen

carbon + oxygen = carbon dioxide

sulphur + oxygen = sulphur dioxide

Pupils should spot:

acid + metal produces hydrogen

acid + carbonate produces carbon dioxide

burning produces an oxide / dioxide

**Challenge:** Ask pupils to think about any common patterns in the 3 types of reaction,
acid + metal, acid + carbonate, and burning.

**Links to plenary:** Discuss the fact that being given either reactants or products helps to
work out the other!

**Badger Key Stage 3 Science Starters**

# Reactions: before and after

hydrochloric acid + calcium =

hydrochloric acid + magnesium =

sulphur + oxygen =

carbon + oxygen =

sodium carbonate + hydrochloric acid =

calcium carbonate + hydrochloric acid =

sodium hydroxide + carbon dioxide

sulphur dioxide

calcium hydroxide + carbon dioxide

calcium chloride + hydrogen

magnesium chloride + hydrogen

carbon dioxide

**Badger Key Stage 3 Science Starters**

# What's in air?

### Objective:

To know that air is a mixture of gases and contains around 21% oxygen.

### Teaching point:

The activity will show the mixture of gases which make up the air and their relative proportions. It may be used to highlight oxygen as part of respiration and carbon dioxide being used for photosynthesis.

### Activity:

Project Copymaster OHT.

Explain that the pie chart shows approximate percentages of each of the following:

oxygen
carbon dioxide
nitrogen
rare gases like argon and neon
water vapour

Ask pupils to suggest which label to write on which sector.

oxygen 21%
carbon dioxide 0·03%
nitrogen 78%
rare gases like argon and neon < 1%
water vapour < 1%

Ask pupils:

Which processes reduce oxygen in the air?
Which processes increase oxygen in the air?
Which processes reduce carbon dioxide in the air?
Which processes increase carbon dioxide in the air?

**Challenge:** Ask pupils to think how human activities that affect air quality combustion can be helpful to plant life.

**Links to plenary:** Discuss the importance of oxygen to burning and carbon dioxide to plant life.

**What you will need:**
Copymaster 59 as OHT.
Whole class activity.

**Time:**
5 minutes

**Badger Key Stage 3 Science Starters**

# What's in air?

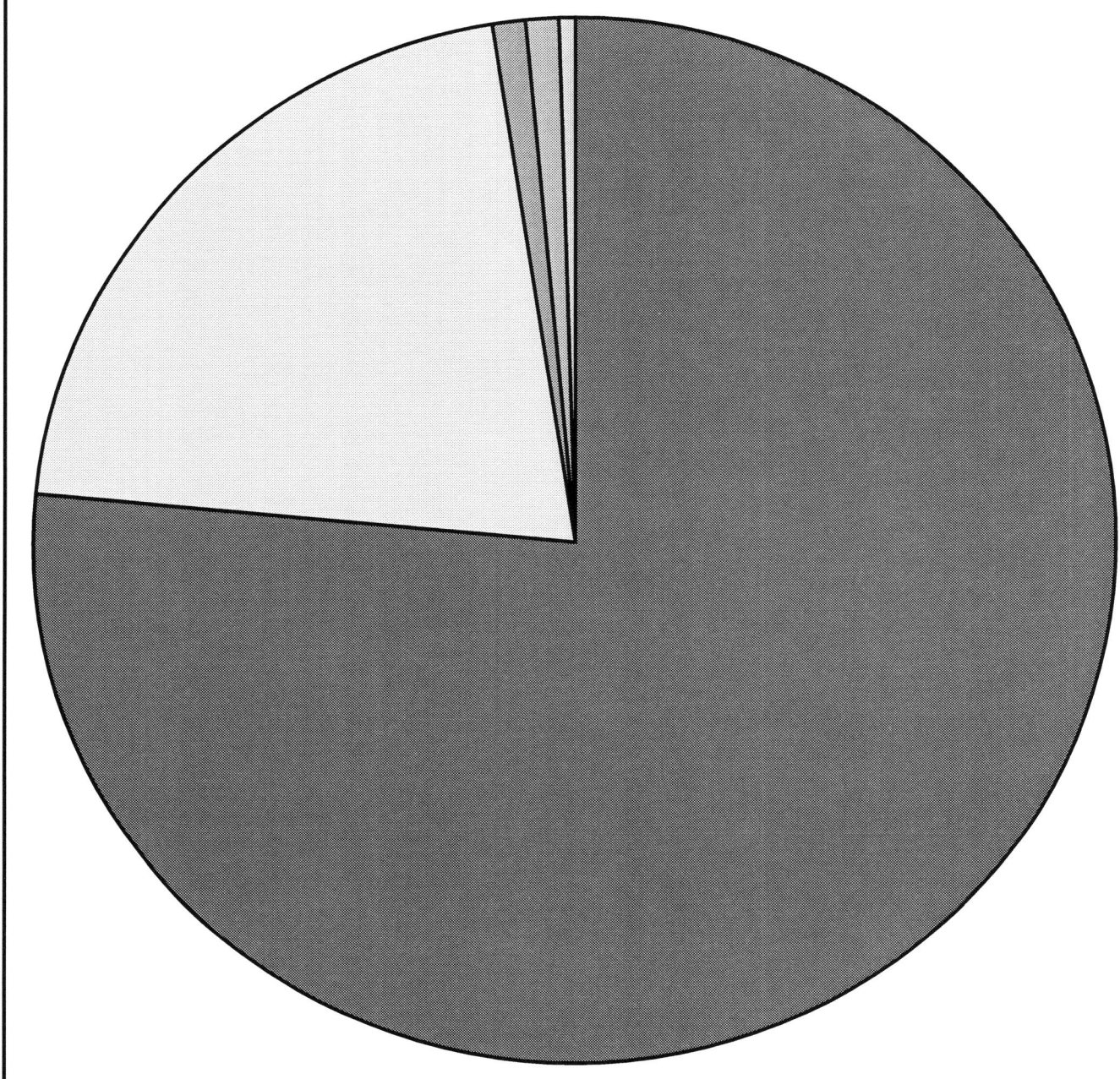

nitrogen

rare gases including neon          oxygen

water vapour          carbon dioxide

# Which fuel?

**Objective:**

To be aware that fuels release energy when they burn and produce carbon dioxide; that methane is a fuel which produces only carbon dioxide and water vapour after combustion.

**What you will need:**
No other resource. Pupils to work in pairs.

**Time:**
5 minutes

**Teaching point:**

The pupils will analyse the table and need to make one decision, to choose the best fuel from the three. The best fuel is B, and is methane, producing no pollutants.

**Activity:**

Draw table below onto OHT or board.

Explain that the task is to choose the best fuel. Pupils should write down the reason(s) for their selection.

A and C are fossil fuels and produce a greater number of products, some pollutants. B is methane, highlight this fact with pupils.

methane ➜ water + carbon dioxide

Point out that fossil fuels are rich in carbon, being based on organisms which lived previously, and that when a fuel produces sulpher dioxide, it produces acid rain as a consequence.

| Substance | Energy released | Carbon dioxide | Water vapour | Sulphur dioxide | Nitrogen oxides |
|-----------|-----------------|----------------|--------------|-----------------|-----------------|
| A | high | ✓ | ✓ | ✓ | ✓ |
| B | high | ✓ | ✓ | ✗ | ✗ |
| C | high | ✓ | ✓ | ✓ | ✗ |

**Challenge:** Ask pupils to research names of a range of fuels used around the world.

**Links to plenary:** Discuss the future use of "clean burn" fuels such as methane, hydrogen.

# Is it solid, liquid or gas?

**Objective:**

To be able to use particle theory to explain the structure and properties of solids, liquids and gases.

**Teaching point:**

The differences between solids, liquids and gases can be explained in terms of the particles. By observing diagram and text cards based on particle theory, pupils can link structure to properties. Pupils follow the clues. Correct statement lists under each diagram will help them position the final cards, **solid**, **liquid** and **gas**.

**Activity:**

Explain that pupils will be given the diagrams, statements and words (solid, liquid and gas) printed on card.

The diagrams show models of the particles which make up a solid, liquid and gas. To identify which of the models is solid, liquid or gas the pupils put each statement under the appropriate diagram.

The statements hold clues which will help them decide how to classify each statement. One statement is repeated to highlight similar property.

Give out solid, liquid and gas cards at the end of the activity for the final identification.

Pupils report back with findings to whole class. Answers given on Copymaster 61b OHT.

**What you will need:**
Enough copies of Copymaster 61a cards.
Pupils work in pairs.

**Time:**
10 minutes

**Challenge:** Name ONE substance in the home which can be a solid, a liquid and a gas. Can the pupils suggest the condition responsible for these changes?

**Links to plenary:** Pupils could classify a number of household substances into solid, liquid or gas. Each state can be explained in terms of particle theory.

**Badger Key Stage 3 Science Starters**

# Is it solid, liquid or gas?

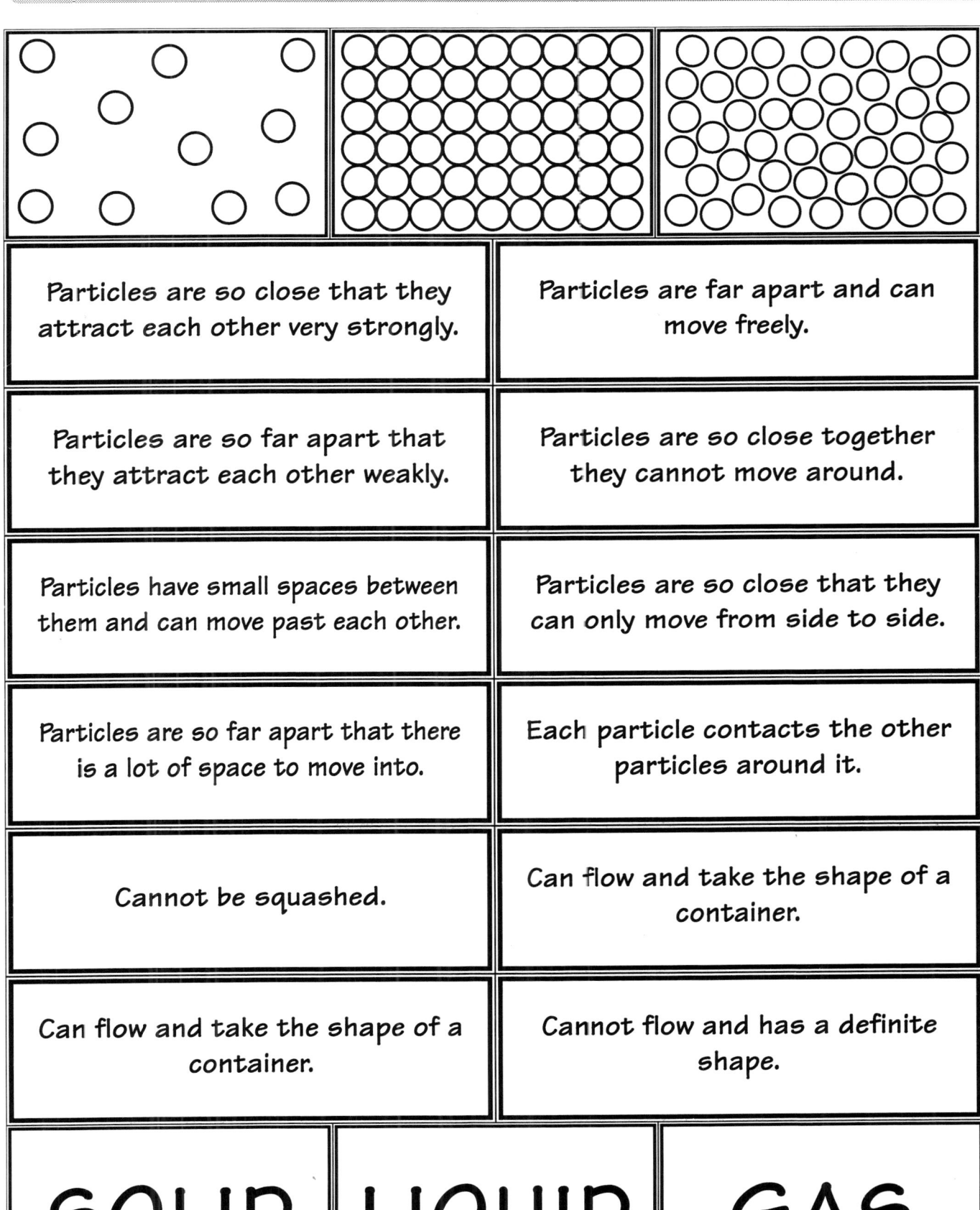

Particles are so close that they attract each other very strongly.

Particles are far apart and can move freely.

Particles are so far apart that they attract each other weakly.

Particles are so close together they cannot move around.

Particles have small spaces between them and can move past each other.

Particles are so close that they can only move from side to side.

Particles are so far apart that there is a lot of space to move into.

Each particle contacts the other particles around it.

Cannot be squashed.

Can flow and take the shape of a container.

Can flow and take the shape of a container.

Cannot flow and has a definite shape.

# SOLID  LIQUID  GAS

## Is it solid, liquid or gas?

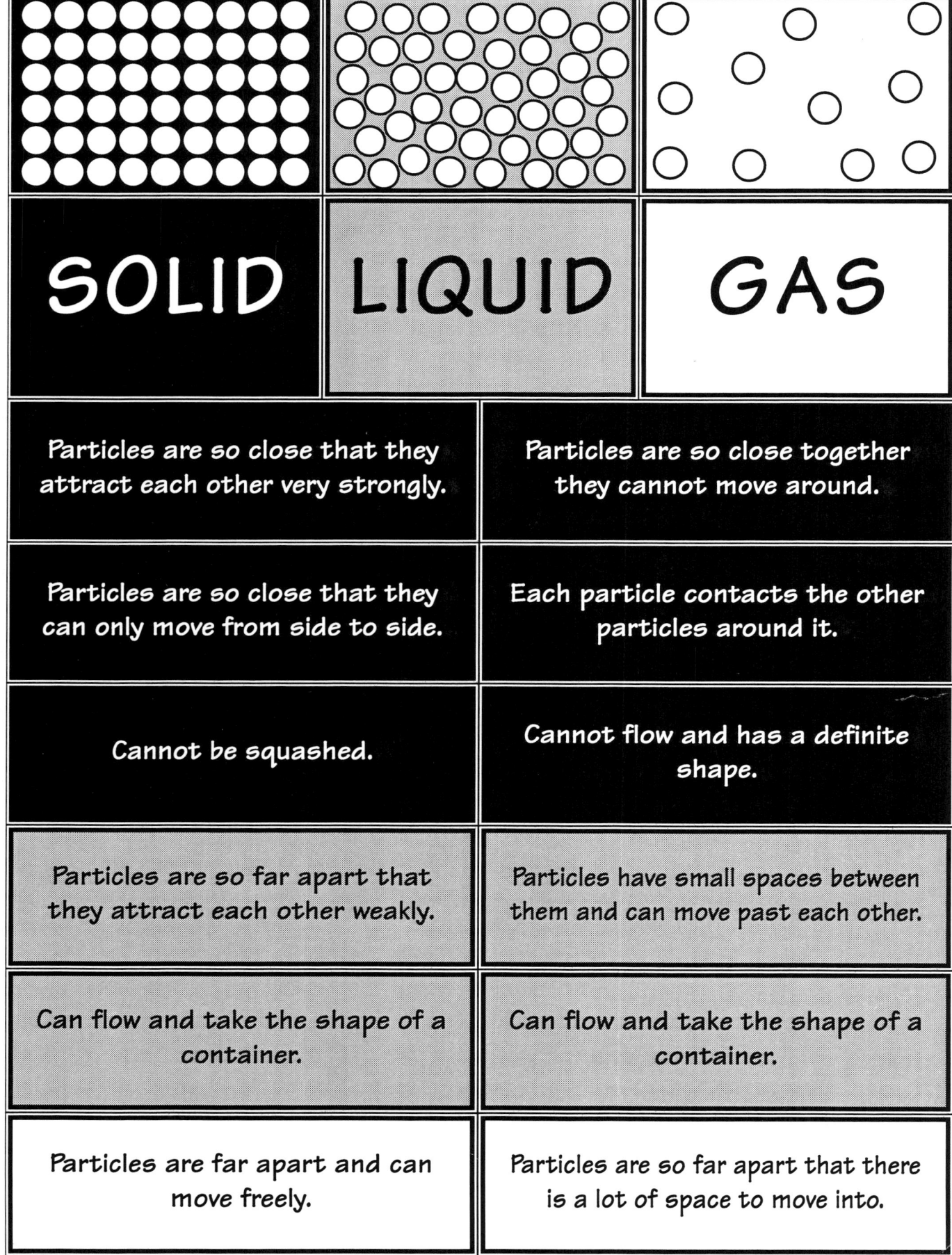

| SOLID | LIQUID | GAS |
| --- | --- | --- |
| Particles are so close that they attract each other very strongly. | Particles are so close together they cannot move around. | |
| Particles are so close that they can only move from side to side. | Each particle contacts the other particles around it. | |
| Cannot be squashed. | Cannot flow and has a definite shape. | |
| Particles are so far apart that they attract each other weakly. | Particles have small spaces between them and can move past each other. | |
| Can flow and take the shape of a container. | Can flow and take the shape of a container. | |
| Particles are far apart and can move freely. | Particles are so far apart that there is a lot of space to move into. | |

# The effect of temperature on a gas

## Objective:

To be able to use particle theory to explain how a gas responds to temperature change.

**What you will need:**
Copymaster 62 as worksheet. Pupils work in pairs.

**Time:**
10 minutes

## Teaching point:

Effects of different temperatures on a gas can be explained in terms of:
(i)  changes in distance between one particle and another.
(ii) the speed of movement of the particles.

## Activity:

Give one activity sheet to each pair of pupils.

Give background information:

- The hot air balloon is shown at two heights, 1000m and 5000m.
- The substances like oxygen and nitrogen are shown as particles.
- The balloon has a burner which can be used to warm the air in the balloon.

Reserve information – it may be necessary to suggest that at the greater height the burner has been used to warm the air.

Explain that the task is to analyse the diagrams and write down the *differences* shown.

Each pair of pupils discuss the *reasons* for each difference they observe. They should note:

- The particles are further apart at the greater height.
- The balloon has a greater width or volume at the greater height.
- The balloon is lighter at the greater height.

**Challenge:** Explain what would finally happen if the balloon went even higher.

**Links to plenary:** Discuss ideas of temperature increase giving more energy for the particles to move quickly away from each other, and to collide with the sides of the balloon. The greater the energy, the greater the force on the sides, so the balloon's volume gets bigger.

**Badger Key Stage 3 Science Starters**

# The effect of temperature on a gas

## Going up? The flight of a hot air balloon

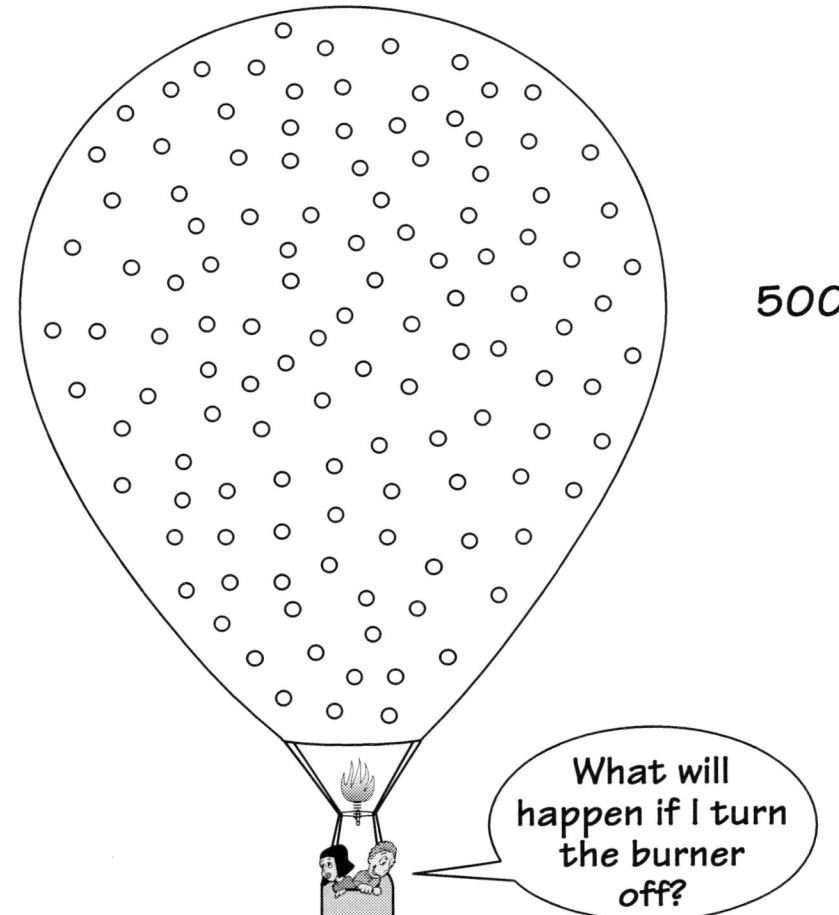

5000m above the earth

1000m above the earth

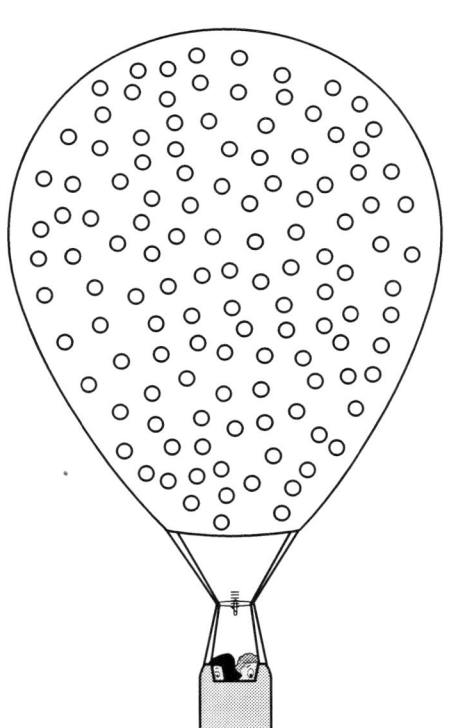

⊙⊐ **KEY POINT**

# Changing state

**Objective:**

To understand why substances change state and to explain in terms of particle theory.

**Teaching point:**

The activity involves analysis of a diagram showing an ice cube, flowing tap water and steam. The diagrams offer an opportunity to explain change of state in terms of the distances between particles.

**What you will need:**
Copymaster 63 as OHT.
Whiteboards and pens.
Pupils work in pairs.

**Time:**
5 minutes

**Activity:**

Project Copymaster OHT.

Explain that the diagrams show water in three different states.

Ask them to write down one word only which indicates the factor responsible for the changes. *(temperature)*

Once temperature has been established ask the pupils to write down the ways in which water vapour (steam) in the diagram could be changed to liquid, then ice.

Ask pupils to explain what happens in terms of the distances between particles.
*(Steam - particles are a maximum distance from each other; Water – particles are closer together: Ice – particles touch.)*

**Challenge:** Ask pupils to find out about substances which change reversibly from solid to gas, e.g. iodine.

**Links to plenary:** Compare the change of form of water to other substances, e.g. the cooling of propane / butane to liquid in gas cylinders, and cooling of nitrogen to form "dry ice."

**Badger Key Stage 3 Science Starters**

# Changing state

SOLID

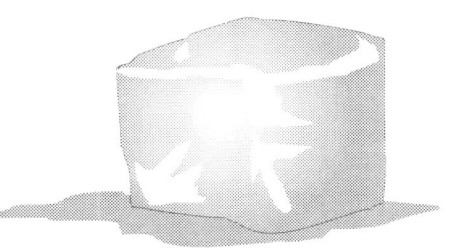

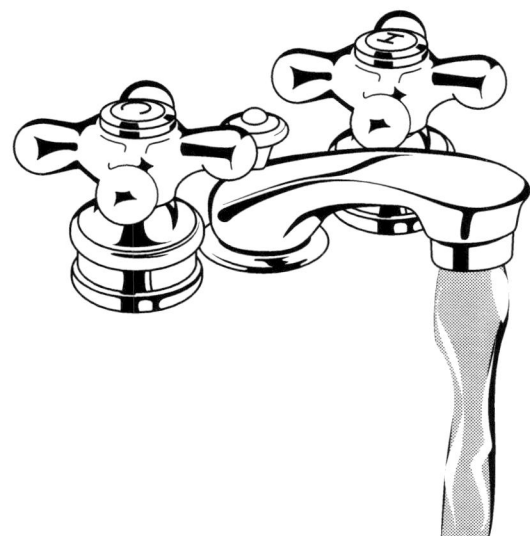　　LIQUID

GAS

# Diffusion

### Objective:

To be aware that diffusion takes place in liquids and gases.

### Teaching point:

The diagrams show bromine diffusing from one gas jar to another. Models are given, from which to select the one which shows diffusion.

**What you will need:**
Copymaster 64 as worksheets. Pupils to work in pairs.

**Time:**
8 minutes

### Activity:

Give out Copymaster worksheets.

Explain that the diagrams show what happens when bromine gas is in contact with another containing air.

From the models shown only one shows what happens. Ask the pupils to choose the correct one.

- The process will only take place from high to low concentration. ✓

- So the low to high is wrong. ✗

- And the model showing the same concentration at either side is wrong. ✗

Ask if any pupil knows what the process is called.

Particles move from high to low concentration and the process is **diffusion**.

**Challenge:** Ask pupils to explain what happens as a spoonful of sugar is added to a beaker of water.

**Links to plenary:** Discuss diffusion in a number of different contexts, e.g. perfume in air.

**Badger Key Stage 3 Science Starters**

# Diffusion

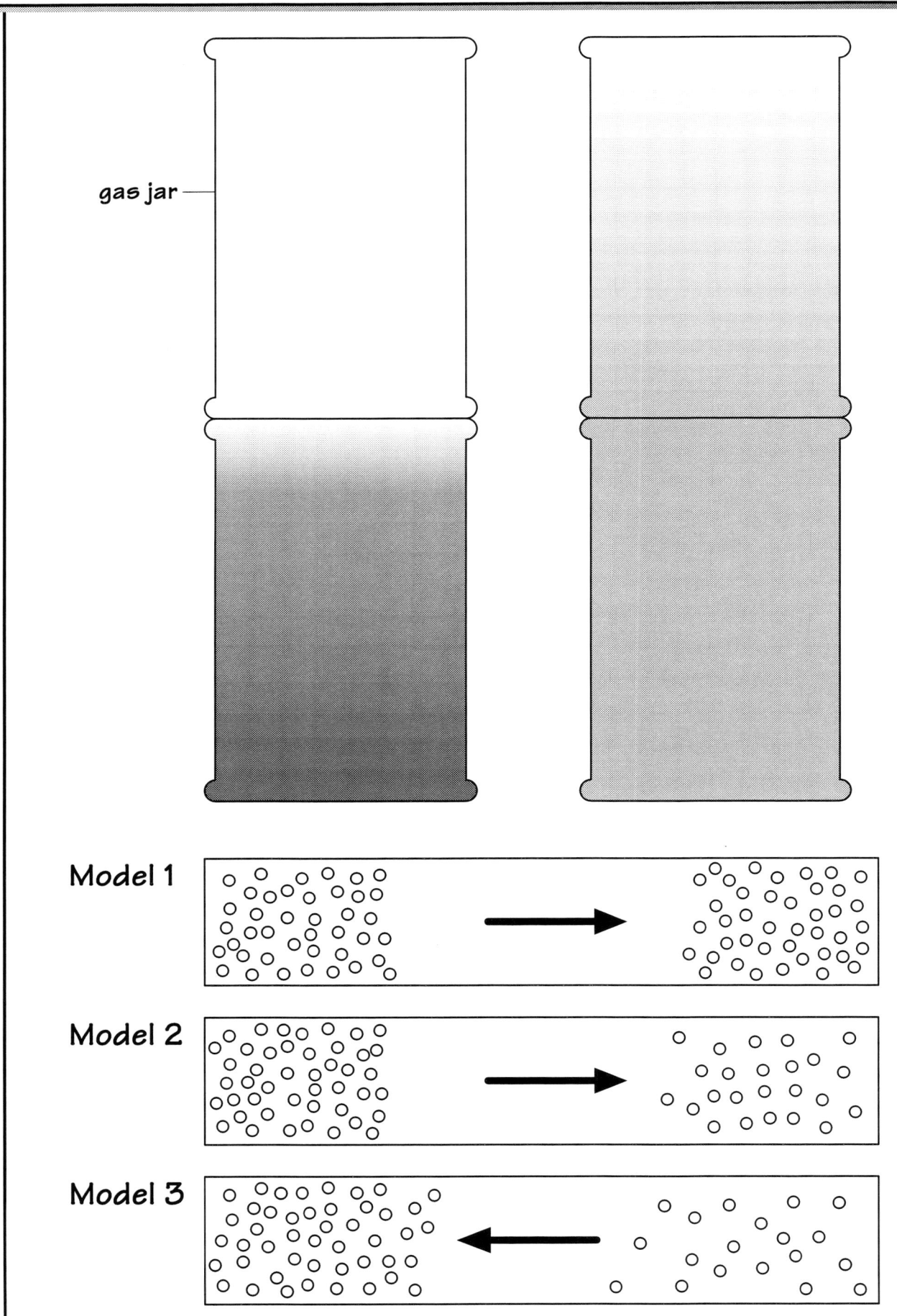

gas jar

Model 1

Model 2

Model 3

⊶ **KEY POINT**

# Air pressure

### Objective:

To be aware of the reasons why air exerts a pressure.

### Teaching point:

The diagram will stimulate consideration of why the tyre tube increases in volume as the foot pump is applied. The activity is a cloze exercise. Correct use of the list of words supplied will lead to a consideration of air pressure in a tyre inner tube.

**What you will need:**
Copymaster 65 as worksheets. Pupils to work in pairs.

**Time:**
8 minutes

### Activity:

Give out Copymaster worksheets.

Explain that the diagram shows someone pumping up a car tyre. Inform pupils that gas molecules move randomly in all directions.

Ask the pupils to write in the gaps, choosing words from the list.

**Answers:**

The foot pump is pressed down. This pushes <u>air</u> through a connection into the tube of the car tyre. As the pump is used, more and more air is pushed into the tube. The more air pumped into the tube, the more the molecules in the air <u>push</u> on the tube sides. This causes the <u>volume</u> of the tube to increase. At the same time, the pressure of the air in the tube also increases. <u>Pressure</u> of air in the tube is caused by molecules in the air colliding with the sides of the tyre tube. The more they collide, the <u>higher</u> the pressure.

**Challenge:** Ask the pupils to explain how pressure is caused by the propane inside a gas cylinder. Inform them that propane is a gas at room temperature.

**Links to plenary:** Discuss the exertion of air pressure in tyre inner tubes and balloons. Highlight the random movement of gas molecules and collisions with containing walls.

**Badger Key Stage 3 Science Starters**

# Air pressure

## volume    higher    pressure    air    push

The foot pump is pressed down. This pushes . . . . . . . . . . . .

through a connection into the tube of the car tyre. As the pump

is used, more and more air is pushed into the tube. The more air

pumped into the tube, the more the molecules in the air

. . . . . . . . . . . . on the tube sides. This causes the . . . . . . . . . .

of the tube to increase. At the same time, the pressure of the air

in the tube also increases. . . . . . . . . . . . . of air in the tube is

caused by molecules in the air colliding with the sides of the tyre

tube. The more they collide, the . . . . . . . . . . . . the pressure.

# A solution or not?

### Objective:

To be able to find out if a given liquid is a solution or not.

### Teaching point:

The activity is based on 2 beakers containing liquids. One is water and the other is (salt) solution. By applying evaporation to both the correct deduction can be made.

**What you will need:**
Copymaster 66 as OHT.
Whole class activity.

**Time:**
5 minutes

### Activity:

Project Copymaster OHT.

Explain that Jamie investigated 2 liquids, A and B. One was known to be a solution and the other was not.

Ask pupils to:

Select which is the solution.

Give a reason for the selection.

The idea of water evaporating should be given by pupils.

After pupil responses as a class have been shared explain that:

- salt is the solute
- water the solvent
- the mixture of the two is solution.

**Challenge:** Ask pupils to give a list of substances which dissolve in water.

**Links to plenary:** Discuss the use of solutions in the home.

**Badger Key Stage 3 Science Starters**

# A solution or not?

## A solution of salt?

Liquid A                             Liquid B

**1.**
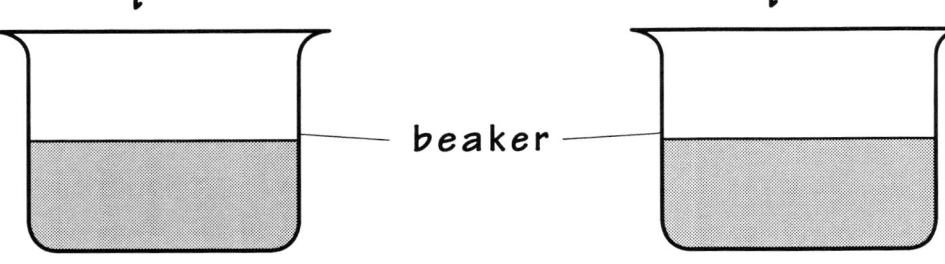
beaker

**2.**

**3.**
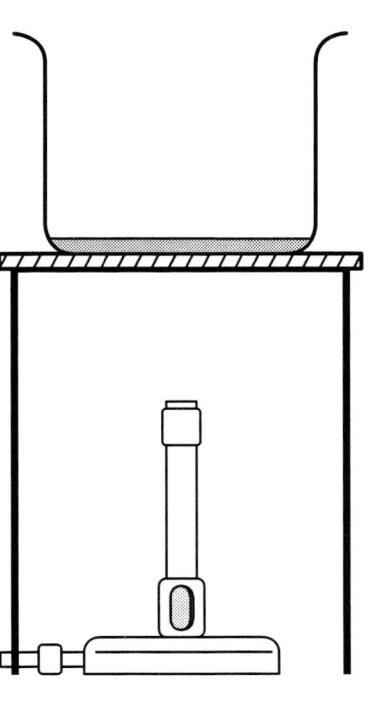
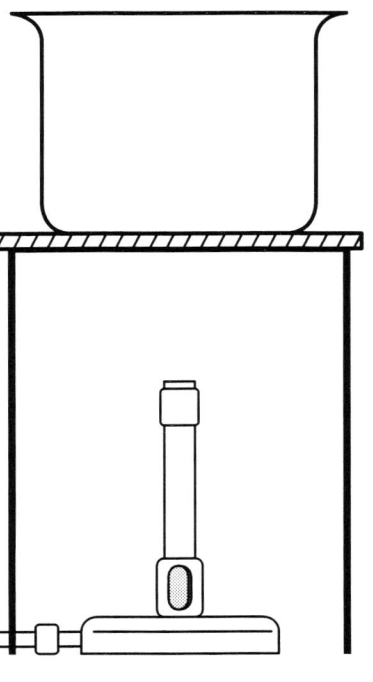

# Separating sand and salt

### Objective:

To understand how to obtain samples of sand and salt from rock salt.

### Teaching point:

The activity is based on a successful separation of sand and salt from rock salt. It incorporates dissolving, filtration, evaporation. Pupils should re-sequence the given statements.

**What you will need:**
Copymaster 67 as worksheets. Pupils to work in pairs.

**Time:**
8 minutes

### Activity:

Give out Copymaster worksheets.

Explain that the statements should be cut from the worksheet. Tell pupils that the aim is to re-sequence the statements correctly to explain how pure sand and pure salt were produced from a lump of rock salt.

**Answer:**

The sample of rock salt was crushed then put into a beaker with water.

This produced a brown liquid which was heated and stirred.

This helped the salt in the brown liquid to dissolve.

Filter paper was put into a funnel.

The brown liquid was poured through the filter paper.

A clear liquid dripped through, and pure sand was left behind.

The clear liquid was poured into an evaporating dish.

The clear liquid was heated to evaporate off the water.

Pure salt was left behind.

**Challenge:** Ask pupils to design a method to separate two liquids which do not mix together like cooking oil and water.

**Links to plenary:** Discuss the way that a number of different techniques were used in the separation technique.

**Badger Key Stage 3 Science Starters**

# Separating sand and salt

## Statements

| | |
|---|---|
| Filter paper was put into a funnel. | Pure salt was left behind. |
| This produced a brown liquid which was heated and stirred. | The clear liquid was heated to evaporate off the water. |
| A clear liquid dripped through, and pure sand was left behind. | The brown liquid was poured through the filter paper. |
| This helped the salt in the brown liquid to dissolve. | The clear liquid was poured into an evaporating dish. |
| The sample of rock salt was crushed then put into a beaker with water. | |

# Is mass conserved when substances dissolve?

### Objective:

To know that mass is conserved when substances dissolve to form solutions.

### Teaching point:

A sequence of three diagrams shows that mass does not change when a solution is produced. A balance display is shown and the mass of constituents is constant. Oil is added to show that when no evaporation takes place the mass is static.

**What you will need:**
Copymaster 68 as OHT.
Whole class activity.

**Time:**
5 minutes

### Activity:

Give prompt questions before projecting Copymaster OHT:

Do you think that mass changes when copper sulphate is added to water?

Why do you think this is?

Project Copymaster OHT.

Explain that the sequence of diagrams shows a solution of copper sulphate being produced.

Inform pupils that oil was used after the copper sulphate was dissolved in the water. This was to prevent any evaporation and will not change the solution at all.

Ask the pupils:

What do you think happened to the mass?

Why do you think this is?

After analysing the diagrams they should write a conclusion about the **mass of substances when a solution is formed**.

The simple conclusion **mass does not change** should emerge if calculations are carried out.

**Challenge:** What would have happened to the mass if oil had not been used?
What effect would this have on the concentration of the copper sulphate?

**Links to plenary:** Discuss the fact that mass is retained when a solution is formed, even though the molecules in the solution are re-arranged in some way.

**Badger Key Stage 3 Science Starters**

# Is mass conserved when substances dissolve?

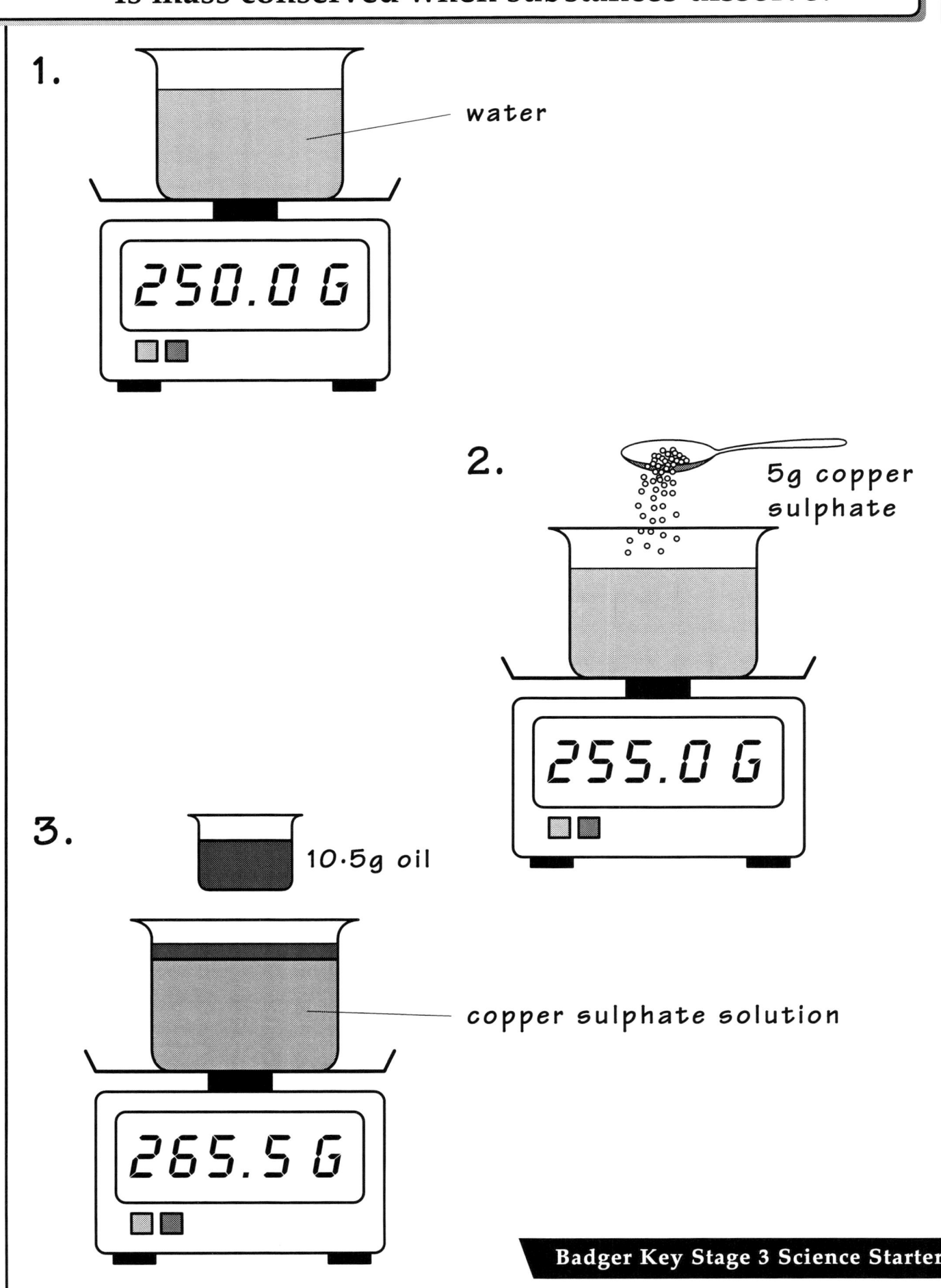

1. water — 250.0 G

2. 5g copper sulphate — 255.0 G

3. 10·5g oil — copper sulphate solution — 265.5 G

# Distillation

## Objective:

To understand the process of distillation; show that distillation can be used to separate a liquid from dissolved solids.

## Teaching point:

The Copymaster shows a diagram of a Liebig condenser being used to distil ink. This together with a key word list gives clues to aid explanation.

**What you will need:**
Copymaster 69 as OHT.
Whole class activity.

**Time:**
10 minutes

## Activity:

Project Copymaster OHT.

Explain that the apparatus shown was used to prove that ink is made from a coloured solid and water.

The activity is to write down how the apparatus can be used to separate the solid (solute) pigment from the water (solvent). It gives key words which the pupils should incorporate into their explanation. Key words are in random order so will need to be correctly sequenced.

The explanation should include:

- Bunsen used to <u>boil</u> ink.
- Water <u>evaporates</u>, changing from liquid to gas (<u>steam</u>).
- The steam is <u>cooled</u>, and <u>condenses</u> back to liquid water.
- <u>Pure water</u> is collected in a beaker.
- Coloured <u>solid</u> left behind in the flask.

Inform pupils that this is distillation.

**Challenge:** Ask pupils to research how distillation is used in the alcohol industry.

**Links to plenary:** Explain that the sequence of evaporation followed by condensation can be used to separate solutes from solvents, and that this combination is known as distillation.

**Badger Key Stage 3 Science Starters**

# Distillation

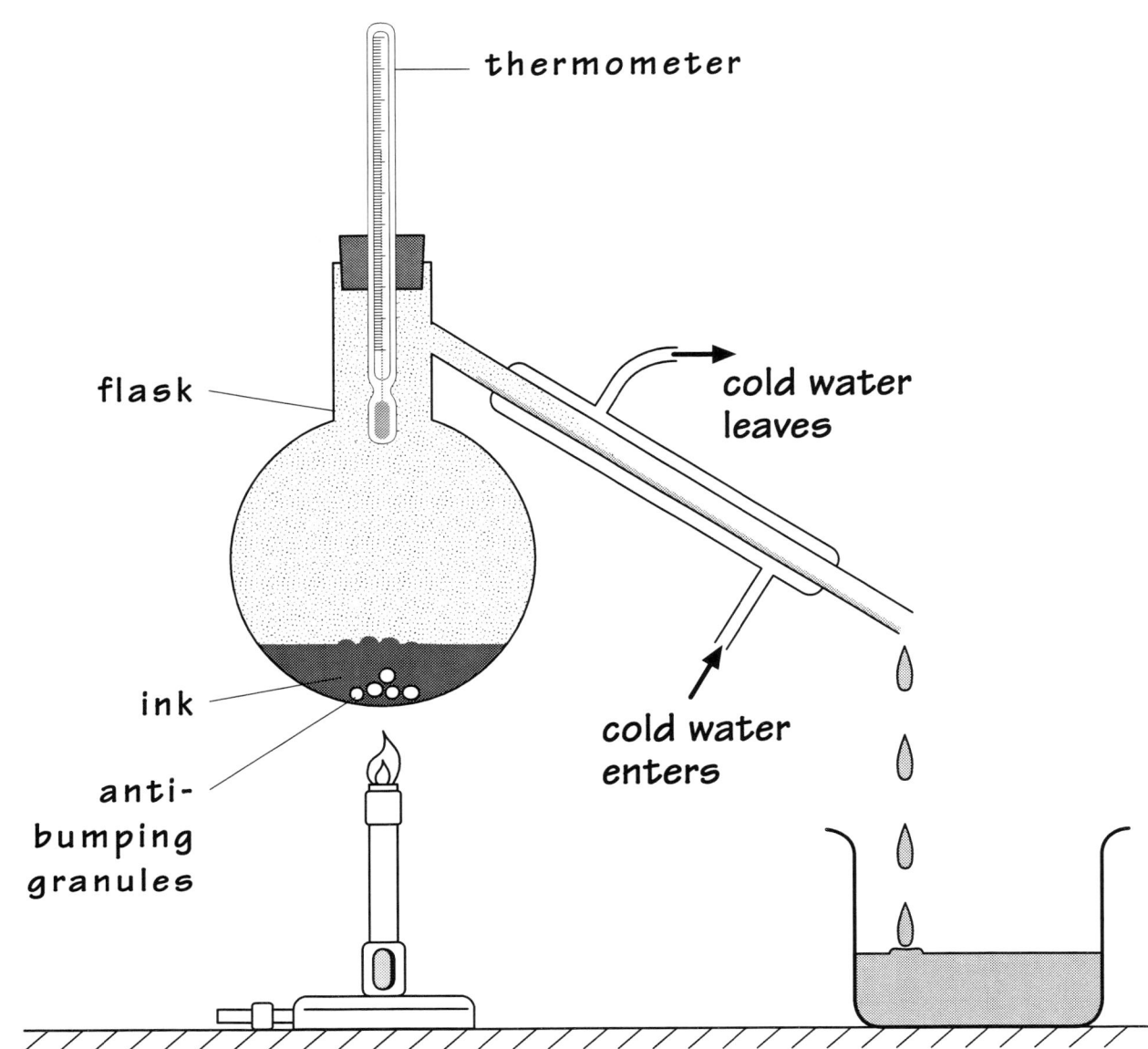

- thermometer
- flask
- ink
- anti-bumping granules
- cold water leaves
- cold water enters

## Distillation apparatus

pure water
cooled
boils
condenses
evaporates
heat
solid
steam

# Chromatography

### Objective:

To know that two or more solutes can be separated using chromatography.

**What you will need:**
Copymaster 70 as worksheets. Pupils to work in pairs.

**Time:**
8 minutes

### Teaching point:

The activity is in two parts. Firstly the diagram of the chromatography apparatus is given to elicit an explanation of how it works. This is followed up by a chromatogram used to show the differences in the ink from three different felt-tip pens.

### Activity:

Give out Copymaster worksheets.

Explain that the diagram shows typical chromatography apparatus.

Ask the pupils to explain how the process enables the separation of solutes. You may wish to give further guidance with questions:

Why is the solvent acetone used?
*(To help the solute molecules move.)*

Why is the start line drawn in pencil?
*(Otherwise it could produce moving colour spots as well.)*

Why should the ink dots not be drawn at or below the solvent level?
*(Ink would dissolve into the acetone.)*

In which direction do the solvent molecules move?
*(Up)*

Pupils share ideas, and you should highlight the above information.

Tell pupils that purple is a mixture of blue and red. Ask the pupils to enter the spot for red on the worksheet. *(In line with highest purple dot.)*

**Challenge:** Chlorophyll can be extracted from plants and consists of a number of pigments. Ask pupils to describe how this could be proved.

**Links to plenary:** Ask pupils to give a repeat explanation of chromatography. Ask how it may be used in forensic work.

**Badger Key Stage 3 Science Starters**

# Chromatography

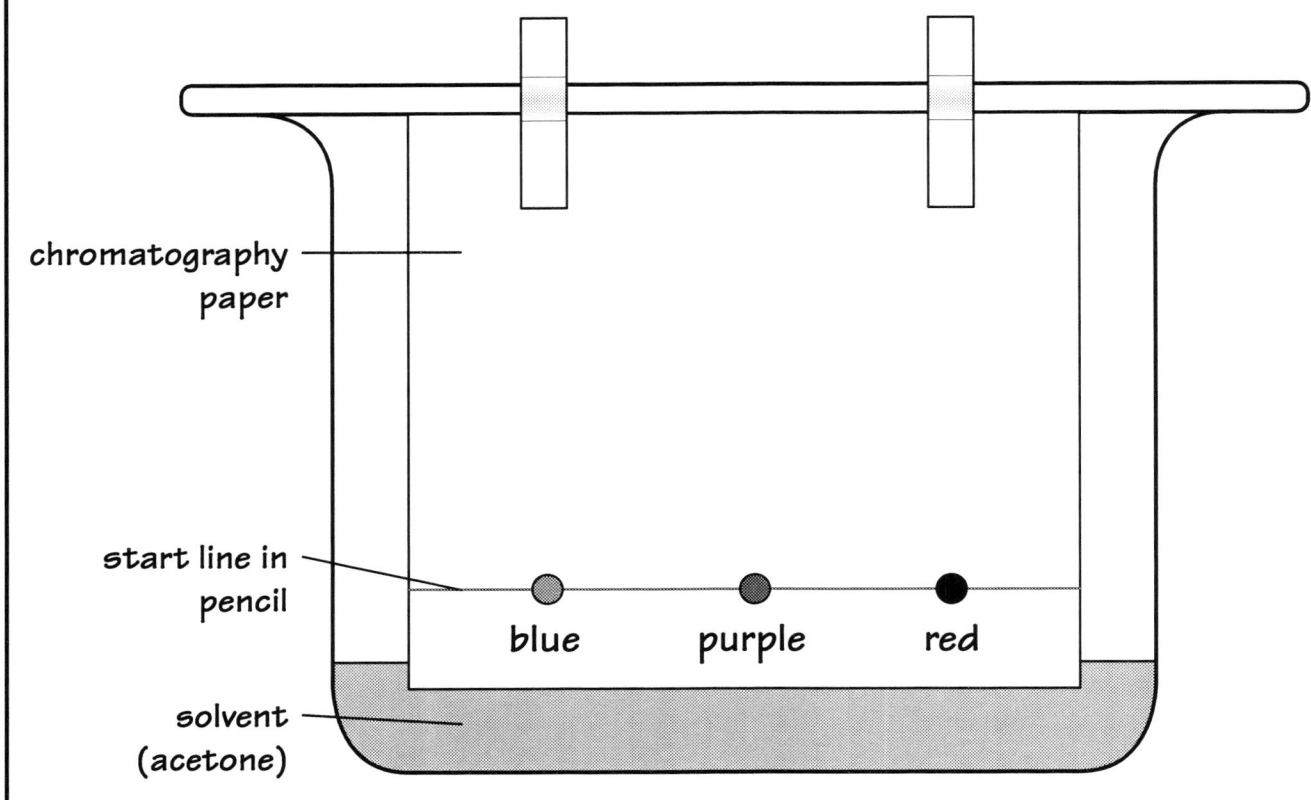

chromatography paper

start line in pencil

blue    purple    red

solvent (acetone)

## Chromatography apparatus at start

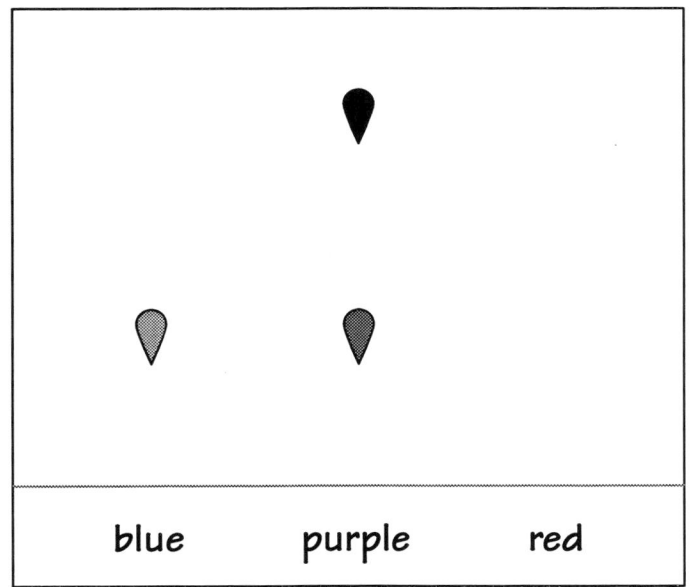

blue    purple    red

## The completed chromatogram

**Badger Key Stage 3 Science Starters**

# Does temperature affect solubility?

## Objective:

To show that substances tend to be more soluble at higher temperatures.

## Teaching point:

Copymaster 71a shows the solubility curve of copper sulphate. The pupils will analyse the graph and may conclude that solubility increases with temperature.

## Activity:

Give out Copymaster worksheets.

Explain to pupils that the graph shows how much copper sulphate dissolves in water at a range of different temperatures.

Ask pupils to analyse the graph then answer the questions below the graph.

Answers are provided on Copymaster 71b OHT.

Highlight the final answer. Explain the term **saturation**, as when no more solute will dissolve, so any addition copper sulphate would show up as crystals.

**What you will need:**
Copymaster 71a as worksheets. Pupils to work in pairs.

**Time:**
10 minutes

**Challenge:** Ask pupils to explain what would happen if a saturated solution of copper sulphate at 70°C was cooled to 10°C.

**Links to plenary:** Discuss the pattern of the solubility curve of copper sulphate and inform that different substances have different solubility. In fact some do not dissolve at all.

**Badger Key Stage 3 Science Starters**

# Does temperature affect solubility?

Daisy and Dino dissolved as much copper sulphate as they could at the following temperatures 10°C, 20°C, 30°C, 40°C, 50°C, 60°C, and 70°C.

The graph shows the pattern of their results.

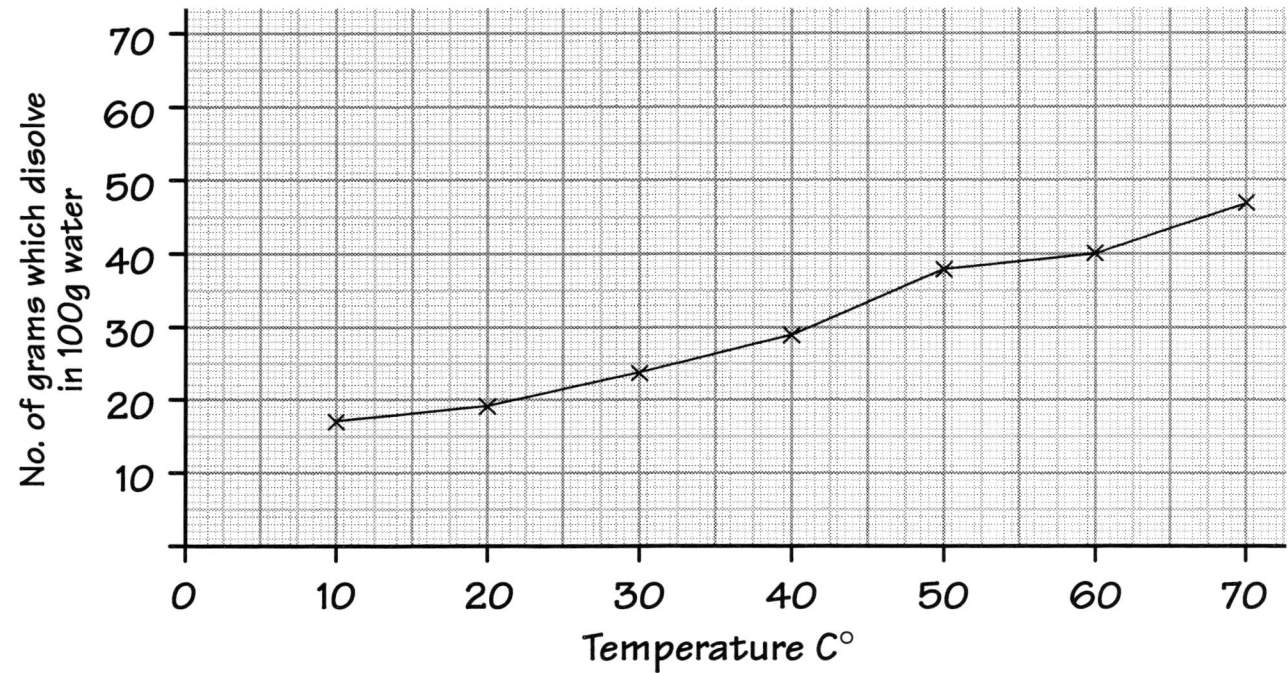

Use the graph to help you answer the following questions:

(a) How much copper sulphate dissolved at 35°C?

(b) At what temperature would 22g copper sulphate dissolve?

(c) Daisy and Dino did not measure how much copper sulphate dissolved at 80°C. Use the graph to help you to make a prediction.

(d) What would Daisy and Dino have seen in the beaker to show them that no more copper sulphate would dissolve?

(e) What term is given to a solution which will dissolve no more of a solute?

# Does temperature affect solubility?

## Answers:

(a) How much copper sulphate dissolved at 35°C?

*26g*

(b) At what temperature would 22g copper sulphate dissolve?

*25°C*

(c) Daisy and Dino did not measure how much copper sulphate dissolved at 80°C. Use the graph to help you to make a prediction.

*53 or 54g*

(d) What would Daisy and Dino have seen in the beaker to show them that no more copper sulphate would dissolve?

*crystals / solid*

(e) What term is given to a solution which will dissolve no more of a solute?

*saturated*

# Which fuel?

### Objective:

To investigate which fuel releases the most energy, using fair test principles.

### Teaching point:

Different fuels release different amounts of energy. The activity will develop pupil investigative skills in the planning of how to compare fuels. Additionally it underlines the nature of a fuel.

**What you will need:**
Copymaster 72 as OHT.
Pupils to work in groups.

**Time:**
10 minutes

### Activity:

Project Copymaster OHT.

Explain that the spirit burner works by the wick dipping into a liquid fuel. The activity is to plan, using fair test principles, an investigation to find out which fuel releases the most energy. Energy released is to be measured by heating up water.

Groups write down their ideas.

Stimulus questions:

How much fuel should be put into the spirit burner?
*(Equal amounts)*

How can the conditions be kept the same?
*(Same room temperature etc, no wind to blow flames)*

How much water should be heated up?
*(Equal amounts)*

Which equipment should be used?
*(Boiling tubes, measuring cylinder, thermometer, stop clock, safety goggles)*

How can you make the investigation safe?
*(Use goggles)*

Is some heat energy wasted? If so, how can this be kept to a minimum?
*(Insulate boiling tube, quickly commence heating of water once the flame ignites)*

These questions could be reproduced as worksheets to help plan an investigation.

**Challenge:** Ask pupils to research "fuels" which supply energy inside the human body. Additionally ask them how the energy is released.

**Links to plenary:** Discuss the aspects of this plan that can be transferred to other investigations. Highlight that a fuel contains energy which can be released.

**Badger Key Stage 3 Science Starters**

# Which fuel?

## Spirit burner

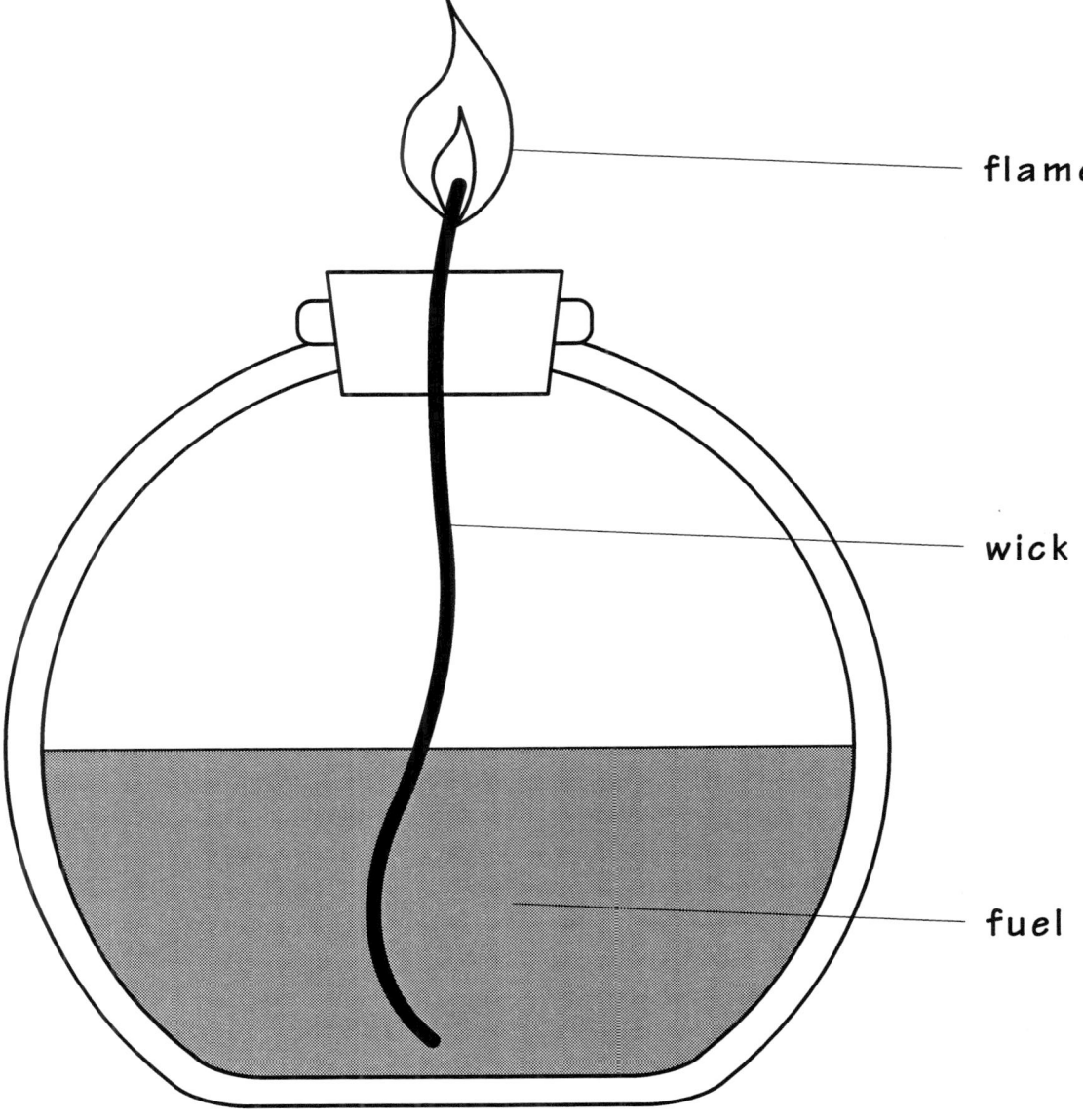

flame

wick

fuel

# How were fossil fuels produced?

### Objective:

To know how fossil fuels were formed from organic origins.

### Teaching point:

A diagram linking a scene from millions of years ago to deposits of crude oil and natural gas provides a stimulus for a cloze exercise. Pupils will complete the text to give a description of formation.

**What you will need:**
Copymaster 73 as worksheets. Pupils to work individually.

**Time:**
10 minutes

### Activity:

Give out Copymaster worksheets.

Explain that the diagrams show deposits of oil and gas. The activity is to use the information and their own knowledge to complete the cloze exercise.

Millions of years ago lived microscopic plants and <u>animals</u>. When they died they did not rot down. They probably became covered in some way so that conditions lacked <u>oxygen</u>. Over many years they became trapped by rock layers and were changed into <u>crude oil</u> and natural gas by heat and <u>pressure</u>. They are called fossil fuels because they formed from dead organisms. They are <u>non-renewable</u> because it would take millions of years before they could form again.

Highlight the answers to help pupils to understand the process of formation.

**Challenge:** Ask pupils to list other sources of energy.

**Links to plenary:** Discuss the depletion of fossil fuels, including coal and the disadvantages of using them.

**Badger Key Stage 3 Science Starters**

# How were fossil fuels produced?

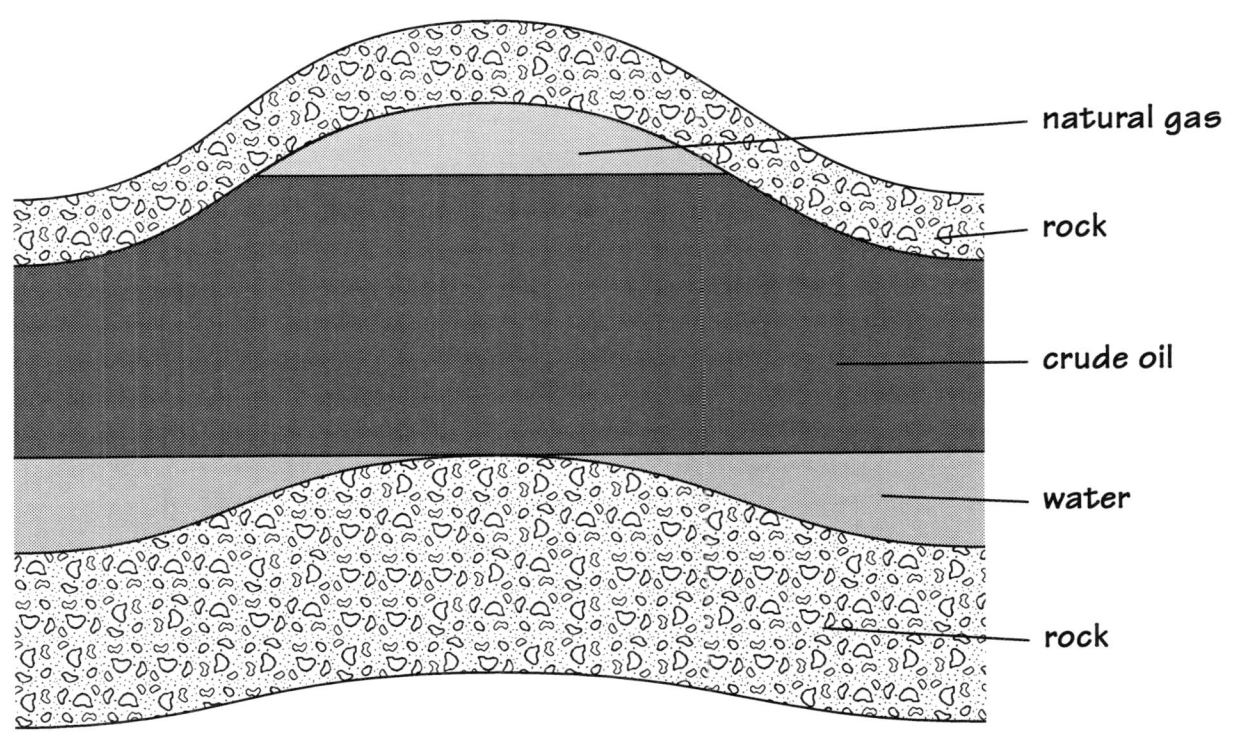

fossil          pressure          non-renewable
oxygen          animals           crude oil

Millions of years ago lived microscopic plants and . . . . . . . . . . . . . . .

When they died they did not rot down. They probably became covered in

some way so that conditions lacked . . . . . . . . . . . . . . . Over many

years they became trapped by rock layers and were changed into

. . . . . . . . . . . . . . . and natural gas by heat and . . . . . . . . . . . . . . .

They are called . . . . . . . . . . . . . . . fuels because they formed from

dead organisms. They are . . . . . . . . . . . . . . . . . . . . because it would

take millions of years before they could form again.

# Renewable energy?

### Objective:

To be aware that sunlight can be harnessed as a renewable energy source.

### Teaching point:

The diagram of the renewable energy house shows 4 different ways to harness the sun's energy.

**What you will need:**
Copymaster 74 as OHT.
Whole class activity.

**Time:**
10 minutes

### Activity:

Project Copymaster OHT.

Explain that the aim of the devices is to supply useful energy without polluting the Earth.

Ask pupils:

Give one word which links each of these devices.
*(sunlight)*

The solar panels are black and have water pipes going through them. How do they work?
*(Heat the water system of the house; give hot water - being black they absorb more heat energy.)*

What is the energy source of the calculator?
*(light, sunlight)*

How does this power the calculator?
*(Light is converted to electricity by a photoelectric cell.)*

How does the wind turbine give power to the home?
*(Wind turns the turbine, which generates electricity.)*

**Challenge:** Ask pupils to name three other renewable energy sources and explain how they can be harnessed.

**Links to plenary:** Review the methods and ask how the energy source can be regarded as renewable.

**Badger Key Stage 3 Science Starters**

# Renewable energy?

## The renewable energy house

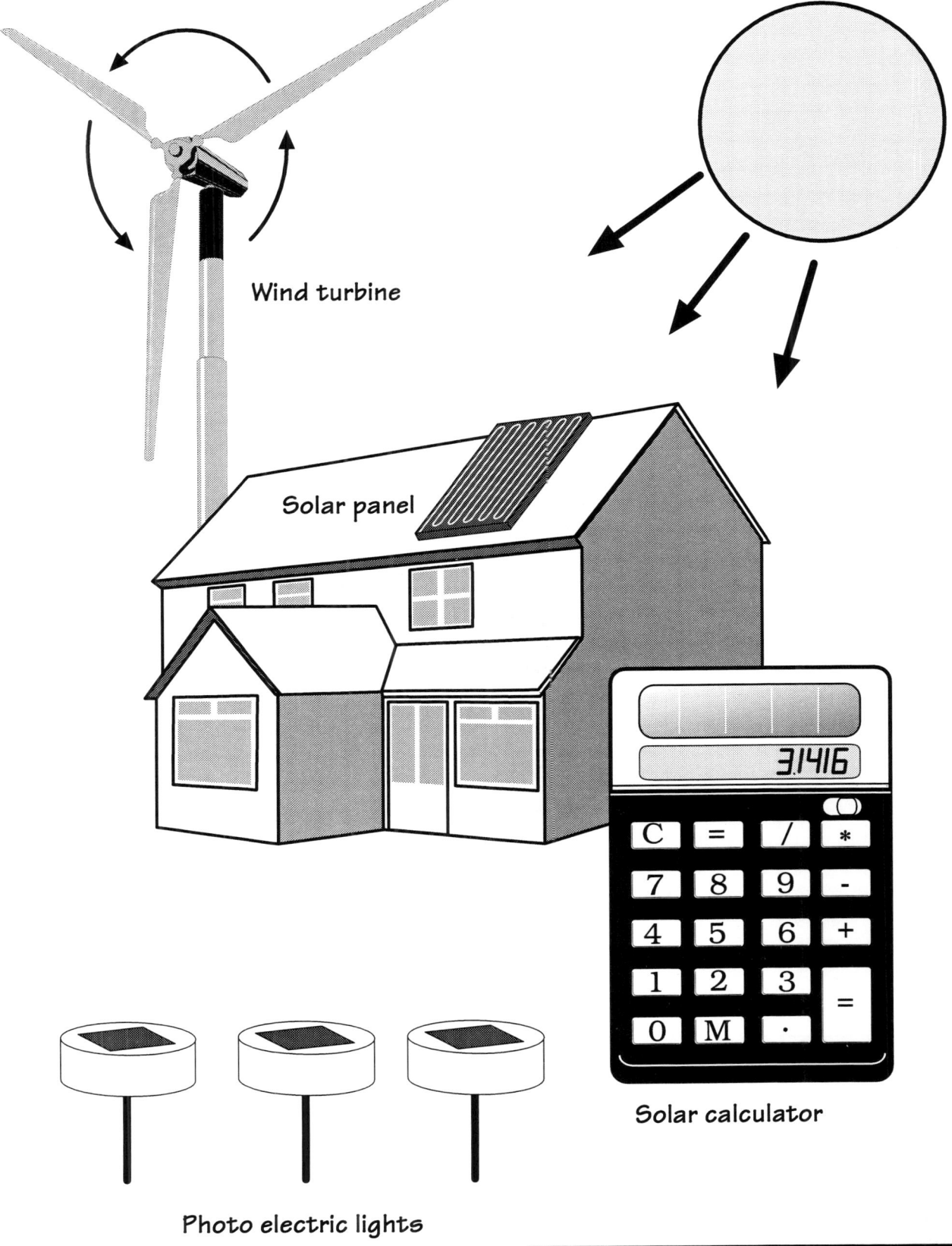

Wind turbine

Solar panel

3.1416

Solar calculator

Photo electric lights

# Measuring energy output of food

### Objective:

To be aware that the energy output of food can be measured.

### Teaching point:

Foods are an energy store and this energy can be released by combustion and respiration. The activity gives a diagram of a calorimeter. Pupils may be able to work out how the energy output of different foods can be measured using the apparatus.

**What you will need:**
Copymaster 75 as OHT.
Whole class activity.

**Time:**
8 minutes

### Activity:

Project Copymaster OHT.

Explain that the calorimeter is used to measure energy output of different foods.

The activity is to give details of how the pupils think it is used.

They should use clues in the diagram.

Ask pupils to write what they think each part is for. Use the following prompts:

(a) electrical heating element
It allows the <u>food</u> to ignite.

(b) oxygen
It allows the <u>food</u> to burn.

(c) stirrer
It mixes the <u>water</u> so that the temperature is the same everywhere.

(d) thermometer
It measures the <u>increase</u> in water temperature.

Once the answers have been discussed, inform the pupils that temperature increase is used in the calculation of joules or kilojoules. Tell them that they will learn more in the future.

**Challenge:** Ask pupils to research the energy output data on a number of different food products.

**Links to plenary:** Discuss how a calorimeter can be used to compare different foods. Highlight the importance of equal mass comparison and repeated readings.

**Badger Key Stage 3 Science Starters**

# Measuring energy output of food

## A calorimeter

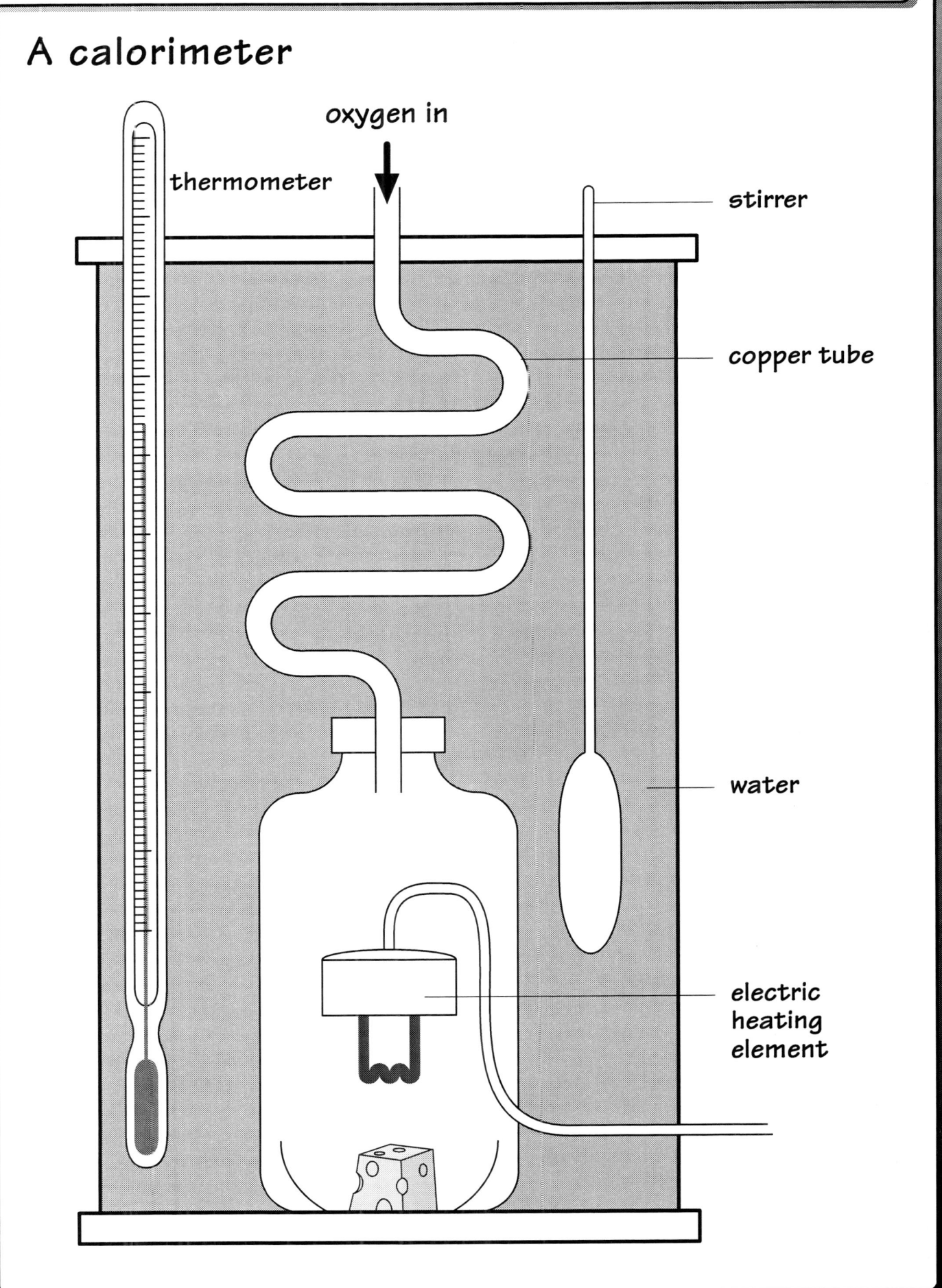

thermometer

oxygen in

stirrer

copper tube

water

electric heating element

# Renewable or non-renewable?

### Objective:

To be able to classify a number of different energy sources.

### Teaching point:

Completion of the table will enable a range of fuels to be classified. For each choice, renewable or non-renewable, reasons should be given. This will allow the pupils to establish the pattern in both types of energy source.

**What you will need:**
Copymaster 76a as worksheets. Pupils to work in pairs.

**Time:**
10 minutes

### Activity:

Give out Copymaster worksheets.

Explain that the aim is to complete the table by writing in renewable or non-renewable for each, and to give a reason for each choice.

You may need to explain the traditional use of peat in parts of Ireland (see table).

Discuss pupil ideas.

Copymaster OHT 76b provides the answers.

Establish the key factor in defining renewable, being the speed of replacement of the source.

Alternatively, use Copymaster OHT 76b to produce cards for pupils to match, to complete the table.

**Challenge:** Ask pupils to add other energy sources not included in the table.

**Links to plenary:** Discuss the advantages and disadvantages of the different types of energy source.

# Renewable or non-renewable?

| Energy source | Is it renewable or non-renewable? | Reason for your choice |
|---|---|---|
| coal | | |
| wave power | | |
| geothermal power | | |
| wood | | |
| wind power | | |
| peat | | |

# Renewable or non-renewable?

## Answers

| Energy source | Is it renewable or non-renewable? | Reason for your choice |
|---|---|---|
| coal | non-renewable | once burned it has released energy; millions of years to form more |
| wave power | renewable | waves available day after day |
| geothermal power | renewable | geothermal power can be tapped day after day |
| wood | renewable | grow more trees; can re-plant |
| wind power | renewable | wind is regular; it returns! |
| peat | non-renewable | once burnt it has released its energy; thousands of years to form more |

# Energy source ~ living organisms

### Objective:

To be aware that the sunlight is the ultimate source of energy for living organisms.

### Teaching point:

The diagram shows a scene involving both plants and animals. The pupils need to trace the source of energy back to the sunlight. This will stimulate further discussion.

**What you will need:**
Copymaster 77 as OHT.
Whole class activity.

**Time:**
8 minutes

### Activity:

Project Copymaster OHT.

Explain that the arrows show the transfer of energy from one organism to another.

Ask the pupils: What is the original source of energy to organisms in the diagram? *(sunlight)*

Draw in the sun after pupils have given their ideas. Show the energy direction.

Potential questions:

How is the sun's energy transferred to the plants?
*(plants make their own food, photosynthesis)*

How is energy transferred from one organism to another?
*(eating)*

In a year when there is a lot of cloud, what effect does this have on the energy available to organisms?
*(reduces energy to plants, so less energy to animals)*

Highlight the importance of the original source of energy, the sun.

**Challenge:** Ask the pupils to list other uses of energy in non-living systems, e.g. use of fuels.

**Links to plenary:** Discuss the consequences if sunlight energy was not available to organisms.

**Badger Key Stage 3 Science Starters**

# Energy source ~ living organisms

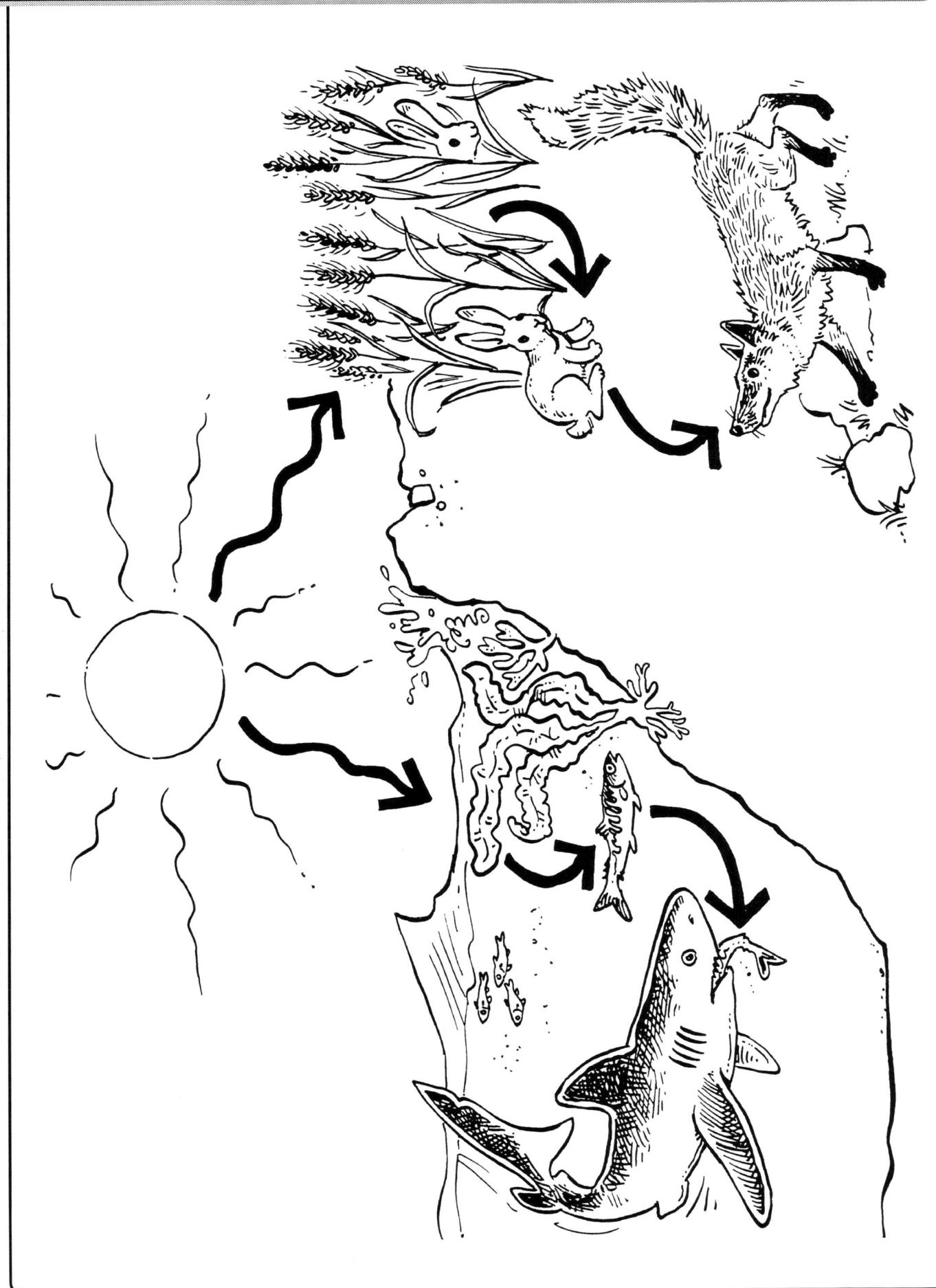

# Running out of fossil fuels!

### Objective:

To be aware that conservation of fuels is important in light of the Earth's diminishing energy resources.

### Teaching point:

The newspaper article states that there are dangers in using fossil fuels and that they are becoming exhausted. Pupils are asked questions which test understanding.

**What you will need:**
Copymaster 78 as worksheets. Pupils to work in groups.

**Time:**
10 minutes

### Activity:

Give out Copymaster worksheets.

Explain that the newspaper article indicates problems in fossil fuels running out. Additionally extraction and combustion have problems. The questions probe knowledge of these aspects.

Ask pupils to answer the questions. Answers provided below:

(a) Give TWO energy sources which are not fossil fuels.
   *Solar energy, wave, wind, running water, geothermal, biomass*

(b) Explain the problems caused by extracting the fossil fuel, coal, from the ground.
   *Disruption of habitats, spoil environment, subsidence*

(c) Explain the problems of burning fossil fuels.
   *Releases carbon dioxide, greenhouse gas, global warming, pollution.*

**Challenge:** Ask pupils to research and write an article about the advantages of using renewable energy sources.

**Links to plenary:** Discuss the issue of energy supply in the future.

**Badger Key Stage 3 Science Starters**

## Read the newspaper article

# Running out of fossil fuels!

People are becoming increasingly concerned that fossil fuels will soon run out. Reserves will last for a further 30 years but then will be exhausted. Alternative energy sources are needed.

An Environmental spokesperson stated that there are problems caused by the extraction and burning of fossil fuels.

We need to use clean sources of energy to heat our homes and supply electricity.

(a) Give TWO energy sources which are not fossil fuels.

1. . . . . . . . . . . . . . . . . . . . . . . . . . . . . . . . . . . . . . . . . . .

2. . . . . . . . . . . . . . . . . . . . . . . . . . . . . . . . . . . . . . . . . . .

(b) Explain the problems caused by extracting the fossil fuel, coal, from the ground.

. . . . . . . . . . . . . . . . . . . . . . . . . . . . . . . . . . . . . . . . . .

(c) Explain the problems of burning fossil fuels.

. . . . . . . . . . . . . . . . . . . . . . . . . . . . . . . . . . . . . . . .

. . . . . . . . . . . . . . . . . . . . . . . . . . . . . . . . . . . . . . . .

**Badger Key Stage 3 Science Starters**

# Electricity: which symbol?

**Objective:**

To recognise electrical symbols used in circuit diagrams.

**Teaching point:**

Pupils need to be aware of the components used in electrical circuits. The activity requires them to link symbols to their correct name.

**What you will need:**
Copymaster 79a as worksheets. Pupils to work in pairs.

**Time:**
5 minutes

**Activity:**

Give out Copymaster worksheets.

Explain that the aim is to link each symbol to its correct name.

Copymaster 79b OHT provides the answers.

Highlight the use of the word "cell" as being equivalent to battery. Clarify that a battery can consist of two cells and would be represented by a two cell symbol.

**Challenge:** Ask pupils to explain which two of the components can break a circuit and then explain how they do this.

**Links to plenary:** Discuss the advantages of using symbols to show circuits rather than "real life" diagrams.

**Badger Key Stage 3 Science Starters**

# Electricity: which symbol?

      voltmeter

      fuse

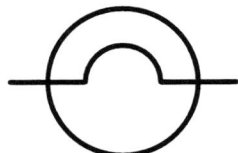      cell

      ammeter

      wire

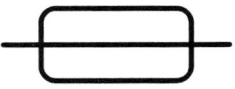      resistor

      switch

      lamp

# Electricity: which symbol?

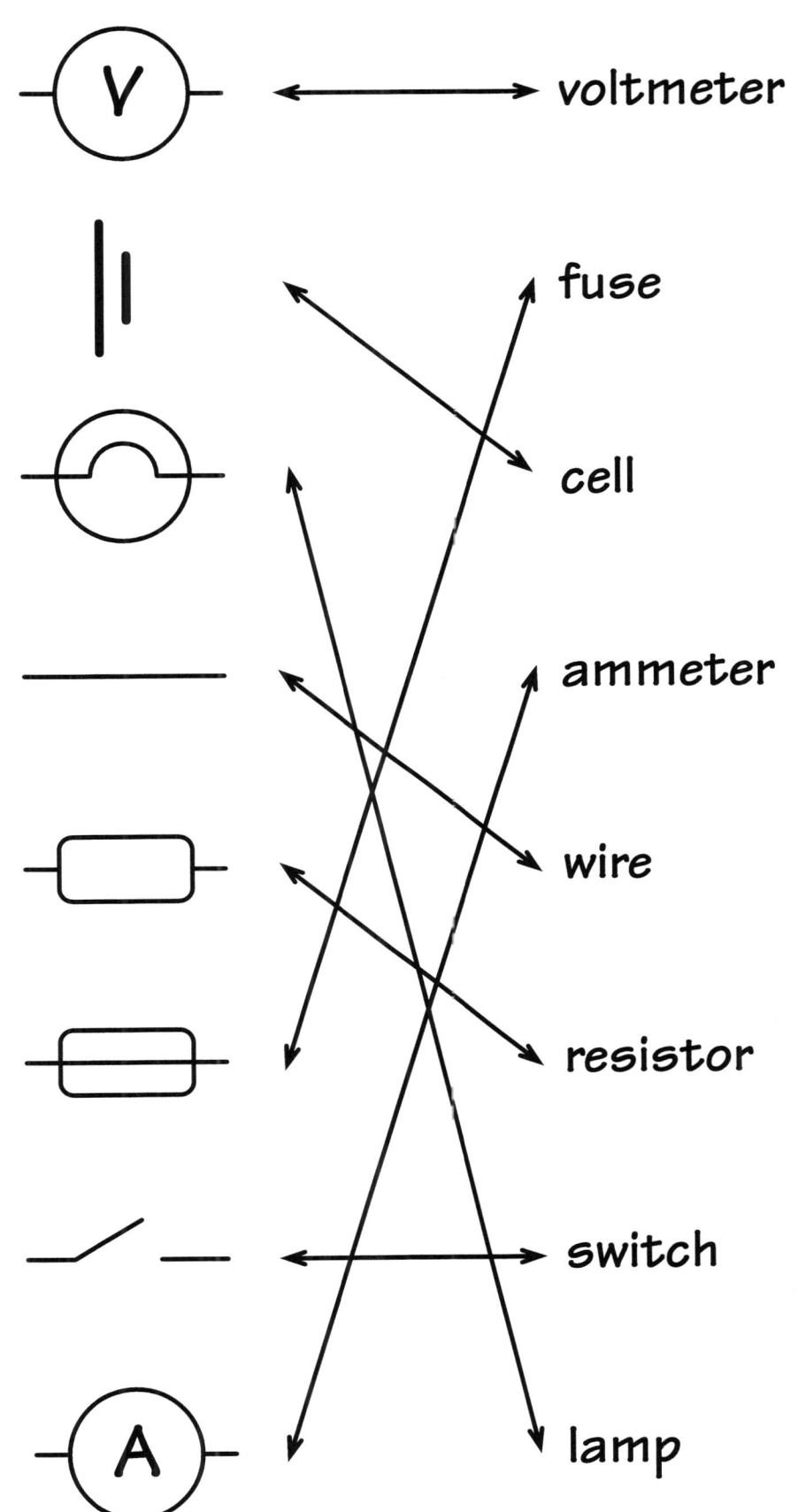

⌐ KEY POINT

# So you think you know the battery symbol?

## Objective:

To recognise electrical symbols for components used in circuit diagrams, and to know their function in circuits.

## Teaching point:

The activity is based on the cell / battery symbols and their functions in a circuit. Pupils will be asked to respond to diagrams, as oral questions are given by the teacher. The activity will make pupils think about the direction of current flow and what the symbol parts actually represent.

**What you will need:**
Copymaster 80 as OHT.
Whiteboards and pens.
Pupils work in pairs.

**Time:**
5 minutes

## Activity:

Project Copymaster OHT. Use partial reveal technique.

1.  Show the diagram of the single cell battery. Ask pupils:

    Draw the diagram and put positive at one end and negative at the other.

    Which is positive? Which is negative?

2.  Ask pupils: How can we represent this cell in a circuit diagram?

3.  Draw the symbol and put positive at one end and negative at the other.

    Which is positive? Which is negative?

4.  Ask pupils: Draw a single cell battery in a circuit. Which direction does the current flow when the circuit is complete? Show this on your circuit diagram.

**Challenge:** Ask the pupils to consider important uses of cells for medical applications.

**Links to plenary:** Discuss the use of 2 cell batteries and the symbols used. Relate the symbol to the direction of current flow.

**Badger Key Stage 3 Science Starters**

# So you think you know the battery symbol?

**1.**

**2.**

+ Positive          − Negative

+ Positive | | − Negative

**3.**

+ || −

# How does the torch work?

**Objective:**

Apply knowledge of circuits to a household device.

**Teaching point:**

By careful observation, pupils can apply knowledge of a simple circuit to work out how the torch works.

**What you will need:**
Copymaster 81 as worksheets. Pupils to work in pairs.

**Time:**
5 minutes

**Activity:**

Give out Copymaster worksheets.

Explain to pupils that the worksheet shows a torch.

Ask pupils to analyse the diagram and then work out how it works.

They should use all of the labelled parts to help explain how it works <u>in terms of an electrical circuit</u>.

Pupils may find it helpful to explain using bullet points.

Important points:

- both cells connected, + to –
- a spring connects to the – of second cell
- this connects to switch on bent metal strip
- switch slides down for "on"
- which pushes bent metal strip onto lamp
- which completes circuit
- so the lamp shines!

**Challenge:** Ask pupils to draw a circuit diagram for the torch.

**Links to plenary:** Ask pupils to imagine that the torch does not work, then give a possible fault list. (This will challenge whether they understand the way it works or not.)

**Badger Key Stage 3 Science Starters**

# How does the torch work?

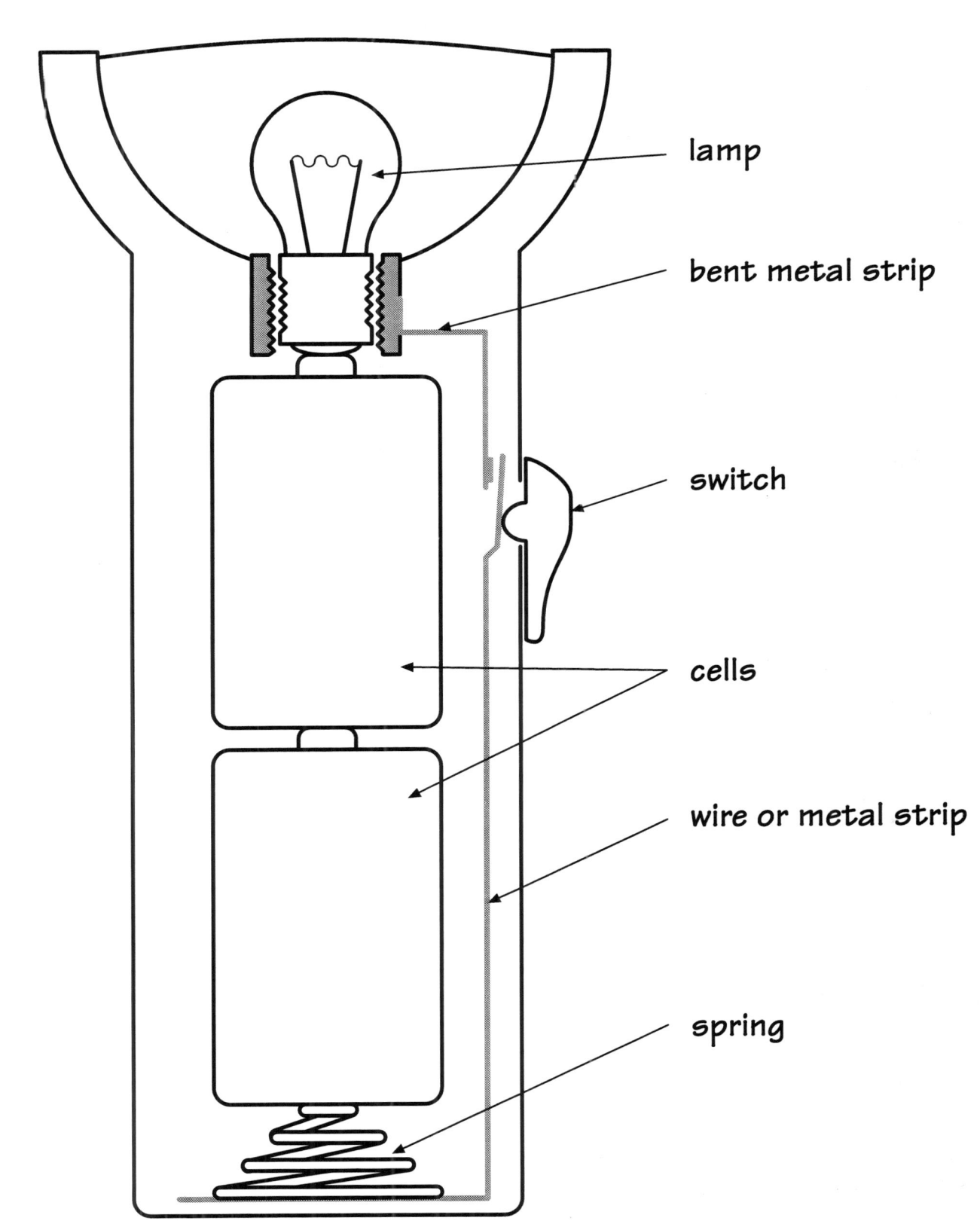

lamp

bent metal strip

switch

cells

wire or metal strip

spring

# Electricity: lets find the fault

**Objective:**

To be aware of series circuits and devise a system to check components.

**Teaching point:**

The Copymaster gives a simple series circuit with a switch and ammeter. Pupils to answer orally.

**What you will need:**
Copymaster 82 as OHT.
Whiteboards and pens.
Pupils work in pairs.

**Time:**
5 minutes

**Activity:**

Project Copymaster OHT.

Explain that Henry has set up a circuit with a new battery. He used:

3 lamps
1 switch
1 ammeter
1 cell/battery
6 wires

The switch was pressed on and the lamps went on; at the same time the ammeter showed a value of 0.5 amps.

Abruptly all of the lights went out. Ask the pupils to devise a fault detection plan.
*(check lamps individually, check connections to ensure circuit complete, check switch is working)*

Answers to be written on whiteboards.

Prompts: Henry thought that one of the lamps had developed a fault.

Ask pupils: Why would all the lamps go out, even if only one was defective?
*(series circuit, circuit passes through lamp filament, so if it is not complete then neither is the circuit for all three lamps)*

Inform pupils that the ammeter reading would be the same, 0.5, everywhere in the series circuit.

**Challenge:** Ask pupils to draw a circuit including 3 lamps, ammeter, and switch in a parallel circuit. Ask what would happen if the switch was on and one of the lamps was defective.

**Links to plenary:** Discuss the disadvantages of a series circuit.

**Badger Key Stage 3 Science Starters**

# Electricity: lets find the fault

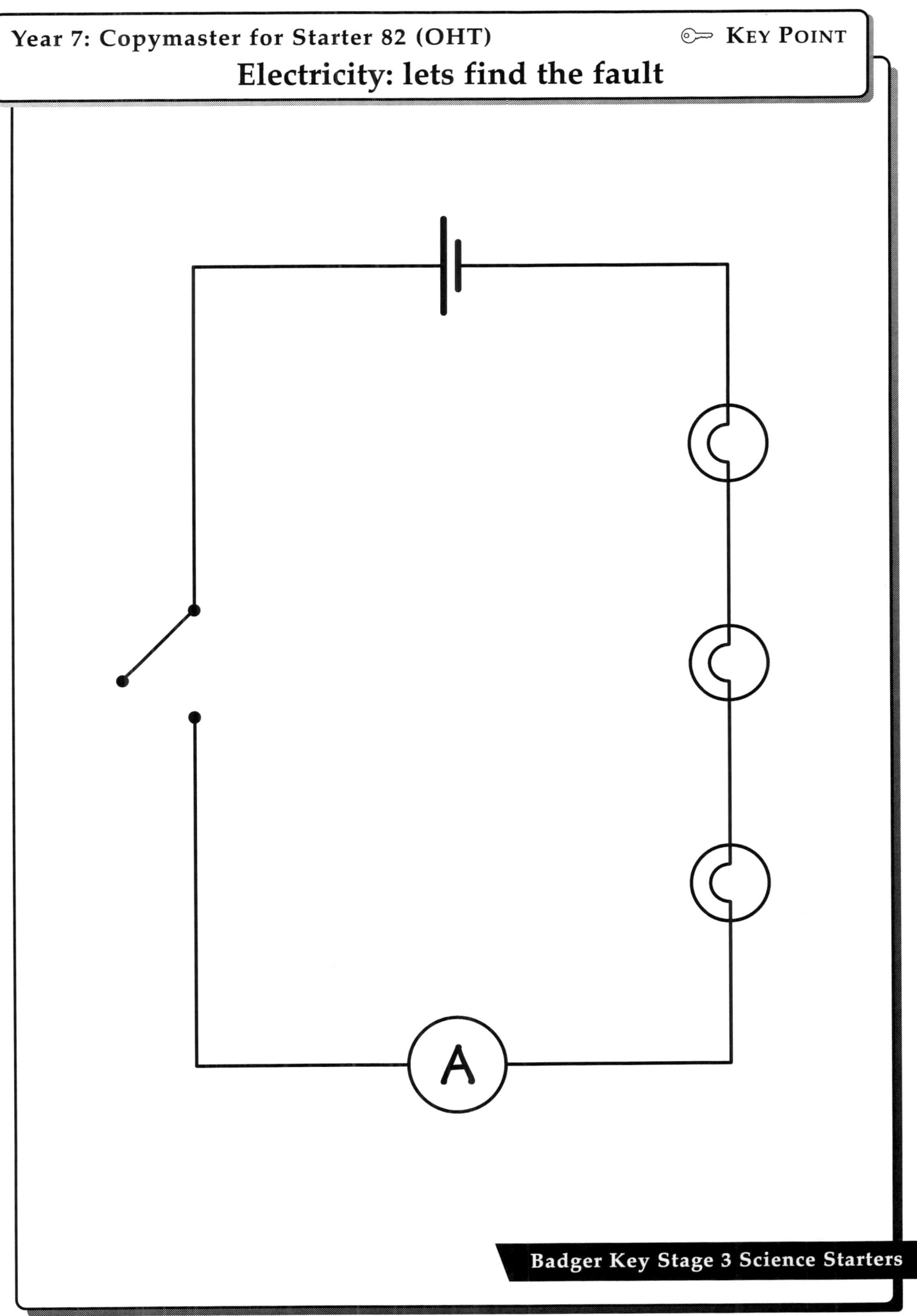

**Badger Key Stage 3 Science Starters**

# Electricity: on or off?

**Objective:**

To understand the functions of circuit components.

**Teaching point:**

The Copymaster shows a circuit diagram where there are 2 switches. The activity is to analyse the diagram and use the information to answer the questions.

**What you will need:**
Copymaster 83a as worksheets. Pupils to work in pairs.

**Time:**
5 minutes

**Activity:**

Give out Copymaster worksheets.

Explain to pupils that the circuit diagram may have more than one possible circuit. Additionally highlight the motor and fan.

Their aim is to draw the circuit to show when:

(a) lamp + motor are on

(b) lamp + motor + fan are on

Which circuit would give the motor a maximum "lifetime"? *(b)*

Ask pupils to give a reason for their answer.
*(because cooling the motor prevents overheating.)*

Answers provided on Copymaster 83b OHT.

**Challenge:** Ask pupils to list electrical devices in a house which has (a) 2 way switches (b) cooling fans.

**Links to plenary:** Discuss the fact that a number of different circuits exist in the home, where individual switches exist in more than one circuit.

**Badger Key Stage 3 Science Starters**

# Electricity: on or off?

Switch X

Switch Y

(M) = Motor

(F) = Fan

# Electricity: on or off?

Answer a

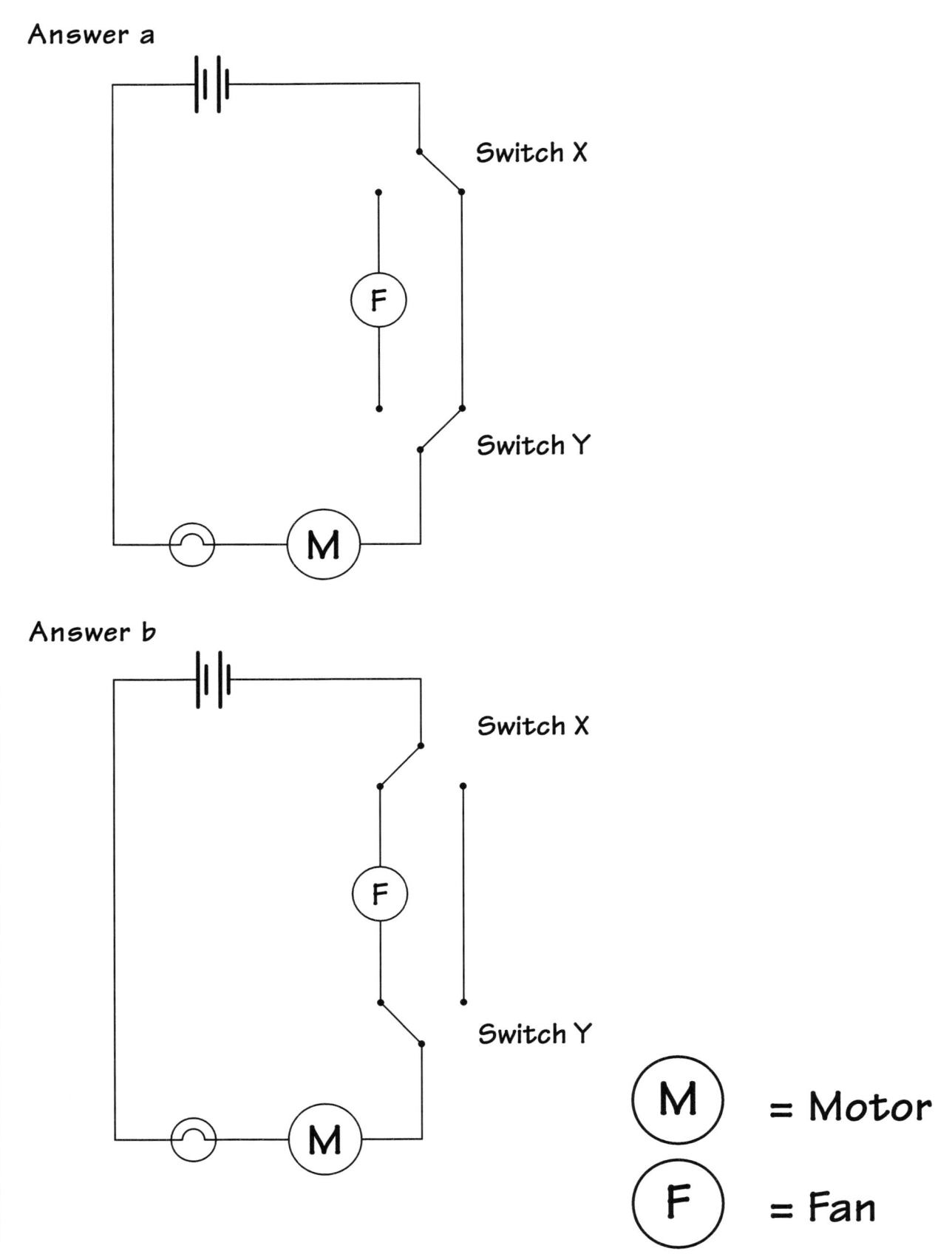

Switch X

F

Switch Y

M

Answer b

Switch X

F

Switch Y

M

M = Motor

F = Fan

# Electricity: measuring current (1)

**Objective:**

To know how an ammeter can be used to measure current.

**What you will need:**
Copymaster 84 as OHT.
Whiteboards and pens.
Pupils work in pairs.

**Time:**
5 minutes

**Teaching point:**

The activity gives a series circuit to the constancy of current value at different parts. Motor and lamp devices are incorporated in the circuit.

**Activity:**

Project Copymaster OHT.

Explain that the circuit diagram shows a series circuit with motor and lamp. It shows 3 positions where an ammeter was connected. The values at those parts of the circuit are shown.

Ask pupils to look at the values and write a list of facts about current flowing through a series circuit on their whiteboards.

- The same amount of current which leaves the battery returns to it.

- Each component in a series circuit receives the same current.

**Challenge:** Ask pupils to produce a rule about current *at every position* of a series circuit.

**Links to plenary:** Discuss the use of the ammeter in different parts of the circuit. Remind pupils of the importance of connecting up the ammeter the correct way around.

**Badger Key Stage 3 Science Starters**

# Electricity: measuring current (1)

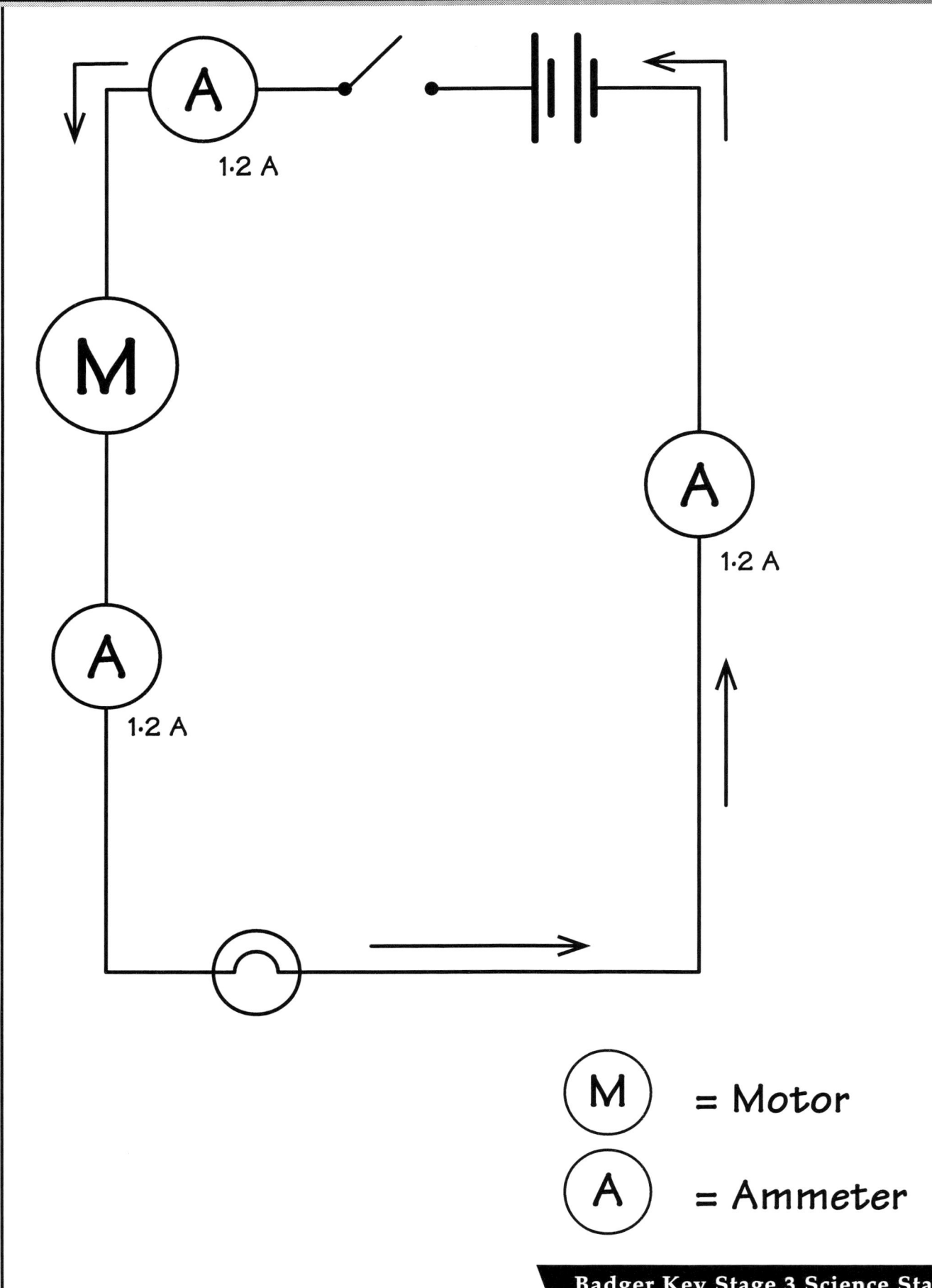

M = Motor

A = Ammeter

☞ KEY POINT

# Electricity: measuring current (2)

### Objective:

To know how an ammeter can be used to measure current.

### Teaching point:

The activity gives a parallel circuit to show differences in current value at different parts; motor and lamp devices incorporated in the circuit.

**What you will need:**
Copymaster 85 as OHT.
Whiteboards and pens.
Pupils work in pairs.

**Time:**
5 minutes

### Activity:

Project Copymaster OHT.

Explain that the circuit diagram shows a parallel circuit with motor and lamp. It shows the 4 positions where an ammeter was connected. The values at those parts of the circuit are shown.

Ask pupils to look at the values and write a list of facts about current flowing through a parallel circuit on their whiteboards.

- The same amount of current which leaves the battery returns to it.

- The motor receives 0·8 amps.

- The lamp receives 0·4 amps.

- The sum of these together give the 1·2 amps which are the return current value.

**Challenge:** Ask pupils to produce a rule about current leaving and returning to a power source.

**Links to plenary:** Compare the current values in series and parallel circuits.

**Badger Key Stage 3 Science Starters**

# Electricity: measuring current (2)

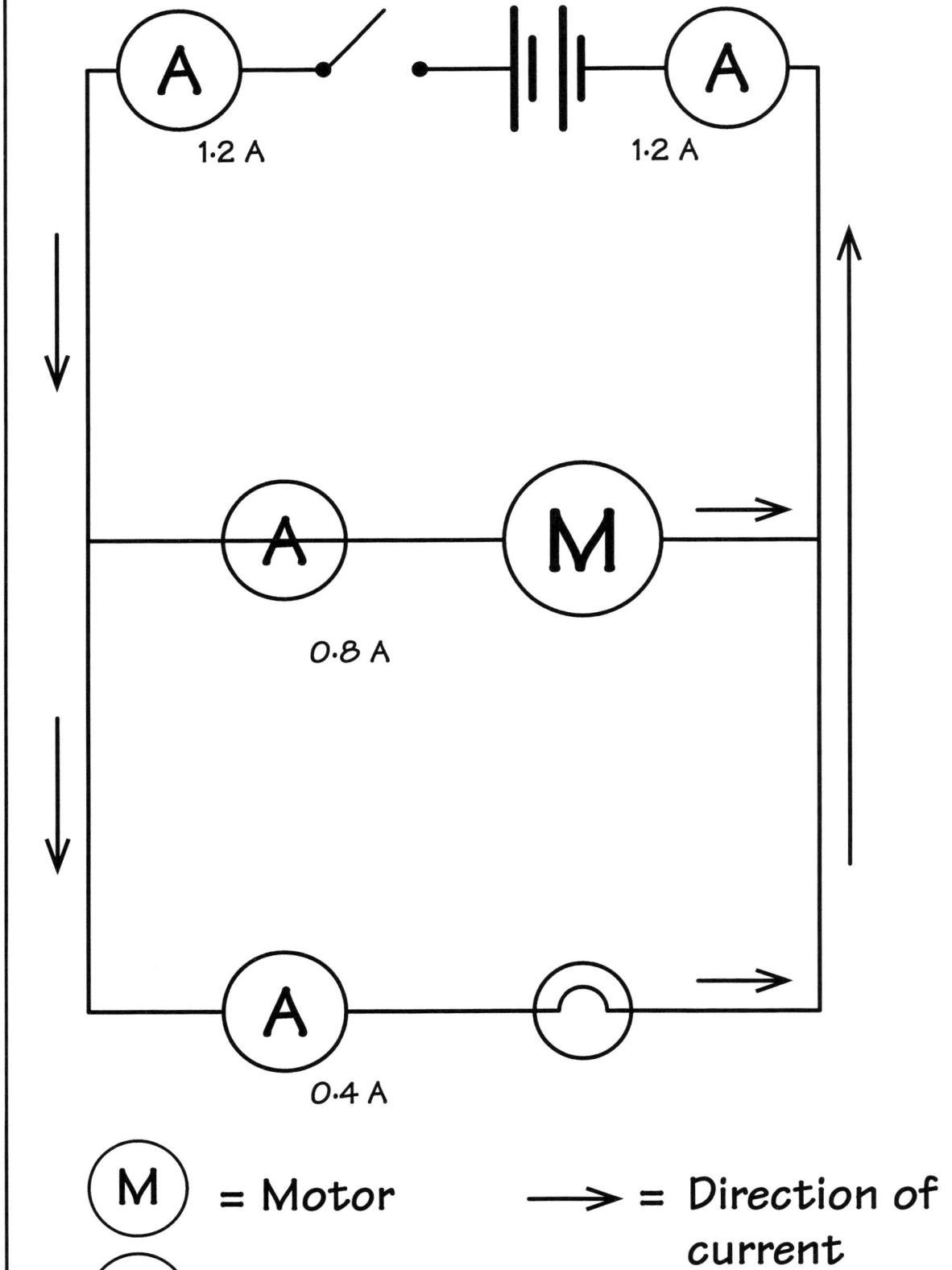

1·2 A

1·2 A

0·8 A

0·4 A

M = Motor          → = Direction of current

A = Ammeter

# The flow of current

## Objective:

To be able to describe current flow through a circuit.

## Teaching point:

The activity is a cloze exercise which supports understanding of current flow through a circuit.

**What you will need:**
Copymaster 86 as worksheets. Pupils to work individually.

**Time:**
5 minutes

## Activity:

Give out Copymaster worksheets.

Explain that the passage is about current flow through a circuit. The pupils should use the supplied words to complete the passage.

**Answers:**

Current in a circuit is <u>not</u> used up. Current which leaves a cell returns to it. Current leaves from the <u>positive terminal</u> and returns to the negative terminal.

The cell is a device which gives <u>energy</u> to components of the circuit. <u>Voltage</u> is what makes the current flow. A battery with a 9V rating will make the same lamp <u>brighter</u> than one with a 4.5V rating.

Devices and wires oppose the flow of current. This is known as <u>resistance</u>.

Highlight the terms *current*, *resistance* and *voltage*.

**Challenge:** Ask pupils to research the relationship between current flow, resistance and voltage.

**Links to plenary:** Discuss flow through a circuit in terms of flow, resistance and voltage.

**Badger Key Stage 3 Science Starters**

# The flow of current

resistance

brighter

energy

not

positive terminal

voltage

Current in a circuit is . . . . . . . . . . . . . . used up. Current which leaves

a cell returns to it. It flows from the . . . . . . . . . . . . . and returns

to the negative terminal.

The cell is a device which gives . . . . . . . . . . . . . to components of

the circuit. . . . . . . . . . . . . . is what makes the current flow. A

battery with a 9V rating will make the same lamp . . . . . . . . . . . . .

than one with a 4.5V rating.

Devices and wires oppose the flow of current. This is known as

. . . . . . . . . . . . . .

⚷ KEY POINT

# Which fuse?

### Objective:

To be aware of the function of a fuse as a protective device and to understand how it works in terms of resistance.

### Teaching point:

The activity involves the diagram of a fuse and supplied information. Pupils should complete a table which includes properties and uses of fuses. Finally a sentence completion exercise should develop further understanding.

### What you will need:
Copymaster 87a as worksheets. Pupils to work in pairs.

**Time:**
5 minutes

### Activity:

Give out Copymaster worksheets.

Explain that fuses are used as protective devices and have wires of different widths / metals inside of them. Too much current beyond their rating and they melt.

Ask pupils to complete the worksheet.

Answers provided on Copymaster 87b OHT.

**Challenge:** Ask pupils to research the alternatives to fuses, circuit breakers.

**Links to plenary:** Discuss a range of devices protected by fuses and their ratings.

# Which fuse?

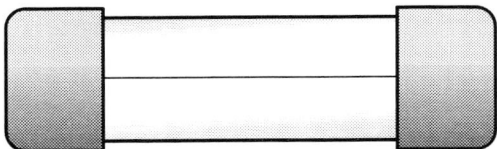

Very thin copper wire has a greater resistance than thicker copper wire. The thicker the wire the lower the resistance.

|  | Fuse | |
|---|---|---|
|  | 5 amp | 13amp |
| How thick is the wire? (thinner or thicker?) |  |  |
| Is the resistance higher or lower? (higher or lower?) |  |  |
| Which device would you use it for? (kettle or mini-disc player) |  |  |

Complete the sentences. Use each word only once!

breaks    melts    protects

If the current flow is too high then the wire in the

fuse . . . . . . . . . . . . . . .

This . . . . . . . . . . . . . . . the device so that components

themselves do not melt.

This . . . . . . . . . . . . . . . the circuit.

# Which fuse?

## Answers:

|  | Fuse | |
|---|---|---|
|  | 5 amp | 13amp |
| How thick is the wire? (thinner or thicker?) | thinner | thicker |
| Is the resistance higher or lower? (higher or lower?) | higher | lower |
| Which device would you use it for? (kettle or mini-disc player) | mini-disc | kettle |

Complete the sentences.

breaks    melts    protects

If the current flow is too high then the wire in the

fuse .melts.......... .

This .protects....... the device so that components

themselves do not melt.

This .breaks......... the circuit.

# The effect of voltage

### Objective:

To understand the effect of different voltages on a circuit.

### Teaching point:

Pupils should understand the effect of voltage on current. The graph gives an illustration of this which pupils can analyse to spot the pattern.

**What you will need:**
Copymaster 88 as OHT.
Whiteboards and pens.
Pupils work in pairs.

**Time:**
5 minutes

### Activity:

Project Copymaster OHT.

Explain that the graph shows voltage plotted against current.
*(Readings were taken under a controlled temperature.)*

Ask the pupils to write down ONE sentence which describes the relationship.
*(The greater the voltage the greater the current which flows. Voltage is directly proportional to current.)*

**Challenge:** Ask pupils to write down one other factor which affects both voltage and current.

**Links to plenary:** Highlight the voltage – current relationship and refer to 240V mains voltage and the need for a range of fuses in the home.

**Badger Key Stage 3 Science Starters**

# The effect of voltage

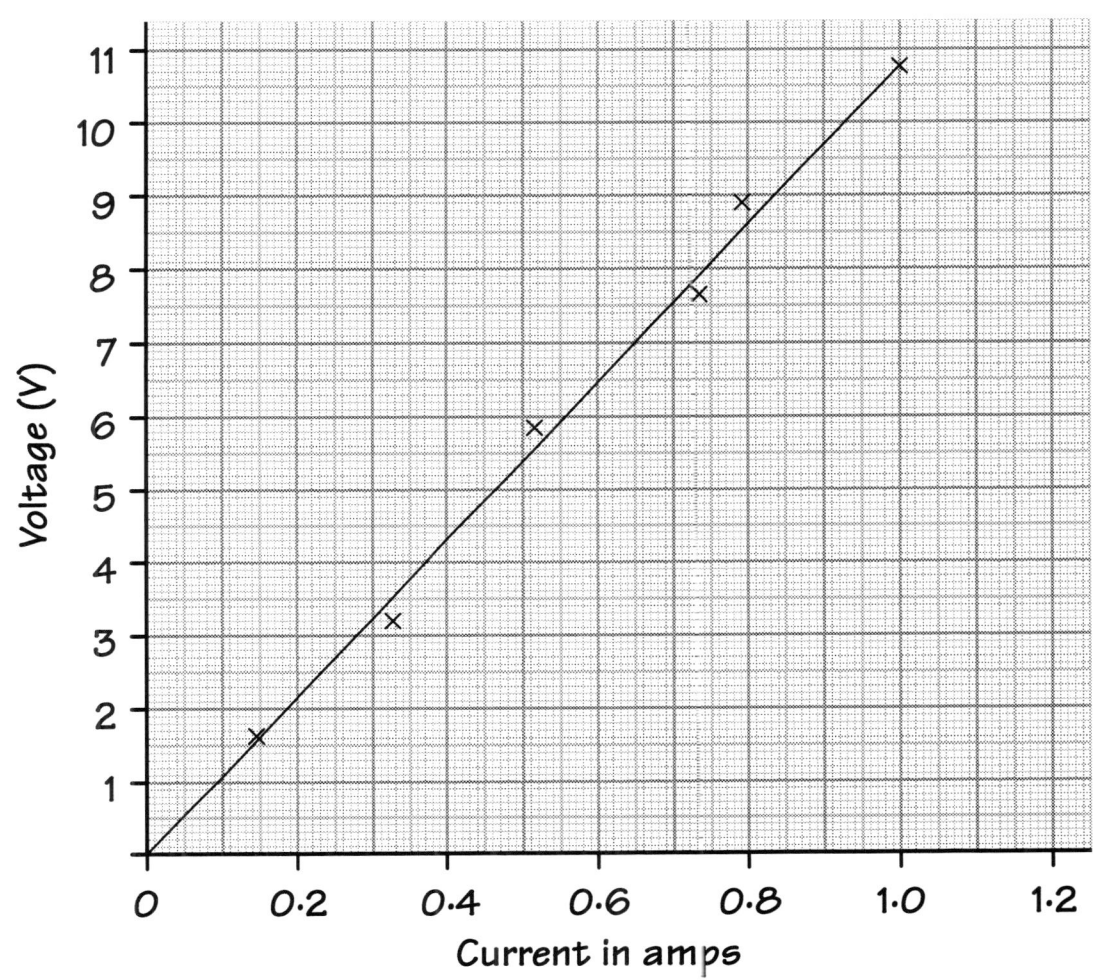

# Electricity and nerves

### Objective:

To know that nerves work by electrical conduction; show one application of nervous conduction: the pacemaker.

### Teaching point:

The passage includes information of the history of early work discovering nervous transmission, leading to a modern day application: the heart pacemaker. The activity will inform that electrical messages pass through nerves.

### Activity:

Project Copymaster OHT.

Explain that the pupils should analyse the passage then answer the questions. The teacher should read through the passage slowly, then pupils can re-analyse. Pupils answer questions.

  (a) How did Galvani begin the discovery that nerves work by electricity?
     *He saw dead frogs' legs moving.*

  (b) Which two metals were involved in the transmission of electricity?
     *iron, copper*

  (c) Suggest why legs can transmit electricity.
     *good conductors*

  (d) What effect does a pacemaker have on the human heart?
     *Helps heart beat at correct rate.*

**What you will need:**
Copymaster 89 as OHT.
Whole class activity.

**Time:**
12 minutes

**Challenge:** Ask pupils to consider why a long term battery should be used in a pacemaker.

**Links to plenary:** Galvani thought that the frogs' legs produced electricity, but it was Volta who realised that the legs and metals developed the electricity themselves. Link Volta to a modern unit!

**Badger Key Stage 3 Science Starters**

# Electricity and nerves

## Fact file:

Galvani, an Italian scientist, was the first to discover that electricity could stimulate the nerves of an organism. He was not sure of why this was! He noticed that dead frogs' legs, hung over an iron fence by a copper hook, seemed to twitch.

Electricity did flow through the legs, for two reasons:

(i)  the use of the 2 metals set up an electrical cell.

(ii) legs are good conductors of electricity.

We now know that electrical impulses pass through nerves so that we can feel things and move our muscles. Even when we have nerve problems then electricity can rescue us!

Pacemakers produce electrical stimulation for the heart so that it beats at the correct rate.

## Questions:

(a) How did Galvani begin the discovery that nerves work by electricity?


(b) Which two metals were involved in the transmission of electricity?


(c) Suggest why legs can transmit electricity.


(d) What effect does a pacemaker have on the human heart?

# Using a force meter

**Objective:**

To know how to measure the force of gravity pulling on an object using a force meter.

**Teaching point:**

Given the image of a force meter attached to a sack, the pupils should interpret what they see and answer the questions orally.

**What you will need:**
Copymaster 90 as OHT.
Whiteboards and pens.
Pupils work in pairs.

**Time:**
5 minutes

**Activity:**

Project Copymaster OHT.

Explain that the diagram shows a sack being held up by the force meter.

Ask pupils to write the answers to the following on their whiteboards:

What is the reading shown on the force meter? (Always give the units!)
*(120 N)*

Which unit does the N represent?
*(Newton)*

Which force is attracting the sack downwards?
*(Gravity)*

The sack is being held above the ground. Which force is opposing gravity?
*(muscular force)*

**Challenge:** Ask pupils to consider other ways of using a force meter to measure forces other than gravitational.

**Links to plenary:** Discuss the major effect of the Earth's gravitational pull.

**Badger Key Stage 3 Science Starters**

# Using a force meter

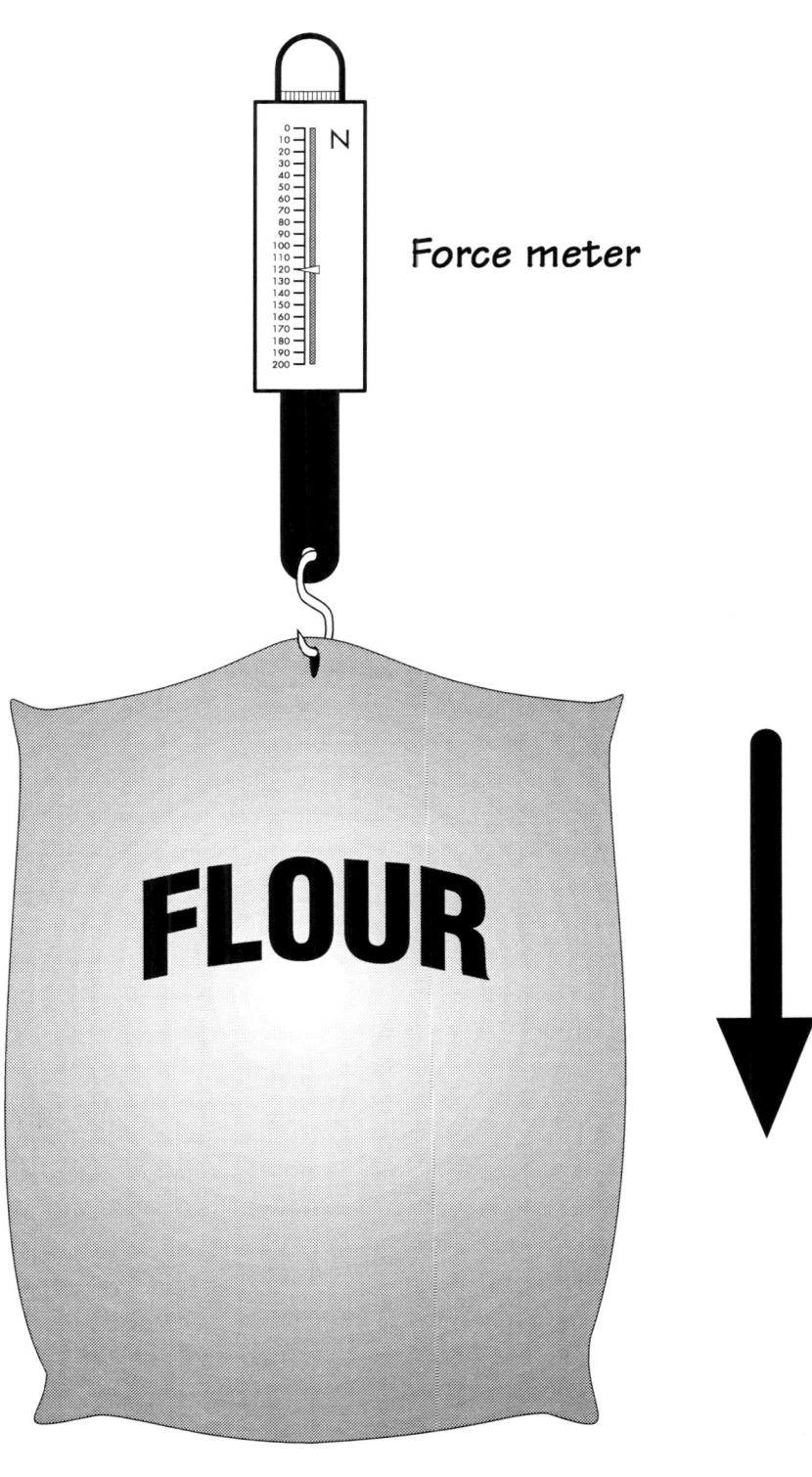

Force meter

# Friction: useful or not?

### Objective:

To show that friction is a force which sometimes is useful and sometimes needs to be reduced.

### Teaching point:

Pupils focus attention on an OHT of a bicycle. Via questioning, pupils volunteer parts where friction is useful and others where motion is opposed, so that the force must be reduced.

**What you will need:**
Copymaster 91 as OHT.
Whole class activity.

**Time:**
5 - 10 minutes

### Activity:

Give background information that friction is a **force** and it **opposes** motion.

Ask in which parts of the bicycle is force of friction useful:

Tyres - good tyres give more grip with the road.

Brake blocks - good brake blocks give more grip with the wheel rims.

Pedals - good pedals give more grip with the rider's trainers.

Seat - a good seat keeps the rider's bottom on the bike.

Handlebar grips – maximum grip, due to maximum friction; very safe.

Ask where on the bicycle should the force of friction be reduced:

Wheel hubs - wheels move easier due to bearings and lubricant.

Brake lever - lower friction through lubricant, easier to apply brakes.

Brake cable - must move easily to transfer force to brake.

Headset bearings - handlebars turn easier due to bearings and lubricant.

Bottom bracket - crank axle goes through bottom bracket, moves easier due to bearings and lubricant.

Pedal bearings - bearings in pedal are lubricated so that pedal rotates easily.

Chain links - each link joins to the next by a pin which is lubricated.

**Challenge:** Ask pupils about the force of friction between tyre and road. What effect would a worn tyre have on friction? What effect does the road surface have on friction? Describe sports which involve the importance of low and high friction.

**Links to plenary:** Bring together points considering both advantages and disadvantages of force of friction in the home.

**Badger Key Stage 3 Science Starters**

# Friction: useful or not?

## Bicycle

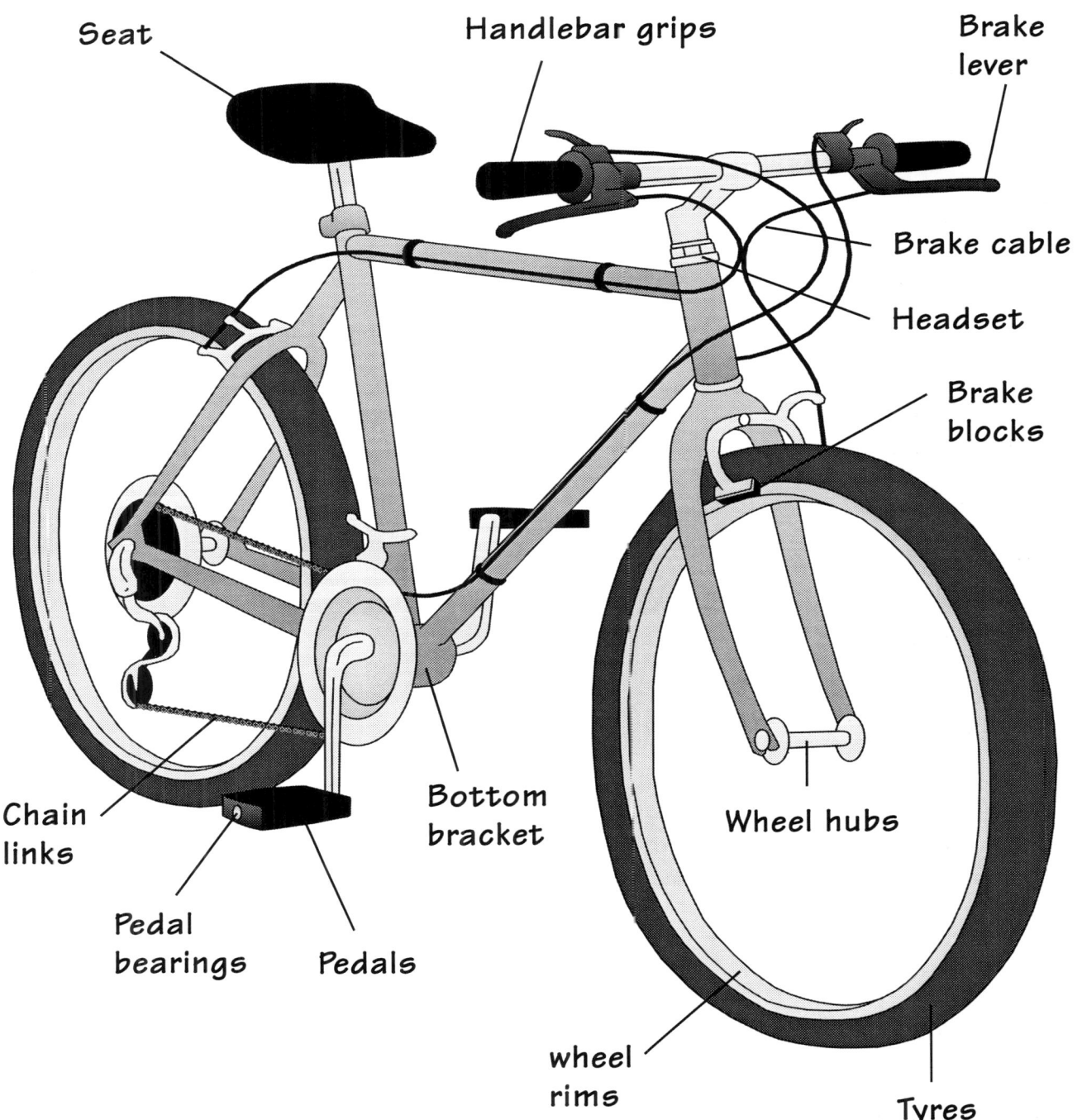

Seat

Handlebar grips

Brake lever

Brake cable

Headset

Brake blocks

Chain links

Pedal bearings

Pedals

Bottom bracket

Wheel hubs

wheel rims

Tyres

# Toy shark

### Objective:

To analyse a given scenario to identify forces.

### Teaching point:

The activity involves the projection of OHT diagram of a magnetic toy. Pupils should be asked to interpret why the shark is "suspended" in the air.

**What you will need:**
Copymaster 92a + b as OHTs. Pupils to work in pairs.

**Time:**
10 minutes

### Activity:

Project Copymaster OHT.

Explain to the pupils that the toy shark was a free gift with a take-away meal. It is plastic on the outside and actually keeps up in the air as shown.

The task is to work out the scientific reason for how it works. Pupils should draw the inside of the toy to show how it may work.

You may wish to give a clue word, forces!

Use the three stage OHT:

1.  No inside showing

2.  Magnets in position

3.  Show the poles

The final OHT confirms both magnetic fields and pole positions! You can project each OHT to superimpose the final identification of poles.

**Challenge:** Ask pupils to consider the forces of magnetic repulsion and gravity.

**Links to plenary:** Discuss the fact that a number of different forces exist, and that pupils should be ready to interpret different interacting forces when given unknown scenarios to analyse.

**Badger Key Stage 3 Science Starters**

# Toy shark

## Can you work it out?

 Key Point

# Toy shark

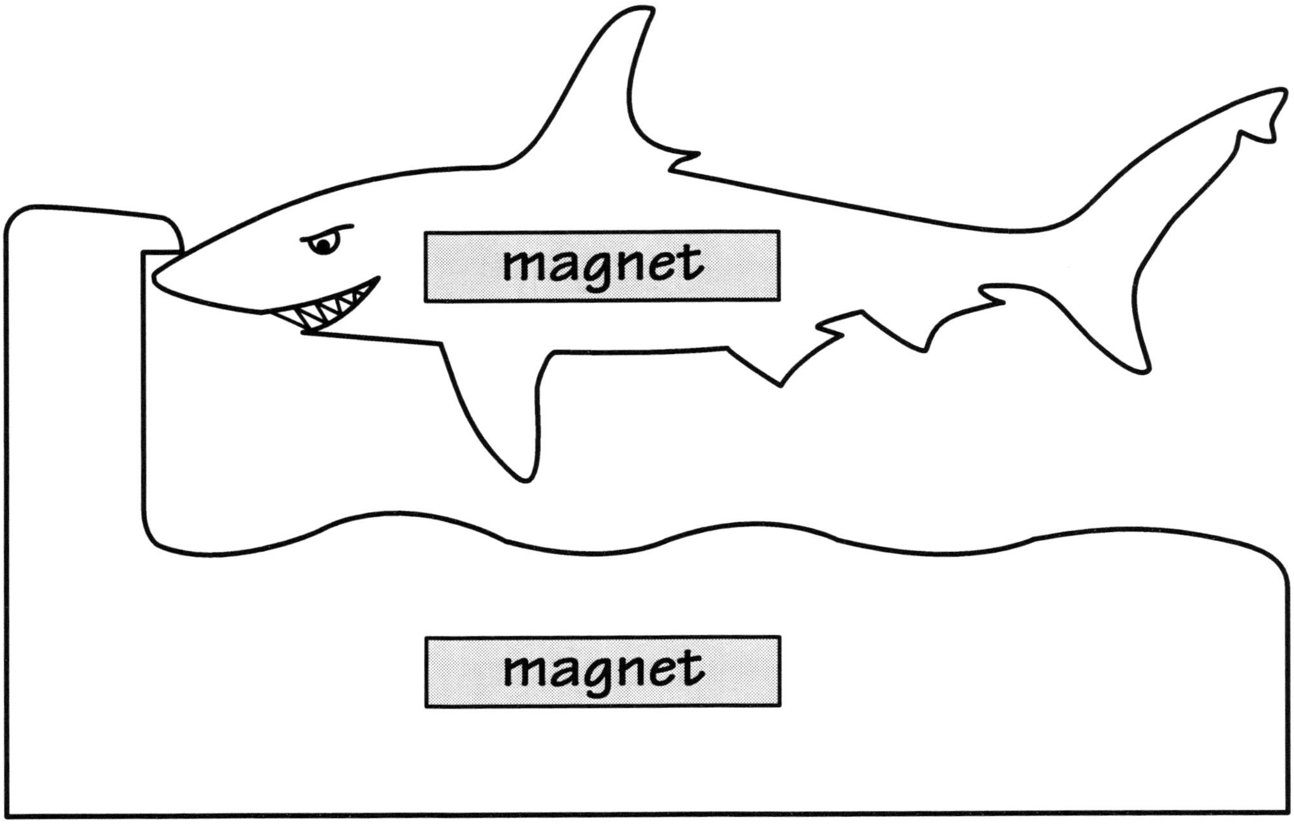

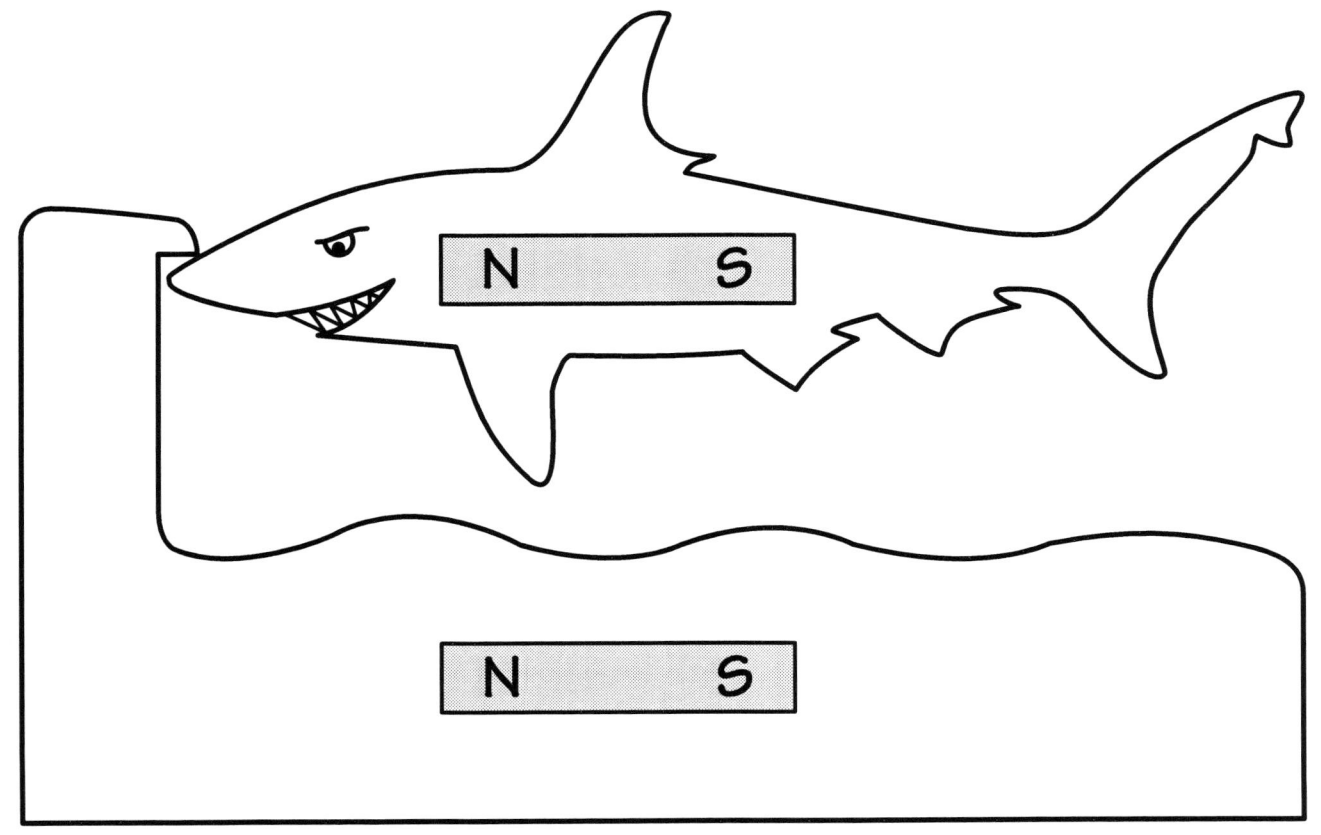

magnet
magnet

N S
N S

# Float your boat

### Objective:

To know that up-thrust exists as an object floats and that up-thrust has different values in different fluids.

### Teaching point:

The activity is based on a diagram which shows a model boat in three situations: suspended by a force meter in air, floating in distilled water, and floating in brine.

**What you will need:**
Copymaster 93 as OHT.
Whiteboards and pens.
Pupils to work in groups.

**Time:**
10 minutes

### Activity:

Project Copymaster OHT.

Explain that the same boat was treated in three different ways:

- suspended by a force meter in air.

- suspended by a force meter and floating in distilled water.

- suspended by a force meter and floating in very salty water.

You may wish to give them 2 key forces, **gravity** and **up-thrust**.

Ask the pupils to analyse the scenario, then make conclusions. Prompts if necessary:

Which force is pulling the boat downwards? *(Gravity)*

What is its value? *(50 N)*

What is the up-thrust in distilled water? *(50N)*

What is the up-thrust in very salty water? *(50N)*

Discuss the fact that when the boat is able to float, then the value shown on the forcemeter is equal to 0N after being 50N in air. In the instance of this experiment, floating takes place in distilled water and salt water.

Distilled water has a lower density than salt water, therefore the volume of water which equates to an upthrust of 50N is of a bigger volume than the salt water displaced by the boat.

**Challenge:** Ask pupils to consider why a block of steel sinks but built into boat shape it floats.

**Links to plenary:** Discuss the values of up-thrust and the fact that it is in direct opposition to gravity.

**Badger Key Stage 3 Science Starters**

# Float your boat

Force meter

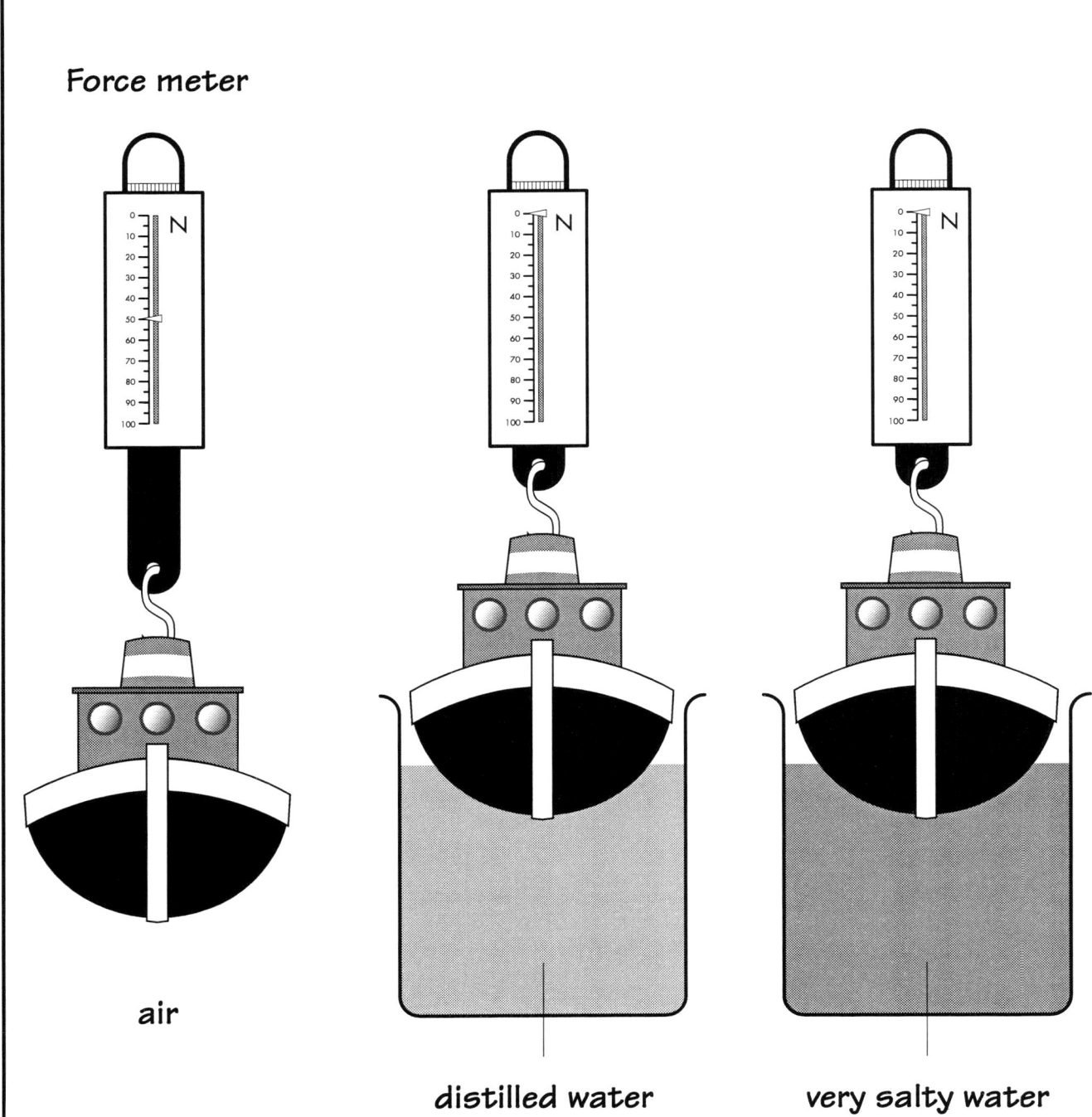

air

distilled water

very salty water

# Floating and displacement

### Objective:

To know that the force of the up-thrust is equal to the weight of water which is displaced.

### Teaching point:

The activity is based on a force meter reading of an object in air, and in water. Using a displacement vessel, the water overspill is collected and gravitational force on this water measured.

### Activity:

Project Copymaster OHT.

Explain that the diagram sequence (1 → 4 ) shows a force meter measuring:

- object in air

- object floating

- beaker

- beaker + water which left spout

Ask pupils to:

1.  Work out the value of the up-thrust in Newtons

2.  Can they give a conclusion which links the force of up-thrust with the force of water which is displaced.

    - Block of wood = 12N in air

    - Beaker alone = 6N in air

    - Water and beaker = 18N in air

    So water displaced = (18 - 6) 12N

    Conclusion - The amount of water displaced weighs 12N, exactly equal to the weight of the block in air. The upthrust is 12N.

**What you will need:**
Copymaster 94 as OHT.
Whiteboards and pens.
Pupils to work in groups.

**Time:**
10 minutes

**Challenge:** Ask pupils to write out a *general* calculation sequence which could be used to test the relationship between water displaced and up-thrust.

**Links to plenary:** Discuss the conclusion in terms of the early work of Archimedes.

**Badger Key Stage 3 Science Starters**

# Floating and displacement

**1.**

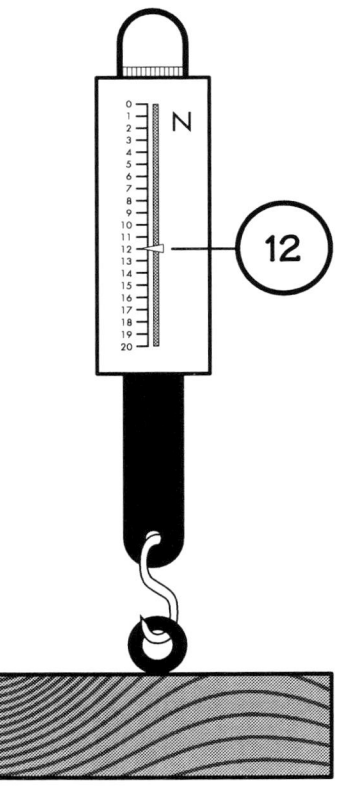

**2.**

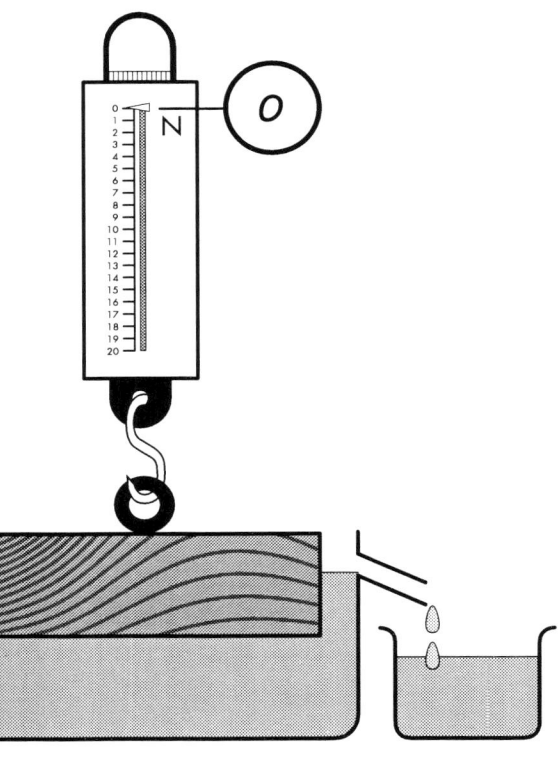

**3.**

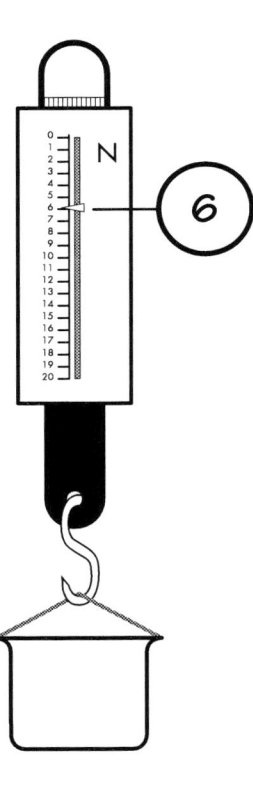

**4.**

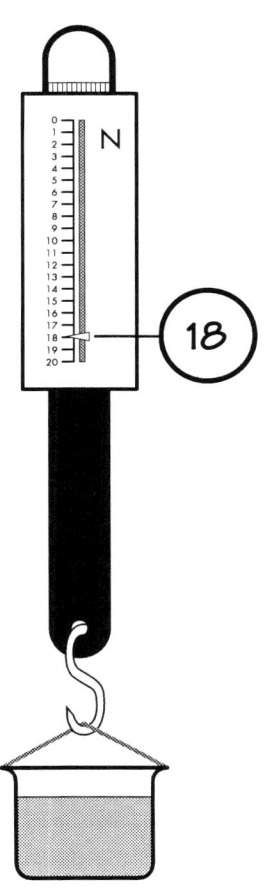

# What is density?

**Objective:**

To be able to calculate density of different materials.

**What you will need:**
Whiteboards and pens.
Pupils to work in pairs.

**Teaching point:**

The activity involves the completion of a table based on mass, volume and density for brick, hardwood and softwood. Brick is given, so the pupils have clues as to how to attempt the calculations.

**Time:**
5 minutes

**Activity:**

Copy table below onto OHT or board.

| object | mass (g) | volume (cm³) | density (g / cm³) |
|--------|----------|--------------|-------------------|
| brick | 3600 | 1200 | 3 |
| Hardwood block | 1800 | 1800 | |
| Softwood block | 1200 | | 0·6 |

Explain that the calculation of density involves mass and volume. Ask pupils if they can work out how density of brick was calculated, then the other values can be written into the table. (*Hardwood 1g / cm³ , softwood 2000 cm³*)

Ask pupils to complete the table then, using the three terms, to write out an equation to calculate density.

(density = $\frac{mass}{volume}$)

**Challenge:** Ask pupils to show the equation manipulated to give mass and volume.

**Links to plenary:** Discuss the idea that different substances have different densities. Link different densities to different substances.

**Badger Key Stage 3 Science Starters**

⌐ **KEY POINT**

# Balanced or unbalanced?

**Objective:**

To interpret situations of balanced and unbalanced forces.

**Teaching point:**

Pupils should analyse a boat in different situations when the tide is coming in. They need to identify forces which interact.

**What you will need:**
Copymaster 96 as OHT.
Whole class activity.

**Time:**
5 minutes

**Activity:**

Project Copymaster OHT.

Explain that the scenes show a boat in two different situations:

1. The tide is coming in strongly.
   The boat is pointing out to sea.
   The engine is on.
   It is stationary.

2. The tide is still coming in strongly.
   The boat is pointing out to sea.
   The boat is moving towards the shore.

Ask the pupils to give details of what is happening in terms of forces, and to indicate if they are balanced or unbalanced.

**Potential answers:**

1. The force of tide coming in equals the force of boat in opposing it.
   The force of the moving propeller is equal and opposite to that of the tide.
   The forces are balanced.

2. The force of tide coming in is greater than force of boat in opposing it.
   The forces are unbalanced.
   So the boat moves towards the shore.
   Perhaps the tide became stronger.
   Perhaps the engine cut out, or gave a lesser force.

**Challenge:** Ask pupils to identify other forces which would be exerted within the scene.

**Links to plenary:** Discuss the identification of the forces "at work" in the scenes. Highlight the idea of detail being important. In future examinations, the more detail given in response to longer answer questions, the higher the level of achievement.

**Badger Key Stage 3 Science Starters**

# Balanced or unbalanced?

⌐○ KEY POINT

# Stretching a spring

**Objective:**

To understand what happens when a material stretches.

**Teaching point:**

The activity is based on a pupil's results showing the length of a spring as a sequence of 10g masses were hung on it. Elastic limit is passed and after this the results show maximum elongation of the wire.

**What you will need:**
Copymaster 97 as worksheets. Pupils to work in pairs.

**Time:**
10 minutes

**Activity:**

Give out Copymaster worksheets.

Explain that a pupil hung a series of 10g masses onto a spring and for every increase in mass the length of the spring was measured.

Ask pupils to answer the questions on the worksheet.

(a) How long was the spring at the start?
*(10cm)*

(b) Comment on the reading for spring length when a 30g mass was hung on it.
(Clue: Does this length fit into the pattern?)
*(No. The result seems wrong. Maybe the pupil did not measure accurately.)*

(c) When 90g, then 100g, masses were hung on the spring both lengths were the same, 24cm. Explain this.
*(Wire / spring would not stretch any more, maybe the wire was close to snapping.)*

(d) After the investigation, do you think the spring would work?
*(No. It would not go back to original length.)*

Comment on the importance of taking enough readings. Stopping at 70g would have given a false impression!

**Challenge:** Ask pupils to research elastic limit.

**Links to plenary:** Discuss the fact that all springs will follow this pattern and beyond a certain limit will not return to original shape.

**Badger Key Stage 3 Science Starters**

# Stretching a spring

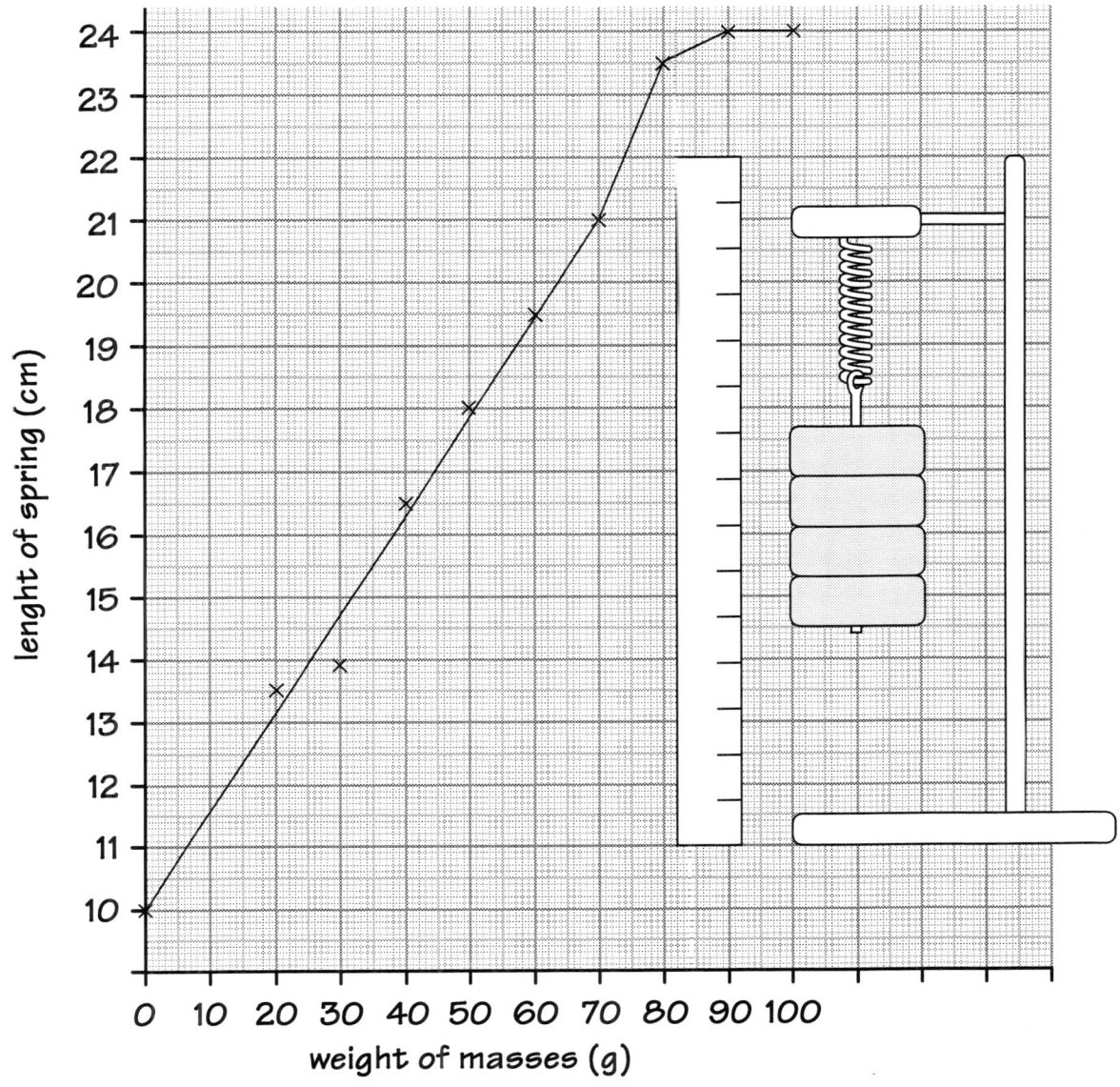

(a) How long was the spring at the start?

(b) Comment on the reading for spring length when a 30g mass was hung on it. (Clue: Does this length fit into the pattern?)

(c) When 90g then 100g masses were hung on the spring both lengths were the same, 24cm. Explain this.

(d) After the investigation, do you think the spring will work? Give a reason for your answer.

⌕ KEY POINT

# Skydiver

**Objective:**

To be able to identify forces exerted and their effects during a given scenario.

**Teaching point:**

The diagram gives a visual stimulus for analysis. There are opportunities to recognise streamlining design and action by the skydiver, and includes air resistance and friction.

**What you will need:**
Copymaster 98 as OHT.
Whiteboards and pens.
Pupils work in pairs.

**Time:**
5 minutes

**Activity:**

Project Copymaster OHT.

Explain that the OHT shows a skydiver in the air. The view is looking down towards the ground level.

The skydiver is wearing a new-design suit with webbing that can be opened out from the body to arms, and between the legs (as shown). The new webbing idea has major advantages to the diver.

Ask these questions:

During flight, how could the skydiver become more streamlined?
*(Put arms to side, put legs together, reduce surface area, dive position rather than horizontal.)*

What effect would this have on the speed of descent?
*(increase)*

During flight, how would the skydiver increase air resistance?
*(Put limbs in an X shape, open out webbing, keep body parallel to ground, activate the parachute.)*

Which force is exerted between the skydiver and the air?
*(friction)*

Which force causes the skydiver to fall?
*(gravity)*

Pupils to write answers on whiteboards.

**Challenge:** Ask pupils what the skydiver would have to do to have the longest time of descent from a height of, say, 5000m.

**Links to plenary:** Discuss the advantages of the new suit and how the skydiver makes a descent. Link each force to its effect.

**Badger Key Stage 3 Science Starters**

# Skydiver

# Remember the planets?

### Objective:

To be aware of the sequence of planets from nearest the sun to most distant.

### Teaching point:

The activity is based on the distance of each planet in the solar system from the sun. Copymaster cards should be given to pupils to put them in the sequence, nearest to furthest. After an initial try, they can be given a mnemonic technique, plus a few minutes to learn it before a re-test.

### What you will need:
Copymaster 99a + b as worksheets. Pupils to work in pairs.

### Time:
10 minutes

### Activity:

Give out Copymaster 99a worksheets.

Ask pupils to cut out planets, to form planet cards. One pupil should test the other to find out if the sequence of planets is correct. Tell them that the planet sizes are **not** to scale.

Give out Copymaster 99b to confirm sequence and show mnemonic technique, or show as OHT.

**My Very Energetic Mum Jumps, Skips Under Nine Planets.**
**Mercury, Venus, Earth, Mars, Jupiter, Saturn, Uranus, Neptune, Pluto**

After the activity, pupils re-testing each other should confirm the sequence has been retained.

**Challenge:** Ask pupils to consider forming another mnemonic which may mean more to them. Encourage the use of the technique for other processes / sequences.

**Links to plenary:** Discuss the sequence from the Sun, Mars etc, in relation to temperature / light and seasons.

**Badger Key Stage 3 Science Starters**

# Remember the planets?

Mercury

Venus

Earth

Jupiter

Saturn

Uranus

Neptune

Pluto

Mars

# Remember the planets?

1 Mercury,   2 Venus,   3 Earth,   4 Mars,

5 Jupiter,

6 Saturn,   7 Uranus,   8 Neptune,   9 Pluto

My Very Energetic Mum Jumps, Skips Under Nine Planets

**Badger Key Stage 3 Science Starters**

# Which seasons?

**Objective:**

To understand the causes of the seasons and link them to the sun.

**Teaching point:**

The activity will involve a Copymaster OHT which tracks the orbit of the Earth around the Sun. The tilt of the Earth's axis gives a clue as to how to deduce the seasons.

**What you will need:**
Copymaster 100 as OHT.
Whiteboards and pens.
Pupils to work in groups.

**Time:**
10 minutes

**Activity:**

Project Copymaster OHT.

Explain that the diagram shows the orbit of the Earth around the sun during different seasons but they are not labelled. The aim is to label the seasons Spring, Summer, Autumn, Winter.

Give them the clues:

(a)  The UK is in the northern hemisphere (marked!).

(b)  The nearer the UK is to the Sun the warmer it is.

(c)  The Earth is at different distances from the sun in different seasons.

Give the pupils thinking time. Ask for the positions.

Answer:

Autumn

Winter          Summer

Spring

**Challenge:** Ask pupils to draw the labelled sequence without any visual clue.

**Links to plenary:** Discuss the orbit and the effect of the Earth's tilted axis on proximity to the Sun.

**Badger Key Stage 3 Science Starters**

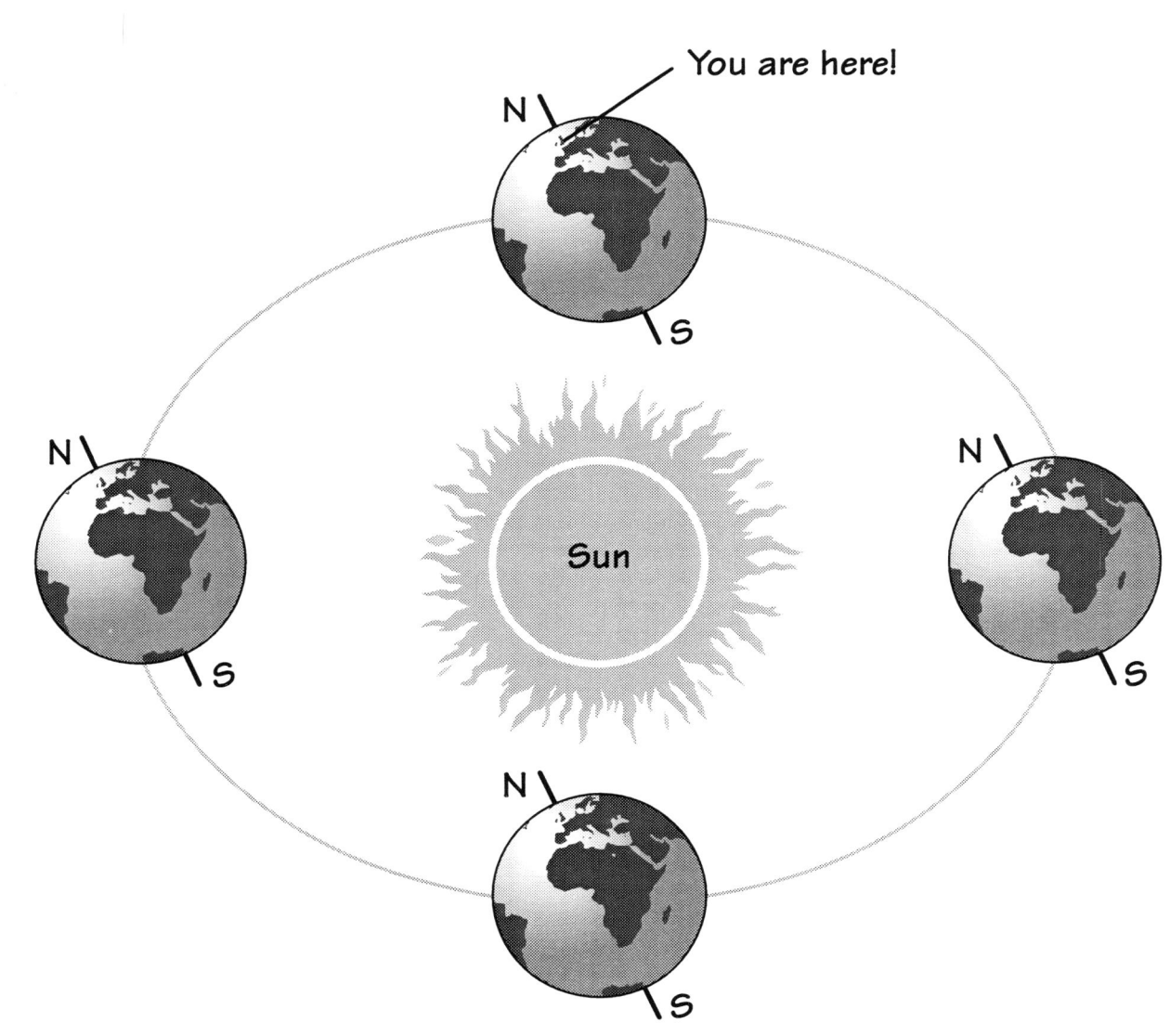

You are here!

Sun

# An eclipse of the Sun

### Objective:

To be aware of how an eclipse of the sun takes place.

**What you will need:**
Copymaster 101 as
worksheets. Pupils to
work in pairs.

**Time:**
5 minutes

### Teaching point:

The activity is based on a diagram showing the Sun, Moon and Earth in alignment. Light rays from the Sun are drawn and the pupils may shade in the total eclipse parts which receive no light.

### Activity:

Give out Copymaster worksheets.

Ask the pupils to analyse the diagram showing the Sun, Moon and Earth. The spots on the Earth represent 2 countries.

Ask the pupils:

    (a) to shade in the area where the Moon stops the light from reaching the Earth. (Where the Sun doesn't shine!)

    (b) to decide for each of country A and B if they have a total eclipse or not.
       *(A does not have total eclipse, B does.)*

**Challenge:** Ask the pupils to explain how a total eclipse shows that the Moon does not, itself, emit light.

**Links to plenary:** Discuss the shading effect of the Moon and indicate the areas of partial eclipse. Highlight the fact that light travels in straight lines and that they should always draw with the help of a ruler.

**Badger Key Stage 3 Science Starters**

# An eclipse of the Sun

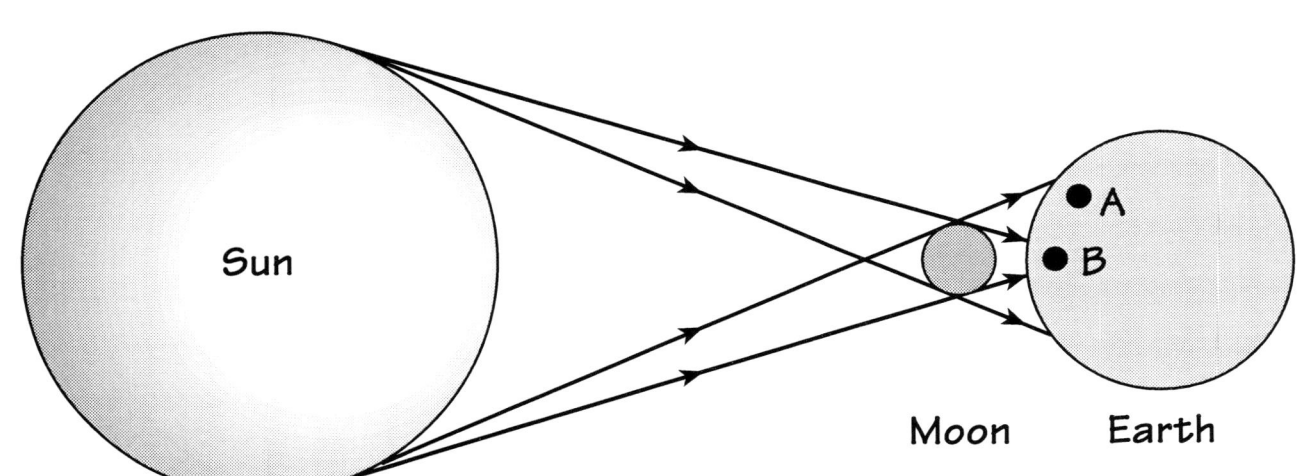

# An eclipse of the Moon

## Objective:

To be aware of how an eclipse of the Moon takes place.

## Teaching point:

The activity is based on a diagram showing the Sun, Earth and Moon in alignment. Light rays from the Sun are drawn and the pupils may shade in the total eclipse parts which receive no light. It will show logically why we cannot see the Moon at all during this phenomenon.

## Activity:

Give out Copymaster worksheets.

Ask the pupils to analyse the diagram showing the Sun, Earth and Moon. The spots on the Earth represent 2 countries.

Ask the pupils:

(a) to shade in the area where the Earth stops the light from reaching the Moon.

(b) to decide for each of country A and B if people in these countries can see the eclipse or not. *(A cannot see total eclipse, B can!)*

**What you will need:**
Copymaster 102 as worksheets. Pupils to work in pairs.

**Time:**
5 minutes

**Challenge:** Ask the pupils to explain how in a lunar eclipse the moon is outlined by a red-orange glow. (Some light is scattered from Earth's atmosphere.)

**Links to plenary:** Discuss the shading effect of the Earth and ask why the Moon is almost not visible to us during a lunar eclipse.

**Badger Key Stage 3 Science Starters**

# An eclipse of the Moon

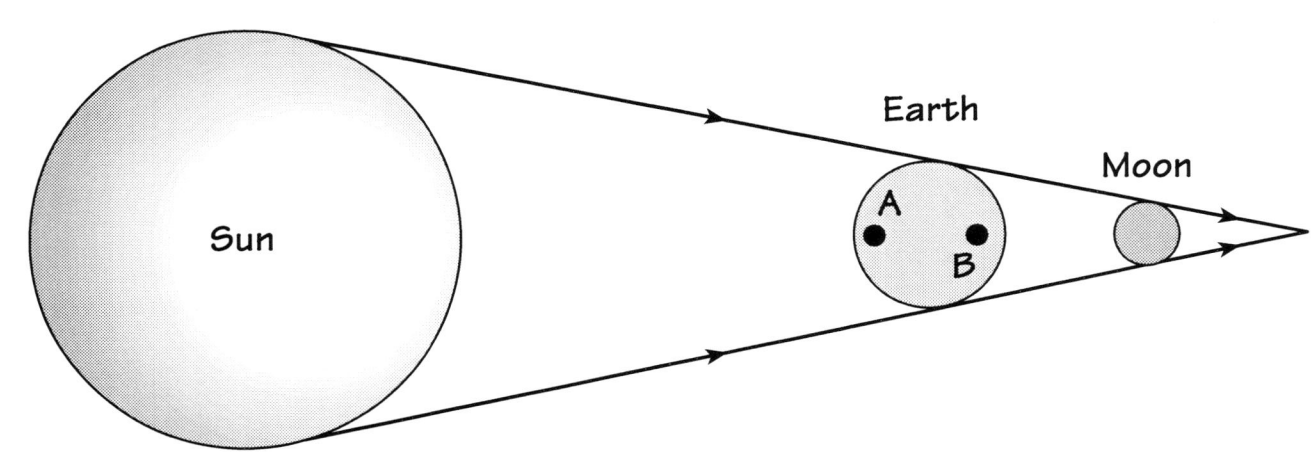

# The solar system

## Objective:

To be aware of a number of features of the stars and planets of the Solar system.

## Teaching point:

The activity is a cloze exercise based on important facts about the solar system. It will clarify some major concepts and help commit to long term memory.

## What you will need:

Copymaster 103 as worksheets. Pupils to work individually.

### Time:
10 minutes

## Activity:

Give out Copymaster worksheets.

Explain that pupils should complete the worksheet. It gives important facts about the solar system but the passage is not complete. Choosing from the word list, the pupils should write in the correct word into each gap.

**Answers:**

When you look up into the sky, bright light shines out from the <u>sun</u>. The sun is the star of the solar system and gives <u>heat</u> and light to all <u>nine</u> planets.

Each planet moves around the sun in a curved path called an <u>orbit</u>. The nearer a planet is to the sun the higher its average <u>temperature</u>. No planet produces its own light. The <u>Moon</u> reflects light from the Sun towards <u>Earth</u>.

Every time a planet spins completely on its axis, this is called a <u>day</u>. Every time a planet completes its orbit around the Sun, this is called a <u>year</u>.

**Challenge:** Ask pupils to predict planets which have a warmer, and those with a colder, average temperature than Earth. They could give reasons for their predictions.

**Links to plenary:** Discuss the time of one year in terms of one orbit, and relate this to longer time for the "years" of planets of a greater distance from the Sun.

**Badger Key Stage 3 Science Starters**

# The solar system

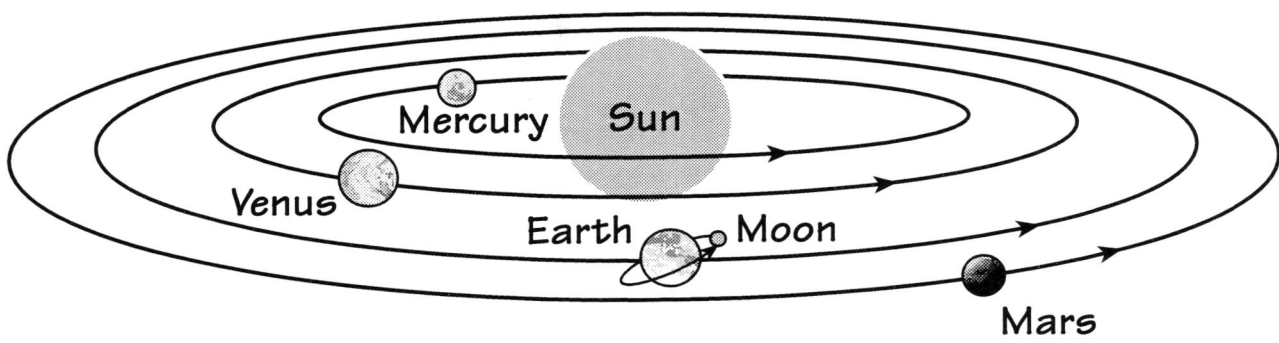

year    day    Moon    nine    temperature
heat    orbit    Sun    Earth

When you look up into the sky bright light shines out from the

. . . . . . . . . . . . . . . . The sun is the star of the solar system and gives

. . . . . . . . . . . . . . . and light to all . . . . . . . . . . . . . . planets.

Each planet moves around the sun in a curved path called an

. . . . . . . . . . . . . . . . The nearer a planet is to the sun the higher its

. . . . . . . . . . . . . . . . No planet produces its own light. The . . . . . . . . . .

reflects light from the Sun towards . . . . . . . . . . . . . . . so we can see

it at night.

Every time a planet spins completely on its axis, this is called a

. . . . . . . . . . . . . . . . Every time a planet completes its orbit around the

Sun, this is called . . . . . . . . . . . . . . .  .

**Badger Key Stage 3 Science Starters**

# Different planets: different conditions

### Objective:

To be aware of facts about the different planets, and relate the different conditions to such factors as proximity to sun and orbit.

### Teaching point:

The activity involves the use of data about the planets of the solar system. Important facts are explored using questions ending in a consideration of conditions needed for life.

**What you will need:**
Copymaster 104 as worksheets. Pupils to work in pairs.

**Time:**
10 minutes

### Activity:

Give out Copymaster worksheets.

Explain that pupils should complete the worksheet. A table gives important facts about the solar system. The table is followed by questions.

Explain that the conditions found on a planet are affected by the distance from the sun.

**Answers:**

The further away from the Sun

  (i)   *the longer it takes to complete a year.*
  (ii)  *the colder the average temperature.*

Which planets orbit the Sun quicker than Earth?

  *Mercury, Venus*

Name ONE planet which may support life. Give a reason for your choice.

  *Mars. Nearest temperature to Earth.*

Apart from temperature, give TWO conditions which would be needed to support life similar to organisms found on Earth.

  *Oxygen, carbon dioxide, water, minerals etc.*

**Challenge:** Ask pupils to work out how many orbits of Jupiter a person would live through if they lived for 78 years.

**Links to plenary:** Highlight the consequences of distance of planets from the sun and the conditions needed for terrestrial type living organisms.

**Badger Key Stage 3 Science Starters**

# Different planets: different conditions

| Planet | Average distance of planet from Sun (million km) | Time to orbit the Sun (years) | Average day temperature (°C) |
|---|---|---|---|
| Mercury | 58 | 0·25 | 350 |
| Venus | 108 | 0·62 | 480 |
| Earth | 150 | 1 | 20 |
| Mars | 228 | 1·9 | 0 |
| Jupiter | 780 | 12 | 150 |
| Saturn | 1430 | 29 | 190 |
| Uranus | 2800 | 64 | 220 |
| Neptune | 4500 | 165 | 240 |
| Pluto | 5900 | 248 | 240 |

Can you spot the patterns? Complete the sentences:

The further away from the Sun

(i)

(ii)

Which planets orbit the Sun quicker than Earth?

Name ONE planet which may support life.

Apart from temperature, give TWO conditions which would be needed to support life similar to organisms found on Earth.

# Distance from the Sun

### Objective:

To be aware of the relative distances of the planets from the Sun.

### Teaching point:

The activity involves using marbles as models of the planets and to space them spatially in a sequence from a model sun. The Sun could be a lamp and in the activity each millimetre represents 1 million kilometres.

**What you will need:**
Copymaster 105 as worksheets. Pupils work in groups.

**Time:**
5 minutes

### Activity:

Give out Copymaster worksheets.

Using a tape measure, pupils should place marbles in a line from the model Sun. Inform the pupils that the marbles represent planets but are NOT to scale. Distance from the model Sun IS to scale.

The line will extend to almost 6m so space is needed!

The data worksheet can be cut down the middle if you wish to give advanced groups the task of working out their own scale.

**Challenge:** After the distance activity ask the pupils to assess the chances of life being supported on Mars and Pluto.

**Links to plenary:** Relate the temperature data and orbit data from Starter 104 to distances from the Sun.

**Badger Key Stage 3 Science Starters**

# Distance from the Sun

|  | million km | cm |
|---|---|---|
| Mercury | 58 | 5·8 |
| Venus | 108 | 10·8 |
| Earth | 150 | 15·0 |
| Mars | 228 | 22·8 |
| Jupiter | 780 | 78·0 |
| Saturn | 1430 | 143·0 |
| Uranus | 2800 | 280·0 |
| Neptune | 4500 | 450·0 |
| Pluto | 5900 | 590·0 |

Badger Publishing Limited
26 Wedgwood Way
Pin Green Industrial Estate
Stevenage, Hertfordshire SG1 4QF
Telephone: 01438 356907
Fax: 01438 747015
www.badger-publishing.co.uk
enquiries@badger-publishing.co.uk


Badger Key Stage 3 Science Starters – Year 7
ISBN 1 85880 353 5

Publisher: David Jamieson
Editor: Paul Martin
Designer: Adam Wilmott
Illustrators:  Juliet Breese & Adam Wilmott


Printed in the UK.

## For details of the full range of books and resources from

# Badger Publishing

including
- Book Boxes for 11-16 and Special Needs
- Full Flight for reluctant readers
- Between the Lines - new course exploring text types at Key Stage 3
- Badger Literacy Starters - Word and Sentence Level - for Years 7 to 9
- Badger Maths Starters - for Years 7 to 9

## See our full colour Catalogue
available on request

## Visit our website
## www.badger-publishing.co.uk
This includes **free sample lesson plans and copymaster pages**
which can be printed out and used in your school.

## Contact us at:

Badger Publishing Limited
26 Wedgwood Way,
Pin Green Industrial Estate,
Stevenage, Hertfordshire SG1 4QF

Telephone:  01438 356907

Fax:  01438 747015

enquiries@badger-publishing.co.uk